STAGING
the
Impossible

The Fantastic Mode in Modern Drama

Edited by Patrick D. Murphy

*Contributions to the Study of Science Fiction
and Fantasy, Number 54*
MARSHALL B. TYMN, Series Editor

GREENWOOD PRESS
Westport, Connecticut • London

Library of Congress Cataloging-in-Publication Data

Staging the impossible : the fantastic mode in modern drama / edited
by Patrick D. Murphy.
     p. cm.—(Contributions to the study of science fiction and
fantasy, ISSN 0193–6875 ; no. 54)
   Includes bibliographical references and index.
   ISBN 0–313–27270–0 (alk. paper)
   1. European drama—20th century—History and criticism.
2. Fantastic drama, European—History and criticism. 3. American
drama—20th century—History and criticism. 4. Fantastic drama,
American—History and criticism.   I. Murphy, Patrick D., 1951–
II. Series.
PN1861.S7   1992
809.2′04—dc20   92–10678

British Library Cataloguing in Publication Data is available.

Library of Congress Catalog Card Number: 92–10678
ISBN: 0–313–27270–0
ISSN: 0193–6875

First published in 1992

Greenwood Press, 88 Post Road West, Westport, CT 06881
An imprint of Greenwood Publishing Group, Inc.

Printed in the United States of America

The paper used in this book complies with the
Permanent Paper Standard issued by the National
Information Standards Organization (Z39.48–1984).

10 9 8 7 6 5 4 3 2

Contents

Staging the Impossible

Introduction
Patrick D. Murphy

In the foreword to *The Poetic Fantastic* I observed that discussion of the fantastic "has been limited primarily to prose" and argued that "critical consideration of the fantastic mode as a whole should not be limited to only one of its generic types or any particular period. In taking up the fantastic, authors have utilized poetic as well as prose genres throughout the history of Western literature and continue to do so. Criticism needs to reflect that reality" (xi). Drama has been neglected by criticism of the fantastic at least as much as poetry. It will become quickly clear that all of the contributors to this volume have had to rely on definitions of the fantastic mode based on analyses of prose fiction, rather than being able to draw on a body of fantastic drama theory. The major purpose of editing *The Poetic Fantastic* was to bring poetry and fantastic criticism together; the purpose of *Staging the Impossible* is to connect drama with that same criticism. This time, however, the focus will be on the twentieth century, in as much as it seems that critics are more willing to entertain the notion that past theatrical periods have been less dominated by realism than the present one, the prominence of the Theater of the Absurd notwithstanding.

Realism was not a concept of much concern to playwrights prior to the nineteenth century. There was a brief period at the beginning of the twentieth century when realism attempted to clear the boards of any competition, but as MaryBeth Inverso notes, "[T]his preeminence of realism (and of the hortatory Shavian and Brechtian models which followed) did not, however, rule out the florescence of various antirealist movements which persisted alongside, or perhaps beneath, as Gothic narrative had always done, the mainstream form" (19). Nevertheless, an amazing number of viewers suffer under the impression that drama means realism, and an uncanny number of critics prescribe for theater, and evaluate it according to, various conceptions of realism.[1] In the minds of critics and theatergoers alike, realism has come to set the standards for evaluating the quality of a dramatic performance; it does not follow, however, that realism is the only genuine theater or that realism is *the* mode in which great drama is written. The 14 original essays collected here serve to dispel any illusion that only the absurd breaks from realism in the modern era.

I am not going to claim that something other than realism dominates theater, whether it be the postmodern, the absurd, or the fantastic. Rather, the general thesis of this volume remains more modest and more demonstrable: the fantastic serves as a significant mode of representation in the modern drama of Western Europe and North America. The former includes Ireland and Britain, and the latter includes the Caribbean. That is all this volume, without becoming too cumbersome, could attempt to treat. Like *The Poetic Fantastic*, *Staging the Impossible* serves as an introductory volume to encourage further research. There is much to suggest that the power of the fantastic is not so geographically limited as the areas these essays survey. Peking Opera has staged and restaged various versions of *The White Haired Girl*, with its mythic heroine, while across the China Sea the people of Taiwan attend various operas that retell popular folktales and ancient myths. In the fall of 1990 I had the pleasure of beholding in Taipei a young woman meet the gods of the mountain forest and then turn from a woman into a man and eventually into a dragon to wreak vengeance on the evil lord who threatened her family. In Africa and in South America magic remains a mainstay of much theater, even as the government of Kenya bans an East African rendition of the allegorical *Animal Farm* from being staged in the streets of a Nairobi ghetto because it is seen as too volatile, and perhaps too ''realistic,'' a production. And around the world, feminist playwrights are engaged in revisioning and rewriting classical myths to reinterpret and challenge patriarchal cultures as in the case of Maria-Joseph Ragué i Arias, whose recent works bear such titles as ''Clitemnestra'' and ''Ritual per a Medea.''[2]

What competes with the realism of the first half of this century and the ''new realism'' of the second half on stages all across the United States and other countries is so varied that any delimiting of it would no doubt omit a valuable addition to our contemporary theatrical repertoire. As these 14 essays indicate, one can find the absurd, the horrific, the supernatural, the mythic, the dream-vision quest, the postmodern, the hyper-realistic, and the science fictional. A recent selection of successful major plays suggests some of this variety, if one were to consider only *The Little Shop of Horrors*, *Cats*, *1000 Airplanes on the Roof*, and *Into the Woods*. Some would argue that while certain elements of the fantastic are stageable, such as the transformation of Dr. Jekyll into Mr. Hyde in the theatrical versions of that story or the appearance of the Eumenides in T. S. Eliot's *The Family Reunion*, they are mainly those identified with the realm of fantasy rather than science fiction. For example, Kathryn Hume, in an otherwise extremely valuable study, asserts that ''science fiction has a minimal stage history; its materials transcend the limits of stage mimesis'' (163), but this only occurs when setting and props are viewed as the primary materials of that genre.

The concluding essay in this volume lays that reasonable, but utterly inaccurate, hypothesis to rest with an annotated bibliography of selected modern science fiction plays—selected because Joseph Krupnik had neither world enough nor time for a comprehensive list, even one limited only to English-language plays.

The variety of manifestations of the fantastic in modern theater once more reinforces the argument that the fantastic must be identified as a literary, and performative, mode rather than a genre. That is to say, it is a perceptual orientation rather than a structural one; a way of getting at significant cultural and psychological issues either unamenable to realistic methods of writing and representation, or else so familiar to average readers that only the horrific, the grotesque, or the absurd could achieve the degree of defamiliarization necessary to make those readers look again at the reality that they thought was before their eyes—hence Hume's minimalist definition: "Fantasy is any departure from consensus reality" (21). And it is in this way that works such as Spalding Gray's *Swimming to Cambodia* and other hyper-realist plays can be understood as part of this fantastic mode. Beyond this volume, what is needed is the type of genre criticism of variations of dramatic productions within the fantastic that Inverso has begun in *The Gothic Impulse in Contemporary Drama*. She begins by defining the "gothic" as it is practiced across the overarching genres of prose fiction, poetry, and drama (specifically melodrama in the nineteenth century). She then defines it in terms of a mode of thought, an orientation toward reality that is characteristic of it as a dimension of the fantastic. Having established such definitions, she looks at contemporary drama, particularly since the 1970s, to analyze specific generic innovations on the stage. The same needs to be done for other generic manifestations of fantastic drama, such as science fiction, horror, myth and folktale adaptations/revisions, fairytales, fantasy musicals, the surreal, the postmodern, and the absurd—although the last category has probably received more attention than all of the others combined. For the contemporary gothic, Inverso's book will be the place to begin.

Here the place to begin is a discussion of the concept of the "fantastic," which may be familiar to some readers. If one were to leaf through the following essays quickly without previous acquaintance with the scholarship on the fantastic, a certain dissonance would probably arise. The reader would find that terms get displaced—fantasy/fantastic/science fiction/horror—and seem to substitute for each other from one essay to the next. And even when the same term is employed, the definition seems to change. Well, that is the way it is. These essays are unified by a concern for an analysis of the manifestations of the "fantastic" in modern drama, but they are not unified by a single definition of that concept. And that is appropriate. This volume is not intended to delimit a single definition of the fantastic that can then be used as a prescription for analyzing whether a particular work is fantastic or whether it succeeds as fantastic art. Rather, it is intended to display the diversity of the fantastic in drama and the variations on that concept that can be applied in drama criticism.

So, two definitions of the fantastic are really necessary at this point in time and will probably remain so indefinitely. The first has to do with the "fantastic" as an umbrella term for all that is not mainstream realism in any genre. Here fantasies, fairy tales, horror stories, mythic literature, heroic fiction, and science fiction can all find a space in which to be discussed as literature. That is the way in the preceding paragraphs that I have used the term. The second has to do with a specific type of literature within the larger mode of unrealistic/anti-realistic writing. Here the fantastic tends to mean works that resist closure; question consensual reality rather than simply producing alternative realities; disrupt generic conventions; rupture the reading contract; and call for reassessments of perception, conception, and communication. This usage can clearly be seen to apply to the Theater of the Absurd and to a great deal of postmodernist drama and performance theater. Yet the basis for the determination of a text as fantastic remains the rub, with theorists and critics approaching the delimitation of the fantastic from various and, at times, contradictory vantage points. This situation gives rise to the divergent definitions within this volume. For the moment, let me distinguish by identifying the phrase "the fantastic mode" as the umbrella term and "fantastic texts" as the narrow term.

One arena in which theorists attempt to define the fantastic mode is the ontological, in which the concern is not simply with realism but with reality as a structure.[3] In analyzing the fantastic mode ontologically, the concern is not only with the relation of the unreal to the real but also the relation of realism and the realistic to reality itself. All realist constructs must necessarily be reductionist, closing down alternatives and possibilities in order to present a certain arrangement of events in a "plausible" series of relationships. As a result, an ontological argument might contend that fantastic texts concern themselves with the inadequacy of the referential dimension of language and with the failure of mimesis to capture the depth of reality rather than merely mirroring its surface appearances. Larry McCaffery, for example, contends that "in the context of Borges's library, it is obvious that the 'reality' against which fantasy, in the most naive sense, sets itself and exists by declaring itself other, is a referential category whose privileged ontological status is arbitrarily determined" (23). McCaffery goes on to use the case of W. R. Irwin's distinction between the fantastic and fantasy, as the former involving an opposition of the "anti-real" and the "established real" and the latter involving rhetorical strategies that make "nonfact" appear factual, to illustrate ontological problems. Irwin relies on consensual notions of "nonfact" and "impossibility" without interrogating the origin of these conceptions and the degree to which consensual views shape rather than reflect the reality in which people participate. And, actually, Irwin's own definition slides from the ontological to the epistemological as it moves from one concept to the other.

McCaffery ends up arguing that fantastic literature is more ontologically accurate than realism or fantasy, because these both require the representation of closed systems based on consensual reality constructs, the former through direct presentation and the latter through "continuous metaphorical relationship to something we have absolutely and arbitrarily designated 'our' world" (37). In contrast, the fantastic remains "open-ended," deconstructing its own genre limitations and refusing the reductions that make author and reader feel that the "chaos" of the universe and one's own life can be ordered and rendered orderly. For McCaffery, then, the fantastic, as distinct from fantasy, is very much embodied by, if not directly arising from, the postmodernist impulse (postmodernism here need not be defined in a chronological period sense but as an "occasion" occurring at various historical conjunctures). The focus, then, should not be on the referentiality of the text but on how, through the generative language games that the fantastic can play out, a text can alter readers' perceptions of the reality they inhabit and on the ways they can shape aspects of that nontotalizable reality.

McCaffery's argument here is similar to others that would define fantasy texts as inherently conservative and fantastic texts as inherently subversive. (If we accept this contention, then the fantastic mode cannot be identified as being either subversive or conservative but necessarily both/neither). Fantasies of whatever genre often follow traditional guidelines and use particularly traditional language with a high degree of emphasis on verisimilitude and internal consistency.[4] In theater, *Peter Pan* comes to mind. At both the ontological and epistemological levels, fantasy dramas reinforce audience beliefs rather than challenging them—children have vivid imaginations and adults should give scope to such imaginings as part of maturation; but adults should not believe such things, and the barrier between worlds becomes impermeable when puberty arrives. The asexual androgyne as lead works perfectly for such a situation. Fantasy, then, like allegory relies on a universe of shared beliefs in which specific beliefs—such as which religion is the true one—may be challenged, but the larger consensus—that a religion can be true—remains unquestioned.[5] This is not to say that fantasies are necessarily lesser works. There are points in time or specific contexts in which precisely the conservative gesture, the recalling of past values, the return of earlier ways, is the most significant statement a playwright can make. I think this would be the case for Halper Leivick's *The Golem*. It is certainly the case for many science fiction plays, which serve as cautionary tales about the loss of certain values or beliefs. The recovery of forgotten or denigrated values or practices can also produce defamiliarization and a reconsideration of what has generally been considered a foregone conclusion.

The fantastic, in contrast, introduces not only a defamiliarization at the ontological level but also an epistemological self-doubt that thwarts a convenient catharsis in the final act, as is the case of Sam Shepard's *Operation Sidewinder*. It may do this through its narrative or dramatic structures—for example, in the works of Beckett and Ionesco where the story unravels rather than unfolds to a climax. Or it may do so through language games—for example, in the plays of Wilde and Cocteau where irony, puns, jokes, and misunderstandings abound. Or it may do so through the interweaving of the apparently "real" and the apparently supernatural to emphasize the necessity for re-cognition—for example, in the plays of Strindberg and Walcott where dreams figure prominently. But in every case, in contradistinction to allegorical fantasy, the fantastic poses a problem, casts a doubt, requires a reconsideration, reorients a perception. Such a stepping past, such a reconfiguring of, acknowledged reality, identity, perceptions, and conceptualizations arises again and again throughout the essays in this collection as a crucial feature of the plays under discussion.

Tzvetan Todorov in attempting a structuralist definition of the fantastic built his argument almost entirely around the word "hesitation." And while he claims that the hesitation between the uncanny and the supernatural has disappeared with the arrival of modern psychoanalysis, I would argue that he has failed to analyze the material at hand. The supernatural continues to appear in modern drama as elsewhere, but it has been stripped of its absolute power and order. The uncanny abounds but does so, as in postmodernist texts, as a depiction of the quotidian that refuses to conform to the dictates of consensual reality, exposing all such realism as social constructs with their own ideologies and social agendas.

As Rosemary Jackson argues, partly in response to Todorov, "a reluctance, or an inability, to present definitive versions of 'truth' or 'reality' makes of the modern fantastic a literature which draws attention to its own practice as a linguistic system" (37). If one moves from this suspension of an alleged mimetic need to imitate "truth" to a concern not with the referentiality of literature but with the affective characteristics of literature, then the fantastic can be viewed as shaping reality without attempting to mirror it: "If one considers literature as rhetoric, significant insofar as it has power to affect an audience, one should be able to admit and recognize fantasy. If swaying the audience is what matters, then any technique which succeeds validates itself" (Hume 26).

Yet as Hume argues through quoting Robert Scholes, no work of literature can completely evade reality, since literature is ineluctably a part of the reality it refuses to reflect mimetically. With drama, that link to audience perceptions of reality which form part of the real in which the work is performed or read becomes far more important structurally than it does in fiction or long poems. On the stage, a dramatist cannot provide a 30-page history of the colonization of the planet that provides the action's setting or lengthy explanations for why Iron Mountain is full of wicked dwarves who hate the pacifist giants of the coast. As a result, fantastic drama more frequently works in the arena of low fantasy rather than high fantasy. This Earth as primary world forms the basis for the essential departures from reality that constitute the work's particularities in low fantasy, while in high fantasy the action occurs entirely on an invented secondary world with no references or linkages to this one. Such a distinction works for science fiction as well. And in the case of both fantasy and science fiction plays, low structure predominates over high, facilitating both staging and reception. Low fantasy structures also make allegorical readings that deny attention to the specifics of the estrangement more difficult. The fantastic as with most other forms of the theater is metonymic as well as metaphoric because, as T. E. Apter contends, "the fantasist's metaphors . . . combine the conflation of vehicle and tenor with strange and new associations; figurative language becomes the only means of making literal assertions, for ordinary meanings fragment, expand, splinter, either because some new, unknown order prevails, or because the former order functions haphazardly or piecemeal" (3). Not surprisingly, many of this volume's contributors give special attention to the idea of the fantastic as a language game.

The preceding remarks are meant to help clarify some ways of thinking about the fantastic when the word comes into view. They are not meant to delimit a controlling definition that would corral all of the various ways literature in general, or drama in particular, thwarts and challenges the realist assurances and would thereby impose a unifying order on this collection of essays. I believe that it is more productive, and more appropriate here, to contend that all of the definitions the contributors provide of the fantastic mode or fantastic texts are necessary but insufficient to help readers cope with the irreducibility of the reactions against the human hubris of universalizing reasons and totalizing discourses. Perhaps none of the definitions proffered should be accepted, or perhaps they all can be used as vehicles, as long as no one expects to arrive at the same place each time. They are departure not arrival definitions.

This volume has come about because I saw a serious gap in the Greenwood series and in the critical work of such conferences as the International Conference on the Fantastic in the Arts, Mythcon, and others. And I heard too many of my colleagues placing themselves in the absurd position of talking about the realism of drama and then teaching *Six Characters in Search of an Author*, *Waiting for Godot*, or *Rosencrantz and Guildenstern Are Dead*. That is to say they talked one thing based on their training and the proclivities of the criticism they read, but they taught another—trying all the while to force those "unreal" plays into the Procrustean bed of reductive realist interpretation. For them, perhaps these essays will prove subversive and liberatory. For me, they have been not only highly educational but also immensely enjoyable. Before turning the reader over to them, let me briefly summarize their more outstanding features.

Susan Taylor Jacobs in "When Formula Seizes Form" begins the assault on the popular notion that drama and realism are synonymous by taking a playwright who would immediately be labeled a realist, Oscar Wilde, and demonstrating his frequent use of "fantastic techniques." Jacobs argues that Wilde is drawn to the fantastic because of his concern with epistemological questions and his doubts about the stability of referentiality. Turning to Sartre, Rabkin, and Irwin for a definition of fantasy that emphasizes its literary function in terms of "a disruption of, or conflict between, rhetorical structures" rather than the more traditional notion of antirealist worlds, Jacobs claims that such a definition "allows us to explore the operations of fantasy even where there is no magic or bizarre other world, as in Wilde's comedies." For example, Jacobs contends that in *Lady Windermere's Fan* Wilde plays with both ironic and traditional theatrical structures to address the question of human identity and the relationship or gap between human nature, identity, and character. Jacobs finds Wilde continuing such an interrogation of identity by presenting "contradictory views of the self" in *An Ideal Husband*. She concludes her study with a detailed examination of *The Importance of Being Earnest*. Here Jacobs finds Wilde transgressing rhetorical conventions in order to disrupt the audience's complacency: "The speed with which Wilde puts together inappropriate ideas and grammatical patterns augments the fantastic fragmentation of sense in the play."

In "A Task Most Difficult," Frederick S. Lapisardi addresses a problem rarely treated in studies of fantastic drama: the difficulty of staging plays in which the supernatural or fantastic hesitation exists. Frequently in such cases, the staging needs to indicate the ambiguity or undecidability of the situation, or it needs to represent simultaneously the conflicting interpretations held by various characters or else held by characters and audience. Lapisardi argues that this has been a significant problem in the production of Yeats's mystical dramas: "The point here is not to prove that Yeats's plays are filled with mythic, fantastic, and supernatural elements. . . . The problem now, as it was when the plays were written, emerges when they are produced on any stage." Lapisardi treats one of the most recent efforts to stage Yeats effectively and retain the supernaturalism that is to be found throughout the corpus. This attempt began in 1989 "when James W. Flannery took up the challenge of producing the full canon of Yeats's dramatic work at the Abbey" and continued into 1991 as Flannery brought play after play to the stage.

Flannery had to go against, according to Lapisardi, years of the Abbey Theatre's being "immersed in realist and largely commercial traditions." The same held true for the actors. Lapisardi concludes that Flannery's productions did not always work but always attempted to depict the fantastic as such, rather than settling for a reductive realism, since "the supernatural is not simply something tacked on to these works: as an integral element in every one of Yeats's plays, the mystical vies constantly against the natural for control. Both must be represented with equal force for the production to succeed."

Peter Malekin's "The Perilous Edge" begins with an analysis of the relationship between madness and the fantastic, building on the argument that "both reformulate reality." And "it is this reformulation that distinguishes the fantastic from mere fantasy, which ultimately leaves the world much as it found it." Malekin finds reformulation at the heart of Strindberg's later plays, particularly *A Dream Play*, which are deeply concerned with metaphysical issues. He contends that "the probing of appearances and opinions is carried further in *A Dream Play*" than in *The Ghost Sonata* due to its more coherent symbolism. Malekin then details this symbolism from the design of the opening curtain to production's end. But he warns his reader not to become too enraptured by his own symbolic tracings, since "the dramatic impact of the play is different from the symbolic structure that can be extracted from it." And from the viewpoint of this volume's thesis, Malekin argues a preeminent place for Strindberg among the authors studied here, because his plays "brought back into western drama much that had been excluded for centuries. They could not have done so without the techniques of the fantastic, and they did so by using the full technical range of the modern theater. *The fantastic thus moved back into the mainstream of modern drama as a powerful weapon*" (my emphasis).

So far the authors studied are clearly canonical playwrights: Wilde, Yeats, Strindberg. Kent W. Hooper takes us farther afield with his essay, "Wassily Kandinsky's Stage Composition *Yellow Sound*," and not only introduces a figure associated more with painting than with drama but also a multimedia rather than traditional dramatic production—published in 1912 but not premiered until 1982. Hooper necessarily begins by addressing the problem of critical analysis of "artistic multiple talents" who worked in more than one medium and adopts a semiotic approach to multiple talent critique. Noting the crucial role that the fantastic plays not only in *Yellow Sound* but in the works of expressionist multiple talents in general, he argues that this has caused problems for viewers and cultural historians alike since they have remained largely unprepared to consider the peculiarities that result from its being generated in the fantastic mode. Utilizing Eric Rabkin's arguments, Hooper contends that critics of *Yellow Sound* generally could not figure out the "ground rules of Kandinsky's narrative world."

Any study of the fantastic in drama would be incomplete without some attention to the Theater of the Absurd. Elizabeth C. and Ian M. Hesson provide the first essay on playwrights associated with the absurd in "Ionesco and *L'insolite*." Working from the playwright's own comments on theater, they suggest that Ionesco's term "*insolite*," the unusual, is more appropriate than "absurd." They then develop a psychoanalytic interpretation of Ionesco's fascination with *insolite* throughout his career. They argue that in the early plays "the fantastic reflects Ionesco's contemplative view of humankind." By the time of such tragic farces of the 1950s as *The Chairs*, Ionesco's perception of reality and his use of the fantastic have changed, revealing an involvement with character not previously displayed. And in *The Killer*, Ionesco "has a much greater emotional involvement in Bérenger than in any previous character," because he represents so clearly the author's own "ambivalence" about helping others. Not until *A Stroll in the Air*, according to the Hessons, does this character develop beyond Ionesco's earlier dualism of "the involved and the detached." The Hessons conclude that "Ionesco's '*insolite*' is a function of perception, as is the fantastic . . . and it also suggests that the absurd can represent an emotional reaction to existence as much as an intellectual one."

Ralph Yarrow in "Ambiguity and the Supernatural in Cocteau's *La machine infernale*" treats another French playwright, but unlike the Hessons he treats a single play. Yarrow writes of this work from the vantage points of both literary critic and producer and focuses his attention on Cocteau's achieving of ambiguity—"the living-on-the-edge, which comes from the juxtaposition of dream and daytime reality, of myth and social form, of the repressed and the admitted." The techniques of the play, an oscillation of styles, are crucial to this achievement. The supernatural and the mythic, according to Yarrow, serve primarily to represent inner psychic states which the main characters repress throughout the play. As a result, they are unable to learn from their own situation but offer an opportunity to the audience; only if, however, the audience is willing to cross the threshold of consensual reality. Yarrow argues that in *La machine infernale*

the borderline and the alternative kinds of knowledge that might be available from beyond it are clearly present in characters and manifestations . . . in the key metaphor of blindness and seeing . . . in the changes of mood, tone, and language; and in the shifts between and among the four acts. The acts taken together suggest knowledge as a complex process of interchange.

Samuel Beckett has been analyzed, reanalyzed, and overanalyzed, often in futile interpretive gestures beyond even the imaginings of one of his own characters. Yet Lance Olsen provides an orientation toward Beckett's work in "Beckett and the Horrific" that enables a rethinking of a number of his plays in terms of their informing mode. He argues persuasively that "Beckett's plays function within the horror tradition in drama"; what separates them from other dramatic horrors is their postmodernity in which physical horrors are transformed into antihumanist metaphysical ones. Olsen argues that a prime example of this shift can be found in the two-part structure of many of Beckett's plays in which one finds a "near-eternal recurrence," but only "near" due to the promise of entropy. This point is developed through analyses of such famous works as *Waiting for Godot*, *Endgame*, and *Krapp's Last Tape*, as well as analyses of other productions, particularly the minimalist ones, such as *Play* and *Breath*. In the end, Olsen defines such productions as "dyscatastrophic horror," appropriate for a culture that believes itself to be in crisis, in between-times, and "post-" without necessarily any promise of being "pre-" as well (decidedly not well).

The treatment of such a gloomy prognosticator as Beckett would be a hard act to follow unless one reversed direction. Peter N. Chetta's essay, "Multiplicities of Illusion in Tom Stoppard's Plays," does just that, with a much more upbeat assessment of another postmodernist. Chetta sees Stoppard as making a decisive break with the absurdists in *Rosencrantz and Guildenstern Are Dead* through his use of Shakespearean characters: "The sense of disbelief is suspended to a different degree, certainly a more intense degree, when a new frame of reference has to operate for characters that previously existed in another work." Chetta is careful to explain how Stoppard's innovation differs from the historical use of known literary characters among the ancient Greeks, their use by such authors as Cervantes, and the work of Restoration playwrights; he also distinguishes Stoppard from other modern playwrights, such as Pirandello and Williams. He then attends to the specifics of *Rosencrantz and Guildenstern Are Dead* as well as Stoppard's later play *Travesties*. Here Chetta finds the same kind of linguistic play that Jacobs highlighted in regard to Wilde's plays, which seems utterly appropriate since Stoppard "borrowed" some of Wilde's characters to write his play.

Carl Schaffer's essay, "Leivick's *The Golem* and the Golem Legend," turns the spotlight on one of the crowning achievements of Yiddish verse. It also suggests the degree to which the myths of a people remain a significant component of fantastic drama throughout the twentieth century. But Schaffer does not only provide readers with the mythical background for this play; he also provides them with its crucial cultural context: the Russian persecution of Jews. Schaffer points out that like all preceding golems, Leivick's is also flawed, but unlike its predecessors "its defect is of a different kind; it comes from a flaw within its creator, and this is the impetus for much of the action of the drama." That flaw is "hatred." The play, as Schaffer demonstrates with exceptional erudition, is deeply imbricated with Golem legends and fundamental tenets of Jewish mysticism, but it is not primarily a play about tradition. Rather, it speaks from a recognition of the unspeakable tragedies of the past toward the dangers and the possibilities of the contemporary human condition: to attempt to destroy others is to destroy oneself.

With Robert Willis's "*Dream on Monkey Mountain*," we cross the Atlantic to look at the work of the Caribbean author Derek Walcott. Walcott's hero is based on a childhood memory but stands for "all poor West Indians" who wage a tragic struggle against colonialism and its myth of racial inferiority. Willis defines *Dream on Monkey Mountain* as a "mythic drama," thus sharing elements with the works of Yeats and Leivick, which combines "fantasy, obeah, music, dance, and poetry to expose the deeper, unconscious sources of identity and the nature of freedom." Under colonialism and neocolonialism, freedom is always defined as a fantasy and, as here, is often experienced only in dreams. The structure of the play owes something to Cervantes' *Don Quixote* but also appears indebted to the Chinese legend of the Monkey-King, while its theme builds on the psychological theories of Fanon and upholds the African heritage of the West Indians. Willis observes that "Walcott dismisses revenge as uncreative," a lesson that the protagonist of *The Golem* learned too late.

The next three essays in this volume, by Jessica Prinz, Theodore Shank, and Veronica Hollinger, treat new experimental and performance theater of the 1980s, with its postmodernism, its hyper-realism, and its exposure of the illusionary fantasy that has served as the basis for "realist" theater for centuries. In "Spalding Gray's *Swimming to Cambodia*," Prinz elucidates a single work of a single performance artist to get at the characteristics of "the new performance mode that Gray is helping to generate." The fantastic in this mode is not the creation of an imaginary world or the drama vision of a hero, but rather the fantastic characteristics of the historical world in which contemporary humanity is attempting to live out its collective existence. In the case of Gray's play, it is the "fantastic but nevertheless true and tragic history of Cambodia." In this sense, Prinz's definition of the fantastic is very much akin to Ionesco's *insolite* that the Hessons detail, as well as the hesitation felt in the shifting conceptions of reality that Cocteau's "ambiguity" evokes. But whereas Jacobs addresses the fantastic in Wilde's work through attention to rhetoric, Prinz gets at the fantastic in Gray's work through attention to gesture. And in the gestures that Gray makes in the course of playing himself on stage, Prinz argues that Gray "calls presence into question" and with it, necessarily, any sense of consensual reality.

In "The Shock of the Actual," Shank argues that theater audiences have become too accustomed to perceiving the illusionary as the real. As a result, "one of the ways of presenting something startling or fantastic in the theater is to direct the audience to focus on actuality, which is something we do not expect to see on the stage." This recognition has led to the following: "Much of the experimental work in the theater since the 1950s has involved disrupting the theatrical illusion by framing actuality in various ways that cause us to perceive it as fantastic." Shank develops this argument in some detail, including a discussion of early experimentation beginning with Duchamp, before turning to a treatment of such groups as The Living Theatre, which initiated task performance in the mid–1960s, building on the "Happenings" of the 1950s. Shank argues that in the 1970s John Fox, director of Welfare State International in England, took task performance a step further when he "incorporated both created illusion and actual surroundings into the fictional frame of his environmental productions," such as a tracing in reverse of the route of King Arthur that ends with Lancelot and company boarding an actual submarine. The Squat Theater, which relocated from Hungary to New York in the 1970s, provides an example of a group that blurs the line between illusion and actuality in its performances, including the use of participant audiences.

Veronica Hollinger begins her essay, "Playing at the End of the World," by discussing the influence of the kind of performance theater that Shank analyzes on the cyberpunk novels of William Gibson. Specifically, Gibson is influenced by a San Francisco–based group Survival Research Laboratories, whose performances, according to Hollinger, "may be read as particularly extreme responses to the problematization of the concept of theatrical presence in contemporary theater." Hollinger argues that such extremities result from the general failure of dramatic realism, a failure apparently as of yet unremarked by many theater critics, and invokes Derrida to help explain why "presence" has become theater's present-day petard. She also ranges across leading dramatic avant-gardists, such as Artaud and Beckett, as well as other contemporary theorists, such as Blau and de Man; and then uses Beckett's *Endgame* to develop a distinction between traditional science fiction (SF) and "specular SF," its postmodernist permutation. This discussion continues in her treatment of "millennarianism" and "American Apocalypses," including a critique of Sam Shepard. Hollinger's argument here displays a certain mutated kinship with Olsen's notion of "dyscatastrophic horror," which one can see certainly operative in *Einstein on the Beach*. Hollinger closes with her own apocalyptic warning: "Given, however, that—like the Elizabethan world—all the postmodern world is indeed a stage, it makes a very great difference whether we submit to the seductions of the imagery of resolution or manage to maintain an ironic distance from our own (on-stage and off-stage) productions."

This volume closes with a brief essay and a lengthy annotated bibliography by Joseph Krupnik, " 'Infinity in a Cigar Box.' " If this essay served only to abolish the shibboleth that there are no science fiction plays, then it would have served its audience well. But it does far more than that. In only a few pages, Krupnik outlines the key critical features of this prejudice against SF on the stage, pointing out that in English alone "the number of science fiction plays that are available in published versions is sizable, well over 100." And while these vary in quality, of course, Krupnik concludes that "both the playwrights and their science fiction plays deserve wider and more serious recognition than they have so far received." To facilitate such recognition, Krupnik annotates 40 plays, including ones by such figures as Candice Bergen, John Guare, John Jakes, Arch Oboler, Elder Olson, I. A. Richards, Sam Shepard, Upton Sinclair, Gore Vidal, and Edmund Wilson. Blinded by the light of movie sets and Hollywood screenings, critics of science fiction and the fantastic have tended to remain ignorant of science fiction drama. As a result of Krupnik's work, however, they may plead ignorance no longer.

The foregoing has, I hope, served to arouse the interest of this volume's readers not only to read the specific essays that address their special interests and concerns but also to peruse the entire range of the modern dramatic fantastic treated throughout these pages. But enough of introductions; the curtain is about to rise on analyses of this century's efforts at staging the impossible.

NOTES

1. Judith Roof sees this penchant for realism, at least in U.S. theater, as being the result of "a privileging of a masculinity narratively bound up with images of creativity, potency, and truth. . . . [M]ainstream American drama and dramatic criticism celebrate one another and the illusory authenticity which anchors their approaches" (106).

2. Kathleen McNerney discusses Ragué i Arias's plays in "Reinterpretations of the Classics: What's Old and What's New in Catalonia."

3. Please see the selected bibliography at the end of the volume for a list of works that attempt to define "fantasy" and the "fantastic."

4. Darko Suvin has long made the same kind of contention for science fiction. Using "cognitive estrangement" as his pivotal criterion, Suvin dismisses most works labeled science fiction as regressive, escapist fantasies and reserves the term "science fiction" for only those kinds of extrapolative speculations that McCaffery and others would define as "fantastic."

5. This orientation would seem to be the basis for Ann Swinfen's approach to the mode in *In Defence of Fantasy*, where she relies heavily on Tolkien for her working definition of "fantasy."

WORKS CITED

Apter, T. E. *Fantasy Literature: An Approach to Reality*. Bloomington: Indiana University Press, 1982.

Hume, Kathryn. *Fantasy and Mimesis: Responses to Reality in Western Literature*. New York: Methuen, 1984.

Inverso, MaryBeth. *The Gothic Impulse in Contemporary Drama*. Ann Arbor: UMI Research Press, 1990.

Irwin, W. R. *The Game of the Impossible: A Rhetoric of Fantasy*. Urbana: University of Illinois Press, 1976.

Jackson, Rosemary. *Fantasy: The Literature of Subversion*. New York: Methuen, 1981.

McCaffery, Larry. "Form, Formula, and Fantasy: Generative Structures in Contemporary Fiction." *Bridges to Fantasy*. Ed. George E. Slusser, Eric S. Rabkin, and Robert Scholes. Carbondale: Southern Illinois University Press, 1982. 21–27.

McNerney, Kathleen. "Reinterpretations of the Classics: What's Old and What's New in Catalonia." *Studies in the Humanities* 17 (1990): 172–78.

Murphy, Patrick D., and Vernon Hyles, eds. *The Poetic Fantastic: Studies in an Evolving Genre*. Westport, Conn.: Greenwood Press, 1989.

Roof, Judith. "Testicles, Toasters and the 'Real Thing.' " *Studies in the Humanities* 17 (1990): 106–19.

Suvin, Darko. *Metamorphoses of Science Fiction: On the Poetics and History of a Literary Genre*. New Haven: Yale University Press, 1979.

Swinfen, Ann. *In Defence of Fantasy: A Study of the Genre in English and American Literature since 1945*. London: Routledge, 1984.

Todorov, Tzvetan. *The Fantastic: A Structural Approach to a Literary Genre*. Trans. Richard Howard. 1973. Ithaca, N.Y.: Cornell University Press, 1975.

1

When Formula Seizes Form: Oscar Wilde's Comedies

Susan Taylor Jacobs

Though fantasy has been dismissed by many academics as a genre of marginal literary value, it attracts artists as well as readers. Indeed, one reason why a consensual definition of literary fantasy eludes us is that authors working in many genres draw upon it, smudging generic boundaries.[1] Oscar Wilde was one of these writers.

Wilde appreciated the mind's power to make its own meanings, and he was skeptical of epistemologies, including his own. He used fantastic techniques, particularly those underscoring epistemological questions, although for him problems of knowing the phenomenological world were less interesting than problems of understanding a literary text. Given the complex, irrational subjectivities of authors and readers, he argued, no literary work could be perfectly understood. Moreover, the ultimate inability of a reader to perceive an author's exact meaning represented opportunities for both in expression and aesthetic pleasure. Wilde pursued such opportunities even in such seemingly conventional forms as the plays that made his fortune, temporarily, in the first half of the 1890s.

This discussion covers some of those plays. Often called Wilde's comedies, they actually conform to conventions of the "well-made play" (sometimes called "society" drama) and a related type, the problem play. The typical well-made play involved the inexorable disclosure of secrets. The problem play, in the hands of an Ibsen, could be made to challenge the status quo; in it, a character facing a moral dilemma would examine his or her heart, which may have been obscured by a life spent subservient to social convention. Wilde's imagination responded to the most conventional elements of these types of plays, particularly their sentimentalization of human nature while formally and ideologically suppressing it.

A discussion of the uses Oscar Wilde made of fantasy in these plays should clarify the differences between fantasy and any genre that is its host, yet critics disagree on fantasy's definition. Fantasy is metamorphic. Like literature in general, it takes on issues and symbols that matter most to an author and her culture, so that many descriptions and prescriptions of fantasy are contaminated by ethnocentricity. Traditionally, fantasy has been defined, as it is in Holman and Harmon's *A Handbook to Literature*, as a genre whose stories contradict reality by describing impossible events, creatures, and places. Such a definition does address what most readers intuit is fundamental to fantasy literature, yet ''reality,'' either as a word or concept, is an unstable criterion. Our understanding of the world is influenced by our education, our experience, and the religious and scientific axioms of our particular culture or society. Some critics concur with Jean-Paul Sartre that magic and otherworldy settings are not essential to fantasy:

So long as it was thought possible to escape the conditions of human existence through ascesticism, mysticism, metaphysical disciplines or the practice of poetry, fantasy was called upon to fulfill a very definite function. It manifested our human power to transcend the human. . . . After the long metaphysical holiday of the post-war period, which ended in disaster, the new generation of artists and writers . . . had returned, with much ado, to the human. This tendency had an effect on fantasy itself . . . [which] in order to find a place within the humanism of our time . . . is going to become domesticated, will give up the exploration of transcendental reality and resign itself to transcribing the human condition. (62–63)

Rosemary Jackson and Leo Bersani are among those to offer psychological, structural, and formal examination of nontranscendental fantasy.

Some critics and writers of fantasy regard it as a disruption of, or conflict between, rhetorical structures.[2] For instance, Eric Rabkin describes fantasy as a text that introduces, then contradicts, ground rules governing how the reader interprets the fictional world. Drawing on Huizinga's theory of play, W.R. Irwin defines a fantastic ''world'' as a place designated by a rigid set of rules and distinguished from those defining the reader's culture. The focus of recent critics like these on the rule-making mind allows us to explore the operations of fantasy even where there is no magic or bizarre other world, as in Wilde's comedies.

Lady Windermere's Fan, produced in 1891, made Wilde's fortune and enhanced his reputation. It is the story of a woman's encounter with the mother who had abandoned her. Lady Windermere's mother has come back, calling herself Mrs. Erlynne and blackmailing the husband, Lord Windermere, who wishes to spare his wife the truth about her mother. Believing that the two are having an affair, the angry Lady Windermere resolves to elope with an admirer, Lord Darlington. Mrs. Erlynne discovers her daughter's plan, follows her to Darlington's empty apartment, and convinces her to return home. Before they can leave, Darlington enters with his friends, including Lord Windermere and Lord Augustus, Mrs. Erlynne's suitor. The women hide, but Lady Windermere leaves her fan behind. When the fan is discovered, Mrs. Erlynne comes out of hiding, allowing everyone to assume she has come to Darlington for an assignation, and explains that she had taken it by mistake. Wilde undermines the impact on the audience of this sacrifice when she mollifies the resentful Lord Augustus the next day. She and her "protector" depart for Paris without revealing her identity to her grateful daughter.

Though this plot contradicts certain clichés, it does not disorient us or contradict the world view of any but the most authoritarian and rigorous of puritans, and so it is not in itself fantastic. In fact, the plot enacts an assumption conventional to both the problem play and the well-made play, that human beings have an essence, an identity, often concealed behind social masks. To uncover this essence, the plot delivers Mrs. Erlynne's moment of maternal protectiveness, supported by some of the stage directions: "For a moment she reveals herself" and "Hiding her feelings with a trivial laugh" (140). The woman, uncovered, is loving, distressed by her alienation from the human community but brave enough to resist a temptation to claim a love that would cause the beloved pain.

If we look more closely at Mrs. Erlynne and some of the other characters, however, we find that their identities may not have been uncovered after all. Lady Windermere, the one character on stage who comes to see Mrs. Erlynne as good, is untrustworthy. As Morse Peckham has observed, Lady Windermere's change of heart is superficial: "She is one of those who cannot tell the difference between ideals and illusions . . . and she is therefore incapable of true moral growth" (13). Moving Mrs. Erlynne over into the category of goodness does not change Lady Windermere's puritanical division of people into good and bad. She merely excuses Mrs. Erlynne's past, rather than confront and understand it. This morally immature character, kept in the dark to the last on the grounds that she does not have the temperament for truth, brings the play's very axioms into question, since the only character to unmask an identity does so in the unexamined, narrow terms of her idealistic culture. Wilde does not emphasize this irony, and so many spectators simply understand the play's conclusion as further manifestation of Mrs. Erlynne's generosity. Yet the coexistence of ironic and traditional structures examining identity, or character, creates an epistemological ambiguity common in fantasy, for neither human nature nor the nature of the play can be decided.

Mrs. Erlynne's comments further undermine the traditional epistemology of this kind of play. Rejecting the characterization of her that the plot has been making, she cavalierly denies that the moment when she nearly sacrifices herself to save her daughter defines her: "I lost one illusion last night. I thought I had no heart. I find I have, and my heart doesn't suit me, Windermere" (141). We can read "my heart doesn't suit me" as a pathetic cynicism, a protest against the pain that comes with living, but "my heart doesn't suit me" has another implication. Though she does not regret saving her daughter (partly because she does not suffer materially), she is openly repelled by her spontaneous gesture, which, ironically, threatens to encapsulate her—inside an identity. "I want to live childless still'' (40), she cries, denying the power of physical fact to force an identity on her. What she did was an emotional impulse, and impulses, she insists, do not necessarily define oneself.

The lack of identity that Mrs. Erlynne preserves is, like her childlessness, an emptiness that is filled incessantly by experimental play. That is, she is a fantasist, responding to the lack implied in the ideal Victorian identity by creating a character for herself the audience would consider impossible, a woman who is all potential because she is without essence. Repeatedly she alludes to herself as a role-player. Gazing at a picture of herself as a young woman, she muses, "Dark hair and an innocent expression were the fashion then, Windermere!" (139). To the spectator, experienced in the kinds of assumptions about human nature promulgated by this sort of play, that photograph is a memento of authenticity, lost when the ingenue entered a hypocritical, dangerous society. But Mrs. Erlynne only claims to see a frame and a pose. To her mind, frame and pose record her as accurately as she can be recorded, for she has no identity, only epochs. Mrs. Erlynne underscores the artificiality of theatrical conventions that purport to disclose the essence of human nature: "Oh, don't imagine that I am going to have a pathetic scene with her, weep on her neck and tell her who I am, and all that kind of thing. I have no ambition to play the part of a mother" (140). The crafty and witty demimondaine may be a mask, but so is the weeping, loving mother that the audience has been expecting to see emerge as the "real" Mrs. Erlynne.

Certainly the play encourages us to see Mrs. Erlynne as revealing a deeper, better self. Yet Mrs. Erlynne's refusal to be a Stella Dallas cannot be entirely dismissed as mere denial. Though in some ways pathetic, deprived of family and dependent economically on men, she is also creative. Hers are the metamorphoses we have seen in myth and fantasy; she makes herself an ingenue, a demimondaine, a powerful mother, and, yes, a Stella Dallas. What Leo Bersani says about "fantasy as a phenomenon of psychic deconstruction" (7) in Baudelaire applies to Wilde as well: "he can be located at that critical moment in our culture's history when an idealistic view of the self and of the universe is being simultaneously held onto and discredited by a psychology (if the word still applies) of the fragmented and the discontinuous" (4). Mrs. Erlynne's dramatic function in the play similarly deconstructs and nostalgically holds onto the culture's idealistic assumptions about identity.

Mechanisms of fantasy often operate through Wilde's epigrams, which can deny the play's premises by creating a bizarre world dominated by surface and style, not heart, or identity. In the Windermere world human nature is constrained by "an idealistic view of the self." Windermere language acknowledges only certain experiences and events, interpreting them only from certain (moral) perspectives. The spontaneous revelation of self that people believe they see in the Windermere world is thus a delusion. The heartlessness, in *The Importance of Being Earnest* that Mary McCarthy complained of (107) is here as well, but not in a moral sense. Heartlessness in the epigrammatic characters is an impersonal wit, with surface and style elevated, in fantasy's exaggerated way, in response to the Windermere idea of heart.

Wilde's contemporary A. B. Walkley noticed that the conversation of dandies in Darlington's rooms took place in a secondary world within the play. Action ceases during the scene, he reported, "but you do not notice its length, for it is a perpetual coruscation of epigrams. Just before the epigrams get boring, the action returns" (122). When action freezes and epigrams take over, the epistemology gestured to by the framing play is replaced by another. The dandies form a community based on epigrams, their conversation a ritual during which they touch and acknowledge one another without learning anything about one another's personal histories or sentiments. There are two exceptions: Lord Darlington, whose love for Lady Windermere has suddenly made him open and earnest, and Lord Windermere, troubled by his blackmailing mother-in-law and furious wife. Neither man speaks or interacts with the other dandies.

An otherwise minor figure, Cecil Graham, underscores the difference between the ludic dandy world and the world of the play enclosing it. When the play is staged rather than read, Graham's importance is clear; besides generating the greatest number of epigrams, he takes up a great deal of space. Starting with the directions "Cecil Graham comes toward him laughing," Wilde sets the character off on peregrinations the principals do not follow. He moves back and forth, lights a cigarette, puts a hand on another man's shoulder, and preens in front of the fireplace. The audience follows his movements, a choreographed display of meaninglessness, and listens to epigrams that reveal nothing about the man inside. During this time, the plot is suspended: Windermere sits thoughtfully, while Darlington writes letters, philosophizes to himself, and finally exits. Only Graham and his frivolous cohorts seem animate in the world that has suddenly come into being, where wit and style, but not heart, dominate. It is the restless Graham who finds the fan and turns it over to Windermere, who exclaims melodramatically over it. Thus the play is handed back to its principals and its principles. Graham moves away and grows still, smirking—perhaps maliciously—from the sidelines.

If Wilde had any reason for giving Graham the name of the friend who commits suicide in "The Portrait of Mr. W.H.," it is that both are alienated from the perspective that informs *Lady Windermere's Fan*. One Graham, the suicide, devotes himself to Shakespeare's poetry and to a theory that articulates stylishly the aesthetic merits of Shakespeare's presumed pederasty. The second, sunny-tempered Graham has an appreciation of comic style that replaces the preoccupations of the rest of the play. Spouting his silly epigrams, this Graham exalts a well-timed jest over moral earnestness and the search for a human essence. The scene at which he is the central figure is thus more than a collection of amusing epigrams: it is a fantastic world insubordinate to the culture's will to define identity, or heart.

At times, then, *Lady Windermere's Fan* contradicts all that the conventional plot encourages us to believe. The play's epistemology is undermined by the fantastic vision that, intruding into it, perceives its subjects from different angles, introduces different assumptions into the story, and in general subverts its structure and direction. The plot concerns a quest for identity, while other elements in the play suggest that identity, at least as it is imagined by the plot, neither exists nor matters. Only the audience's self-delusion, fostered by the more sentimental conventions within the play, can let it believe that at the end it has seen past the facades of the Windermeres and Mrs. Erlynne.

Fantastic structures occur again in *An Ideal Husband* when the moral understanding of identity confronts the heartlessness of wit. Caught in the toils of a blackmailer are an idealistic politician, Sir Robert Chiltern, and his wife, Lady Chiltern. The orange-haired schemer, Mrs. Chevely, wants Sir Robert to vote for a blatantly corrupt canal project. If he obeys her, he will lose his wife's love and the faith of his constituents. If he does not, Mrs. Chevely will publish a letter showing that he sold a state secret at the beginning of his career. His friend, Lord Arthur Goring, a feckless dandy with great reserves of character, learns of Chiltern's predicament. The lucky Lord finds Mrs. Chevely in possession of a bracelet he knows has been stolen, so that he is able to get Chiltern's letter from her. Mrs. Chevely spitefully steals another letter, one from Lady Chiltern to Goring. The wording of the letter is open to misconstruction, and so Lady Chiltern, who has been rather hard on her husband, now must fear him. In the end, Lady Chiltern confesses her error in judgment. With Goring's help, the Chilterns decide to go on with their lives rather than retire from the world in shame.

An Ideal Husband encompasses contradictory views of the self. Representing one view are the Chilterns. They are, in a debased, puritanical form, heir to the Romantic exaltation of experience and the individual. At the end, when their troubles appear to be over, Lady Chiltern assumes that their experience has redeemed and transformed them, declaring optimistically, "For both of us a new life is beginning." Wilde's inclination, throughout his career, was to point out the delusion present in such fits of self-interpretation.

Lady Chiltern and her husband do not possess the wide-ranging, complex minds of the Romantic individual merged with experience whom Keats envisioned in *Hyperion*:

> Knowledge enormous makes a God of me.
> Names, deeds, gray legends, dire events, rebellions,
> Majesties, sovran voices, agonies,
> Creations and destroyings, all at once
> Pour into the wide hollows of my brain,
> And deify me. . . . (113–18)

The god is now a reform minister, and "names, deeds, gray legends, dire events, rebellions" have become, in Lady Chiltern's words, "Factory Acts, Female Inspectors, the Eight Hours Bill, the Parliamentary Franchise" (8: 270–71).

However worthy, these pursuits curb and diminish the infinitely potential self, not only because of their mundanity but also because they represent the Chilterns' assumption that experience is interpretable, factual, and consistent. Without these assumptions, they could not be politicians working to change, or protect, a reality they believe they know.

Lord Goring, the dandy, contradicts the Chilternian epistemology, despite his ultimate usefulness. He creates and inhabits a fantastic world of disengagement, within which experience has no value and self is severed from identity. Illogic, exaggeration, and invention—modes of thought associated with fantasy—are congenial to Goring. Like Mrs. Erlynne, Goring sees himself as self-invented. He mistrusts experience, which does not appear to him to be a dependable, trustworthy agency for personal growth, telling Lady Chiltern that he knows "nothing by experience" of "practical life," though he knows "something by observation" (275). This comment is particularly striking since, as it turns out, he was once engaged to Mrs. Chevely.

In certain moods Goring severs language from experience, preventing the communication of information:

Lord Goring: . . . I am the only person of the smallest importance in London at present who wears a buttonhole.

Phipps: Yes, my Lord, I have observed that.

Lord Goring: (Taking out old buttonhole). You see, Phipps, Fashion is what one wears oneself. What is unfashionable is what other people wear.

Phipps: Yes, my Lord.

Lord Goring: Just as vulgarity is simply the conduct of other people.

Phipps: Yes, my Lord.

Lord Goring: (Putting in new buttonhole.) And Falsehoods the truths of other people.

Phipps: Yes, my Lord. . . . (312–13)

The epigrams resonate with the home truths we have come to expect and enjoy in Wilde. Yet in this exchange, Goring's epigrams also stand as mere parodies of definitive statements, for they lack a receptor. There is only the unmoved Phipps, whose "yes" is not the assent of one who learns. He merely humors Goring, as is Goring's desire, since humoring is in itself a form of noncommunication. This exchange has the rigorous parameters of a game: Goring must declare and Phipps humor, each stoutly maintaining a hierarchy of social power that has no meaning, as it encloses them in solipsism. This solipsistic hierarchy of empty power, where nothing definitive is said, heard, or accepted, contrasts sharply to the Chilterns' world, where power is understood to do good and evil.

In contrast to Goring, the Chilterns treat their pronouncements as being of crucial importance to others:

Lady Chiltern: (Sadly.) One's past is what one is. It is the only way by which people should be judged.

Sir Robert Chiltern: That is a hard saying, Gertrude!
Lady Chiltern: It is a true saying, Robert. (238–39)

Unlike the noncommital Phipps, Sir Robert is influenced and troubled by his wife's words. Moreover, if not for the collusion of her husband, Lady Chiltern would appear as much an egoist when she speaks as Goring. Sir Robert's willingness to be instructed, wounded, and harried by her gives her the illusion that her identity, expressed in words, is confirmed by the world outside her. What she understands to be truth is a protective delusion that allows her to persist in her puritan identity. In the Chilterns' world, what one says matters, since speech concerns an external world which must be explained and acted on. In Goring's world, and even more so in the world of *The Importance of Being Earnest*, where no one crosses over—like Goring—into the puritan world of purposeful action, speech is egoistic and uncommunicative. What one says hardly matters except to oneself, and perhaps not even then.

Rosemary Jackson sees in certain fantasies ''a negation of cultural order, insisting that there is no absolute meaning in the world, no value, and that beneath natural phenomena all that can be dis-covered is a sinister *absence of meaning*'' (57). Without the sinister effect Jackson feels, the negation of cultural order takes place in Goring's cheerfully solipsistic epigrams. Goring's world need not interpret the dominant culture, as in Jackson's view fantasies do; rather, it resists what Huizinga called ''seriousness,'' or the limitation of thought and action to what would illuminate, or be useful to, the ''reality'' implied by culture. Culture and fantasy are alike human creations, Wilde seems to shrug. Therefore, the absence of absolute meaning is not an occasion for angst, as Jackson suggests, but of infinite intellectual and emotional possibility for those ''superficial'' people who do not require an identity.

Goring removes his frivolity, like a coat, to handle Mrs. Chevely or reproach his friends, but he assumes it again when each task is finished. After he proposes to Mabel Chiltern, for example, he abandons his earnestness:

Mabel Chiltern: Do you mean to say you didn't come here expressly to propose to me?
Lord Goring: (Triumphantly.) No, that was a flash of genius.
Mabel Chiltern: Your first.
Lord Goring: (With determination.) My last. (381–82)

Like Mrs. Erlynne's resolution to remain childless, Goring's resumption of his ''disguise'' need not be dismissed as pretense that the play has taught us to see through. The philosophical strength of the disguise, particularly in contrast to the weakness of the characters who represent the cultural world of seriousness that the play also addresses, forces us to at least consider Goring's claim that his usefulness is an aberration and that he will never limit himself to an identity.

It would be most accurate to say that Wilde both confirms and overturns through Goring the epistemology of the Chilterns and the plot. Goring is the ethical center of the play, and, however inept he is at times, he is the chief problem solver. Yet, as in games, the concerns of the commonsense world can suddenly become irrelevant. From the point of view of Goring's frivolity, the play's plot exaggerates the inconsequential—human nature and proper behavior—and glances too casually at the essential—freedom. In this light it is possible to see Wilde's problem plays, with their internal self-contradiction, as the initial phase in a large, perhaps unintentional process that spans several years of Wilde's work. This process culminates in *The Importance of Being Earnest*, Wilde's most coherent, sustained fantastic vision.

The Importance of Being Earnest does not set out to discover what Wilde called, in "The Decay of Lying," "that dreadful universal thing called human nature," (297). Human nature is already known, taken for granted, and put casually into wicked epigrams. Instead, revelations are of superficial features, interchangeable names, and favorite poses. Wilde's purpose in exaggerating the artificiality of his characters is not purely satirical, as Stuart Hampshire observed: "[Wilde substitutes] the superficial for the profound, visible forms for spiritual states as the proper objects of emotion; and this without any satiric intent" (941). The play's artificiality and its exaggeration of style and structure, joined to its psychological improbabilities, produce a ludic, fantasy world in which undefined personality may be mutable and, therefore, freely creative.

In *The Importance of Being Earnest* levity has great influence over reality because of its power over appearance. In one scene Cecily constructs for herself the role of the maiden who enjoys a soothing spiritual influence on those around her. Her guardian Jack is furious with a man she believes is Jack's erring brother, Ernest. After delivering a little speech about the good that is in everyone, Cecily coerces Jack into making the most insincere of forgiving gestures:

Cecily: Uncle Jack, if you don't shake hands with Ernest, I will never forgive you.

Jack: Never forgive me?

Cecily: Never, never, never!

Jack: Well, this is the last time I shall ever do it. (Shakes hands with Algernon and glares.)

Chasable: It's pleasant, is it not, to see so perfect a reconciliation? I think we might leave the two brothers together.

Miss Prism: Cecily, you will come with us.

Cecily: Certainly, Miss Prism. My little task of reconciliation is over.

Chasable: You have done a beautiful action to-day, dear child.

Miss Prism: We must not be premature in our judgments.

Cecily: I feel very happy. (They all go off). (90–91)

Cecily makes for herself a little play, but only Chasable and Cecily speak their lines correctly. Miss Prism's unforgiving prudery and Jack's evident reluctance

mark the unreality of Cecily's sentimental scene, as does the "fact" that the
two men are not brothers. Cecily, however, has the last laugh when in the end
Jack and Algernon are discovered to be brothers after all. In a play whose plot
ostensibly revolves around the truths that people hide from others, a moment in
which people behave insincerely in front of a young girl turns out to be that
girl's triumph. It does not matter that Jack shakes Algernon's hand without real
forgiveness; events need only follow from outward appearance. The self that
lies below manners is entirely inconsequential. The fictional identities people
create for themselves are all that matter, since it is on this fictional plane that
they live and are happy.

In another scene—Jack's proposal to Gwendolyn—Gwendolyn confidently
redesigns the scene to construct for Jack and herself roles that will make them
happy. She starts the proceedings by encouraging Jack to speak his mind, which
he does clumsily: "Miss Fairfax, ever since I met you I have admired you more
than any girl . . . I have ever met since . . . I met you" (33). His is the ineptness
of a conventionally comic lover whose sincerity makes him inarticulate and of
a serious man bemused by a clever, whimsical woman. Likewise, Gwendolyn's
reply derives from the confidence of a certain type of comic heroine, "Yes, I
am quite well aware of the fact," but with a twist, "And I often wish that in
public, at any rate, you had been more demonstrative" (33). She is not so much
concerned for private as for public demonstrations of affection; happiness requires, or is, an audience. Ironically, the relationship she gestures to with the
words "in public, at any rate" is asexual. Indiscreet demonstrations of public
affection are performances, and in performance, not the meeting of two selves
at their most intimate, lies happiness. From the start Jack and Gwendolyn are
literary conventions: Gwendolyn merely elevates their conventionality to a desirable element of love. Identity and essence do not even receive lip service.

After extracting Jack's proposal, she pursues her favorite topic, role-playing:

. . . men often propose for practice. I know my brother Gerald does. All my girlfriends
tell me so. What wonderfully blue eyes you have, Ernest! They are quite, quite blue. I
hope you will always look at me just like that, especially when there are other people
present. (38)

That men propose insincerely, possibly with infamous intentions (or that women
regard the possession of a lover as a mode of self-aggrandizement), is true, but
to Gwendolyn the baseness of human nature is merely an interesting fact, and
facts, from her ludic point of view, do not affect the game. For Gwendolyn,
and for the play as a whole, each person's value lies in his or her power to play
a role, to carry out a little play before others. Jack will help Gwendolyn exploit
certain formal conventions that will allow her, and the others, to get married;
therefore she loves him—and he her. The scene promulgates, then, a fantastic
undermining of the principle of identity: human nature is reduced to the status

of fact, irrelevant in a society in which contentment lies in a game, or performance, well played.

Much of the comedy's fantastic effect derives from Wilde's language play, which elicits, then overturns or deconstructs, our assumptions. Wilde elevates surface by undermining meaning, for which, paradoxically, he has great respect. Because every line in *The Importance of Being Earnest* is at once sensible and absurd, the only way the hearer can digest the play is to be flexible, to take every possible point of view so that she may garner up many meanings. Similarly, words take on several, contradictory meanings, eliciting diverse perspectives from the hearer. By withholding and undercutting a word's standard interpretations, Wilde tries to create in his audience, as always, a state of fruitful uncertainty.

The characters assault the restrictiveness of meaning. Gwendolyn's explanation of her attraction to Jack reverses the normal meanings of the words *safe* and *safety*: "I pity any woman who is married to a man called John. She would probably never be allowed to know the entrancing pleasure of a single moment's solitude. The only really safe name is Ernest" (36). The constant companionship of one's beloved is unendurable. Safety lies not in having a man who can be depended on to stay at home but in having one who can be depended on to leave. Gwendolyn's various other pronouncements and innuendos throughout the play respect her belief that for a woman true safety lies in independence and an interesting instability to the marriage. Her fluid "self" will not be immobilized by an ideal, constant relationship. In the process of substituting her point of view on marriage for a more conventional one (according to which woman's "civilizing" pressure keeps the Huck Finns home), Gwendolyn strains the meaning of safety. It now represents a paradox: security lies in insecurity.

In another speech Gwendolyn multiplies the meanings of the word *develop*. In answer to Jack's romantic declaration that she is "perfect," she exclaims, "Oh! I hope that I am not that. It would leave no room for developments, and I intend to develop in many directions" (27). Gwendolyn's wording hints that her "developments" may not be entirely welcome to those around her. Ordinarily, to develop oneself means to develop one's mind and character, as in continuing one's education, but Gwendolyn puts her pious hope to better herself in spatial terms, "in many directions," as though she were planning to put on weight. Introducing the world of matter into the world of intellect, Gwendolyn's words admit to the mind images of unladylike, willful, and disruptive intrusion. Were she indeed as perfect as Jack says, she would be unchanging, inert; she would lay no claim on space or on the patience of her friends. The vagueness of her words augments her ominous tone, since her developments are unspecified—hence unpredictable and uncontrollable by others. Her words may bring to mind evolution, to the nineteenth-century mind a competitive, sometimes violent, battle of life. All in all, Gwendolyn promises to be no angel in her house.

Other words turn out to have no meaning at all and are thus withdrawn entirely from the effort to promulgate any epistemology. Wilde uses *marry, devotion,* and other such words in ways that are neither cynical nor idealistic, but nonsensical: "But although she may prevent us from becoming man and wife, and I may marry someone else, and marry often, nothing that she can possibly do can alter my eternal devotion to you" (57). Gwendolyn here plays the part of a girl in a conventional romantic situation, torn from her lover but in love with him all her life. The phrase "and marry often" subverts this conventional situation as well as the meanings of "marriage" and "devotion." For one thing, to "marry often" takes from marriage its dreadful permanence. Marriage will not be a barrier between Gwendolyn and Jack if she can slip from one marriage to the next. Furthermore, Gwendolyn's mention of marriage connotes a lusty exuberance that overrides her grief at being separated from Jack. "Marriage" thus stands neither for true love nor exile from love as it does in the conventional stories. Yet Wilde does not subvert the word with an alternate, cynical meaning. His is not the satire of restoration comics; Gwendolyn does not confess here to lust or greed disguised by her willingness to marry often. The play has already established that human qualities such as these are uninteresting facts. They could not, therefore, diminish marriage, as they are merely incidental to it. Marriage simply has no meaning at all, though it has value, since everyone in the play is trying desperately to be married. Each character is simply more complex than are the conventional meanings of marriage, so that marriage becomes in *The Importance of Being Earnest* something sought yet incomprehensible.

Parenthetical clauses often contradict the sentiments and thus the epistemology implied by main clauses. When Jack informs Cecily that she must wait till she is 35 to marry Algernon, she retorts, "waiting, even to be married, is out of the question" (155). Her words are not unexpected, only the structure of her sentence; she ought to have said simply, "waiting to be married is out of the question." Put into the main clause, a general principle receives the weight of her sentence, while her particular desire is relegated to a parenthesis. By taking marriage out of the nominative case and putting it into the parenthesis, Cecily undercuts her romantic posture. She reduces marriage to testing a general rule, the impossibility of waiting for anything. She has asked the question an impetuous romantic never asks, whether the end is worth the frustration. What should have been a passionate cry of resentment reveals a rational weighting of the advantages of marriage over the disadvantages of waiting.

Similarly, the other characters frequently drop their passionate poses to set the facts straight or to speculate, if not always coolly, about their own temperaments and the nature of the universe. Under adversity, Jack collapses into piteous accuracy. He has just admitted to Lady Bracknell that as an infant he was discovered in a handbag at Victoria Station.

Lady Bracknell: The cloak-room at Victoria Station?

Jack: Yes. The Brighton line. (46–47)

Accuracy transforms passion into illogic when Gwendolyn declares to Jack, "If you are not too long, I will wait here for you all my life" (162). In all this, Wilde inverts the commonplace that civilized demeanor conceals an emotional nature. Rather, our nature is rational. In our most passionate moments our uncontrollable reason and self-discipline assert themselves. The irrepressible unconscious is not tumultuous with feeling. It is measured and measuring, like the revealing sentences that the characters construct. Romance thus is not founded in instinct, though it is no less desirable, in *The Importance of Being Earnest*.

The speed with which Wilde puts together inappropriate ideas and grammatical patterns augments the fantastic fragmentation of sense in the play. Algernon's advice to Jack shifts focus in every phrase: "If you ever get married, which seems to me extremely improbable, you will be very glad to Bunbury" (8: 24). He posits Jack's marriage, casts doubt on its ever occurring, and insinuates that Jack will be glad to get out of it, all in one sentence. Each new idea would elicit emotion, but the sentence does not allow Jack to respond. Should he contemplate the idea of his marriage, he must tear himself away from that happy daydream to consider with angry frustration what may prevent it. He must then ponder irritably why Algernon thinks he should want to flee from Gwendolyn and what sort of retort to make. His mind has no time to do the thinking Algernon's loaded phrases require. They become, as a result, effectively meaningless.

The pacing of Jack's account of his history to Lady Bracknell augments the impact of its absurdity:

The late Mr. Thomas Cardew, an old gentleman of a very charitable and kindly disposition, found me, and gave me the name of Worthing, because he happened to have a first-class ticket for Worthing in his pocket at the time. Worthing is a place in Sussex. It is a seaside resort. (45)

Each line introduces a point of view that contradicts others. Mr. Cardew's "charitable and kindly disposition" encourages us to expect a sentimental story about a powerful fatherly figure who, as in stories like *Oliver Twist*, seems placed by a purposeful providence to save and rear the orphan. Cardew's casual manner of naming the baby after a sea resort undercuts his stature, however, by implying a certain wooly-mindedness about him. Trying to tell these objectionable truths, Jack becomes absorbed in facts. They are worthless facts; that Worthing is a seaside resort adds nothing to his cause or to anyone's knowledge of him. Thus, during his speech he takes the audience far from a sentimental point of view to one that explores inadequacy and helplessness. Jack's final inability to communicate parallels the inability of the initial sentimental viewpoint to transcend, control, and stabilize the meaning of Jack's history.

The fantastic elements in these comedies contradict the view that love, not to mention identity itself, is natural and innate. Characters like Gwendolyn and Mrs. Erlynne are conscious that they and their companions play a part in order to feel a sensation, yet they are content to be at once fantasists and forms. Still,

Wilde's vision of humanity as surface is not Wilde's epistemology. That Wilde's characters take the time to choreograph their love affairs may be insightful, but they seem ludicrous nevertheless. Perfect form in human affairs is absurd to the degree that it neglects human spontaneity. Thus, Wilde encourages us to laugh at the perfect symmetry of *The Importance of Being Earnest*, at the three couples clasping at the climactic moment. The natural self is delusion, but its obverse, the artificial self, seems just as ridiculous. The ideal to which the tumbling fantasy of Wilde's comedies truly aspires is expressed finally in R. P. Blackmur's words, "the formula has somehow seized enough life to become form again" (6).

NOTES

1. William Coyle argues that fantasy is a mode, not a genre. See his "Introduction."
2. The danger in this direction is that it becomes increasingly difficult to distinguish fantasy from other genres criticizing social norms and values or exploring various psychological conditions.

WORKS CITED

Bersani, Leo. *Baudelaire and Freud*. Berkeley: University of California Press, 1977.

Blackmur, R. P. *Language as Gesture: Essays in Poetry*. New York: Columbia University Press, 1980.

Coyle, William. "Introduction." *Aspects of Fantasy: Selected Essays from the Second International Conference on the Fantastic in Literature and Film*. Ed. Coyle. Westport, Conn.: Greenwood Press, 1986. 1–3.

Hampshire, Stuart. "Oscar Wilde." *New Statesman* 63 (1962): 941–42.

Holman, C. Hugh, and William Harmon. *A Handbook to Literature*. 5th ed. New York: Macmillan, 1986.

Huizinga, J. *Homo Ludens: A Study of the Play-Element in Culture*. Boston: Beacon, 1950.

Irwin, W. R. *The Game of the Impossible: A Rhetoric of Fantasy*. Urbana: University of Illinois Press, 1976.

Jackson, Rosemary. *Fantasy, the Literature of Subversion*. London: Methuen, 1981.

McCarthy, Mary. "The Unimportance of Being Oscar." *Theater Chronicles 1937–1962*. New York: Farrar, 1963. 106–110.

Peckham, Morse. "What Did Lady Windermere Learn?" *College English* 18 (1956): 11–14.

Rabkin, Eric S. *The Fantastic in Literature*. Princeton: Princeton University Press, 1976.

Sartre, Jean-Paul. "*Aminadab*, or the Fantastic Considered as a Language." *Literary and Philosophical Essays*. Trans. Annette Michelson. New York: Collier, 1955. 60–77.

Todorov, Tzvetan. *The Fantastic: A Structural Approach to a Literary Genre*. Trans. Richard Howard. 1973. Ithaca, N.Y.: Cornell University Press, 1975.

Walkley, A. B. Review of *Lady Windermere's Fan*. *Academy* 5 March 1892: 257–58.

Wilde, Oscar. *The Complete Works of Oscar Wilde*. 12 vols. New York: Doubleday, 1923.

———. "The Decay of Lying." *The Artist as Critic: Critical Writings of Oscar Wilde*. Ed. Richard Ellman. New York: Vintage, 1969.

2

A Task Most Difficult: Staging Yeats's Mystical Dramas at the Abbey

Frederick S. Lapisardi

Yeats's occult studies were as deeply woven into his plays as they were into his lyric poetry and his prose. When he was just 27 years old, the poet wrote to his friend and mentor John O'Leary:

If I had not made magic my constant study I could not have written a single word of my Blake book, nor would *The Countess Kathleen* have ever come to exist. The mystical life is the centre of all that I do and all that I think and all that I write. (*Letters* 211)

This was 1892, the same year Yeats published a poem called "The Death of Cuchulain," later revised and retitled "Cuchulain's Fight with the Sea" (*Variorum Poems* 105), which supplied subject matter, in varying degrees, to three plays—*On Baile's Strand*, *The Only Jealousy of Emer*, and *The Death of Cuchulain*. The last of these was written on his deathbed. In *The Death of Cuchulain*, the dying Cuchulain tells the Blind Man that he sees "The shape that I shall take when I am dead." That vision, "a soft feathery shape," Cuchulain terms "a strange shape for the soul / Of a great fighting-man" (*Variorum Plays* 1060–61). What Cuchulain envisions is consistent with theories expressed by Yeats in *A Vision*, the central philosophical study based largely on occult materials the poet claimed to have gathered through automatic writing. As with so many of his major principles, these occult theories of Yeats's last years, though enlarged by a lifetime of studies, remained a major ingredient in the molding of his dramatic work.

But the problem here is not to prove that Yeats's plays are filled with mythic, fantastic, and supernatural elements. An hour or two skimming through *The Collected Plays* gives ample evidence of that. The problem now, as it was when the plays were written, emerges when they are produced on any stage. The task becomes doubly difficult when the production is at Yeats's own Abbey Theatre where his success at pushing J. M. Synge, Lady Gregory, and Lennox Robinson down everyone's throat resulted in a deeply ingrained tradition of popular, realistic, dialect plays.

In 1989, James W. Flannery took up the challenge of producing the full canon of Yeats's dramatic work at the Abbey, and he began with the Cuchulain Cycle. Loosely based on mythology found in the Irish epic *Tain Bo Cuailnge*, but more directly for Yeats on Lady Gregory's dialect translations *Cuchulain of Muirthemne*, these plays are filled with fantastic elements. A well spews forth the water of eternal life. A challenge from a mythical Celtic figure results in a head for head game similar to that found in *Gawain and the Green Knight*. A power struggle between king and champion culminates in a father/son fight to the death kindled to flame by the fear of witchcraft. Cuchulain's life is saved, at the cost of his love, in a contest between his wife, Emer, and Fand, a woman from the other world. After the death of the legendary Cuchulain, tricked into mortal combat by forces beyond his control, Emer dances amid symbolic severed heads. The cycle ends with a jarring musical time leap into the twentieth century.

In 1990, under the general theme "Masks of Transformation," Flannery offered three more plays: *Cathleen ni Houlihan*, in which, promising certain death, the spirit of Ireland in the guise of an old woman lures a young man from his family and bride-to-be on the eve of his wedding; *The Dreaming of the Bones*, a Noh-influenced dance play about an encounter between a young survivor of the 1916 Easter Rebellion and a pair of 700-year-old ghosts; and *Purgatory*, where an old man, who may himself be trapped in a dream after life, kills his son to free his mother's soul from reliving its own transgressions.

To stage the fantastic elements of poetic drama in a theater so long immersed in realistic and largely commercial traditions[1] requires a large degree of kinship with those souls who, after "the crumbling of the moon," choose "whatever task's most difficult / Among tasks not impossible," as they are described in Yeats's "The Phases of the Moon" (*The Poems* 163–67). James Flannery understands this. In an *Irish Times* interview with Richard Pine (9 September 1989), Flannery spoke of his efforts "to reinstate Yeats in the theater he founded" so that "there will no longer be any question whatsoever as to the viability of Yeats as a dramatist." That is indeed a task most difficult because Flannery knows only too well that Yeats's antirealistic poetic drama, steeped as it is in mythology and the occult, has never gained popular or critical acceptance in Dublin.

With the exception of *Cathleen ni Houlihan*, which haunted Yeats enough to ask, "Did that play of mine send out / Certain men the English shot?" (*The Poems* 345),[2] none of these works was ever a popular success during the playwright's lifetime. Although Yeats thought enough of *On Baile's Strand* to use it on the opening program for the Abbey Theatre in 1904, it earned mixed reviews at best (Hogan and Kilroy 128–31), as did the revised and retitled *The Green Helmet* in 1910 (Hogan, Burnham, and Poteet 24–25). By the time he wrote *At the Hawk's Well*, *The Only Jealousy of Emer*, and *The Dreaming of the Bones*, Yeats had removed himself from the popular stage and had begun writing for small, select audiences.[3] Although he later returned to the stage, he never lived to see some of his best plays produced, no less accepted as good theater.

In *W. B. Yeats and the Idea of a Theatre*, Flannery attributes Yeats's initial failure to weak productions and to unimaginative reviewers:

Yeats suffered because he was still struggling to create an appropriate form for his plays and then to find artists capable of interpreting them, but to an equal extent, his difficulties in finding an audience were caused by the unwillingness or inability of critics to stretch their imaginations far enough to fully comprehend his extraordinary dramatic intentions. (349)

It is those "extraordinary dramatic intentions" that Flannery has explored in his staging of the plays for the W. B. Yeats International Theatre Festival at the Abbey. Although most of the immediate reviews were favorable,[4] Richard Allen Cave's more studied account of the 1989 Cuchulain Cycle in *Theatre Ireland* (Spring 1990), reflected some of the very concerns Flannery mentioned to me when we were in rehearsal for the 1990 Yeats Festival. Cave expresses major dissatisfaction with "the standard of Abbey acting" and asks, rhetorically; "Why is it that Abbey actors, who are happily confident of exploring the poetic dimensions of realistic plays, appear so vulnerable when playing in actual poetic drama?" He found his answer in two production flaws, "the apparent refusal of most of the cast to submit to the discipline of Yeats's verse; to allow its rhythms to work the dramatic effects," and in the lack of physical discipline:

In performance, a physical discipline has to be found to match that verbal stylisation: you can not move naturalistically in expressionist forms of theatre any more than Japanese actors would consider moving naturalistically in Noh. (25)

The only times when Cave found movement in keeping with the subject matter occurred during those moments when unnatural elements took center stage:

. . . the Sidhe because supernatural, the masked characters (the Old Man of *At The Hawk's Well* and the Fool) because symbolic and Cuchulain and Aoife because, presumably, they were deemed strange and "other" with their wild, warrior sensibilities—all moved in a rhythmic and stylised manner. The rest moved naturalistically. (25)

It is never quite clear in Cave's article whether the success in these instances should be credited to the dancer or the dance. The only three actors who seemed to please him from the cast of 16 were Ciaran Hinds as Cuchulain, Olwen Fouere as Aoife, and Derek Chapman as the Old Man. But in singling out their work for praise, he soundly rejects that of the others: "The trouble was that it was glaringly obvious what was wrong, because the few actors who really had the measure of Yeats's stylistic demands made the rest seem worse by comparison" (26).

In a letter to *Theatre Ireland* (3 January 1991), Flannery refuted Cave's claim that the production was "compromised" by the limitation of the Abbey actors. But when he selected the cast and went into rehearsals for the second year of the Yeats Theatre Festival, Flannery took steps to correct related weaknesses he had himself detected. Olwen Fouere returned in the central roles of Cathleen ni Houlihan, Dervorgilla, and the spectral mother from *Purgatory*. Derek Chapman was engaged as co-director. Almost every member of the cast had some musical background. From the first week, rehearsals began with an hour of intensive movement work under the direction of Sarah-Jane Scaife. As composer Bill Whelan completed each piece of music, he brought it in on tape and worked with the cast not only to get the vocal aspects down but to integrate the words and music with Scaife's Bhtoh-inspired stage movement.

The conflict between the actors' natural inclination to play scenes realistically and Flannery's insistence on keeping almost everything—particularly the mythic and supernatural elements—on a strictly expressionistic plane could have developed into a serious problem with a less resilient set of actors and directors. As it was, the players attempted to give Flannery what he asked even when they did not understand the motives behind a move or a particular piece of business. That, for an actor, is also a task most difficult. As literary advisor/dramaturg to the Yeats Festival, I participated in the preparations for staging the plays alongside the players. The cast had spent the first week going over the text word by word, movement by movement, discussing motives and trying phrases with different intonations. Flannery, a singer himself, demanded a range that often began in a barely audible, lower-body rumble and reached a pitch so high that the resulting sound was hardly discernible from the screech of Yeats's lonely seabirds. On the floor, Sarah-Jane Scaife constantly called for slow, flowing movement "from the pelvis" rather than from the head.

In the beginning, as we ran scenes in the immense, sun-drenched (July 1990 was one of the sunniest months on record in Dublin) rehearsal room beside the Abbey roof garden, dark moments—such as Cathleen's triumph over parents and fiancée for Michael and her inevitable and chilling victory over the father for the soul of the boy, Patrick, and the section of *The Dreaming of the Bones* after the ghost of Dervorgilla blows the Young Man's lantern out—seemed fine because we all understood that the physical conditions would change once we moved to the small, dark Peacock Theatre stage. But Flannery did not like what he saw. It was all too realistic.

We went back to the ring of sofas away from the rehearsal room acting area and reexamined every line in all three plays. We reconsidered motives. When, in *Cathleen ni Houlihan* do the parents, Peter and Bridget, realize that they are dealing with something more than a poor old woman and that she will take both of their sons from them? How does Cathleen reveal her true nature to Michael and win his devotion? Why does she win the sons, but not Peter? In *The Dreaming*

of the Bones does the Young Man actually see the ghosts once his lantern is
out? Does he know before he says the words that they are not natural? How
should the ghosts act toward him? Is any of this "real," or is it all something
out of the deeps of the Young Man's mind? And in *Purgatory*, are we witnessing
the Old Man's dreaming back after he is dead, or is he still alive and killing his
son for the first time? Does the audience see what is in the burned-out window
along with the Old Man or only later when the Boy sees it? Do they see anything
at all?

Flannery keeps to Yeats's text. The words do not change. But as he explained
to Christopher Griffin in the first of a two-part interview for *Theatre Ireland*
(September 1989), "To do each one of Yeats's plays, you've got to find out
what is the human thing he is trying to say" (9). To find what he calls the human
element, Flannery goes in search of the play's "inherent dramatic values" (9),
and this entails experimentation with all of the elements of stagecraft. When
Flannery says "to do Yeats justice, you have to invent a theatrical language to
perform him" (6), he does not mean that he is going to alter Yeats's words; he
intends, rather, to throw out all traditional concepts of how those words are
presented. Flannery believes, as he told Griffin, that "Yeats was the great
dramaturg of the whole Irish dramatic movement" (8) and that "Yeats is a
pathway to much of the experimental theatre of our own time" (6).

It was in this spirit that we put the plays back on the rehearsal floor and began
to experiment. Flannery had always seen the chorus, for example, as an integral
part of all three plays, although Yeats only wrote them into *The Dreaming of
the Bones*.[5] But Flannery props one Yeats play against another to build a total
night in the theater. The chorus is a ghostly presence throughout. With Sarah-
Jane Scaife's slow, intense movement, they weave in and out of the action, not
as an intrusion but as a reminder that there is more going on here than the plot
line of the play.

The theme of the entire Second Annual W. B. Yeats International Theatre
Festival was "Masks of Transformation," and in keeping with that idea the
lectures, symposia, art show, poetry reading, lunchtime Beckett plays, and the
central Yeats production, all focused on the changes that had and were taking
place not only in Ireland but throughout Europe and America. There was a sense
behind all this time past, present, and future. Nothing was static, especially our
handling of the Yeats plays. They really never were set. We experimented with
certain lighting effects, for example, right through previews and into the run.
In any production, performance will vary from night to night, but here it was a
more conscious thing. After a performance, we would discuss different aspects
of the production over a few drinks at the Flowing Tide, and the next night these
ideas would usually find their way on stage.

The ending of *Cathleen* never did work right. Early on in rehearsals, John
Olohan, who played the father, went down on his knees and drew young Patrick
to him in a tight embrace when he asked, "Did you see an old woman going
down the path?" (Yeats's stage directions read simply, "to Patrick, laying a

Exhibit 2.1. Olwen Fouere (Cathleen) strikes a pose from the Flannery production of *Cathleen ni Houlihan* for Abbey Theatre staff photographer Fergus Bourke. Photo: Frederick S. Lapisardi.

Exhibit 2.2. Derek Chapman directs an early *Purgatory* rehearsal. Left to right: Conor Mullen (Boy), John Olohan (Old Man), Chapman, and Flo McSweeney (chorus). Photo: Frederick S. Lapisardi.

Exhibit 2.3. Olwen Fouere (Dervorgilla) and David Heap (Diamuid) work out their stylized entrance as the ghosts in *The Dreaming of the Bones*. Photo: Frederick S. Lapisardi.

hand on his arm''); Yann McMahon, as Patrick, delivered what is possibly the most difficult curtain line in all of Yeats's plays: "I did not, but I saw a young girl, and she had the walk of a queen" (*Variorum Plays* 231). The point here, of course, is that the father *wants* the boy to see an old woman rather than the spirit figure of Cathleen who will lead him, as she did his brother, to death in her service. When Olohan grabbed the boy it drove the true meaning of those lines home with all their chilling force, but it also drew attention away from the ghostly figure of Cathleen slowly moving across the stage. Flannery would have none of it. He was dissatisfied with the ending, but he knew that he did not want that much realism. Cathleen moved upstage to blend into the chorus, while the boy moved on a straight line from downstage left to center stage where the father stood. But night after night, the curtain line sounded uncomfortably like Denis Johnston's parody of it in *The Old Lady Said "No!"*: "The Walk of a Quee-in!" (Johnston 47), and the final effect was more ludicrous than chilling.

Over dinner one evening during previews, I suggested a compromise to Flannery. Let the father grab his son as John Olohan had been doing earlier, but then let the boy twist away from him to deliver the last part of that line while we hit just his face with a pinpoint spot which we could hold for about a three count before going to black. We used the light after that, but Flannery still refused to allow the father to grab his son. He was at least half right, of course, but not the half I thought at the time. If the whole point of not embracing the boy is to shift emphasis away from the realistic action of the family and on to the symbolic Cathleen, who herself had a heart-pounding scene during the "It is a hard service they take that help me" speech, the spot should have been fixed on her as she drifted, between father and son, toward the audience, and the boy's line should have come to us out of the darkness. That way we could have built even more on Olwen Fouere's gradual revelation of Cathleen's true supernatural essence and carried *that* into the chorus of *The Dreaming of the Bones* rather than the sense that the unnatural choral figures served merely as a transitional phase as the boy from *Cathleen* merged somehow with the again realistic rebel on the run from the 1916 Easter uprising.

Another unresolved problem developed at the point in *The Dreaming of the Bones* when the ghost of Dervorgilla blows out the Young Man's lantern. Just before this happens, he calls both spirits to him: "Who is there? I cannot see what you are like. / Come to the light." But then Yeats's stage directions read, "The Girl blows out lantern," and the Young Man says, "The wind has blown my lantern out. Where are you?" (*Variorum Plays* 764). It would seem that what follows, until the sun begins to rise toward the end of the play, should be played in near or total darkness. But Flannery, who understands Yeats's theories as well as anyone and better than most, insisted that the entire scene be played in cold, even light, with no change when Dervorgilla's ghost blows out the lantern. There's justification for this. As far back as the publication of *Samhain: 1904*, despite his admiration for Gordon Craig's lighting techniques, Yeats wrote:

Mr. Gordon Craig has done wonderful things with the lighting, but he is not greatly interested in the actor, and his streams of coloured direct light, beautiful as they are, will always seem, apart from certain exceptional moments, a new externality. One should rather desire, for all but exceptional moments, an even, shadowless light, like that of noon, and it may be that a light reflected out of mirrors will give us what we need. (32)

What is more, *The Dreaming of the Bones* is one of Yeats's dance plays. Based on observations he made in the introduction to *Certain Noble Plays of Japan* about the effect of Michio Ito's dancing—"In the studio and in the drawing-room alone, where the lighting was the light we are most accustomed to, did I see him as the tragic image that has stirred my imagination" (*Essays and Introductions* 224)—it would seem obvious that the only way to play the scene is in cold, natural light. But these arguments fall apart when we consider that, by extension, all of the scenes in all of the plays would have to be done with natural lighting, and they were not. In fact, the mostly direct lighting was used for this scene only, and once the principals began to wind their way up the pathway past the ruined Abbey of Corcomroe and the chorus resumed its vocal part, the lights were dropped and the stage was much darker than it had been before.

To add to the problem, when these scenes were done at the earlier rehearsals, David Heap, as the ghost of Diarmuid, offered to help the young rebel as one who understood and even sympathized with his plight, and Conor Mullen, as the Young Man, accepted the help as though he believed the ghost to be a comrade-in-arms. With this reading, there is a double betrayal behind the climactic revelation that these spirits are actually Diarmuid and Dervorgilla who first brought the Normans into Ireland, who are responsible for the 700-year-old crime that remains the root cause of all this youth has rebelled against, and who now seek his forgiveness so they can be reunited at last. The Young Man first trusts them and accepts their help because he thinks they are people both of his world and of his sympathies. When the scene was first played, all of the motives, those of the Young Man and those of the two tortured spirits, could be explained in real terms. That was what the actors liked about the approach, and it was the very thing Flannery objected to. The ghosts seemed too much like real people. The entire interpretation was too realistic. Their whole method of delivering the lines was too conversational. It all had to be changed, and it was.

Flannery's use of cold, bright light was consistent with his reading of the encounter between the Young Man and the two spirits. By leaving the stage lights up during the initial scene, the entire encounter comes into question. Just before the Young Man sees the ghosts, the First Musician, or in the case of Flannery's production, the chorus speaking alternate lines, informs the audience that "He stumbles wearily, and stumbling prays" (*Variorum Plays* 763). He is exhausted, and his mind may be about to play tricks on him. In the same sense that the strange figure out of the sea may be a fiction of the young captain's mind in Joseph Conrad's "The Secret Sharer," these spirits may be born of necessity from the mind of the young rebel in Yeats's play.[6] It is another case of a task most difficult facing not only the director but also the actors who have to understand the interpretation so that they may work out proper readings and enable the audience to grasp the director's intent.

The major problem in all this is that Yeats invariably anchored his supernatural elements in reality. Not only is the Abbey of Corcomroe a real place, but the surroundings are exactly as Yeats uses them in the play. David Heap and Olwen Fouere visited the abbey one weekend and made the trek up the summit that the ghosts and the Young Man make during the action of the play. They brought back pictures to prove that every reference, even to the three natural rest areas where the characters stop, is in reality exactly as Yeats presents it. And Yeats does that in all of his work.[7] He regularly ties the supernatural to the real. There is no doubt that Flannery's reading of this play fits his overall intent to tie Yeats's plays into modern experimental theater, but it is not necessary to eliminate all realistic interpretation and effects to keep from undercutting Yeats's concerns with the supernatural. If anything, the real elements heighten the effect of the unreal. Yeats's work is filled with tension arising from such contrasts. Richard Ellmann pointed out long ago in *Yeats: The Man and the Masks* that, torn between the roles of "dreamer or a heroic man of action," the poet "deliberately magnified his sense of self-division" (289). This sense of division is everywhere in his plays, and, because of it, fantastic elements constantly struggle against realistic ones for control. The key is to keep either one from winning that struggle.

Flannery proved the point himself in his staging of *Purgatory*. None of Yeats's plays better exemplifies his ability to put his dramatic theories into practice.[8] But, despite the importance of the dead mother and her lover to the overall theme, the work can be performed with little or no visual manifestation of these spirits on stage.[9] The lines are so strong that such a production stands in danger of allowing the realistic elements to outweigh the supernatural.

Again, in rehearsal, Flannery saw this danger from the start. John Olohan as the Old Man and Conor Mullen as the Boy brought such power to their roles that we all were swept along with the reality of what unfolded again and again before us. The most chilling moment came with a bit of business Derek Chapman worked out for the scene just after the Old Man stabs the Boy. The Old Man cradles his dead son in his arms and croons the lullaby "Hush-a-bye baby, thy father's a knight, / Thy mother a lady, lovely and bright." As the symbolic tree is bathed in light, Olohan took the limp head of the dead boy between his hands and turned it toward the tree as he delivered the lines: "Study that tree" (*Variorum Plays* 1948–49). Though the effect was electrifying, Flannery was not satisfied. The scene missed on the psychic level. He worked in a counterbalance. The chorus, carrying almost barbaric-looking driftwood branches and a wooden hoop, *became* the tree and the window. The mother and the groom, totally naked and bathed in red light to counter the earlier symbolic white, emerge out of the chorus to act out their part as the Old Man tells his story. They appear again at the end of the play. Flannery's use of light and flesh to represent the supernatural could have tipped the scales in the other direction, but Olohan and Mullen's performances were too strong to be swept aside. Instead, a balance was struck. The play worked.

Flannery, probably the most experienced professional director of Yeats's drama active today, refuses to accept the once common opinion that this is just so much mystical nonsense and that the man would have been better off had he ignored the theater and spent his time writing more lyric poems. Flannery believes in the Yeats plays as living, modern theater, and he understands the enormity of the task he has undertaken in producing all of the plays at the Abbey Theatre.

The Irish have a term, *slagging*, to describe their custom of poking fun only at people they accept and respect. Possibly despite but more likely *because of* those touchy moments described here, which continued through a month of rehearsals, a week of previews, and a three-week run, there was pure "slagging" in the best sense behind Conor Mullen's comment when he expressed the general attitude of the cast toward Flannery and for what he was trying to do in the teeth of the Abbey's almost 100-year-old realistic tradition: "The man's *mad*, but he's a genius! We're all learning something from him."

One of the things we learned was the theatrical importance of the fantastic and the supernatural to Yeats's plays. Every time Flannery refused to accept a realistic reading or piece of stage business, every time he pushed the production away from the ordinary, away from the expected, he acted according to his comprehension of Yeats's "extraordinary dramatic intentions" (Flannery 349).

The supernatural is not simply something tacked on to these works; as an integral element in every one of the Yeats plays, the mystical vies constantly against the natural for control. Both must be represented with equal force for the production to succeed. Flannery's recognition of this internal conflict and his great regard for Yeats's dramatic power drive him back to Dublin each year to attempt what is most difficult among tasks not impossible. It is part of his genius, just as it is part of Yeats's, and it springs from the same source.

Mysticism is that central element that the 27-year-old Yeats wrote about in his letter to John O'Leary. Without it, and without the ensuing constant clash between the realistic and the supernatural, neither Yeats's plays as we know them nor Flannery's daring productions at the Abbey could have ever come to exist.

NOTES

1. Despite its history as the first government-subsidized theater in the English-speaking world, the need for financial stability has never been a topic totally alien to the Abbey directors. In an *Irish Times* editorial (8 August 1990) lauding the appointment of Garry Hynes as artistic director of the National Theatre, the observation was made that the Abbey could not afford to take too many risks because, even with a subsidy, it must fill 70 percent of its seats for every performance to keep its book out of the red.

2. In an interview with Christopher Griffin (*Theatre Ireland* September 1989, 5–11), Flannery explains how in his 1981 production of *Cathleen ni Houlihan* at the Lyric Theatre in Belfast he shifted away from the usual approach to this play as "a simplistic piece of war propaganda" by printing those lines on a large banner and displaying them prominently over the stage. He also dressed Cathleen in "a skull-like mask based upon an actual photo of Maud Gonne's face in old age. . . . The character also wore a blood-red rather than traditional black, cloak."

3. As recently as 28 August 1989, Eric Bentley, quoted in the *Irish Times* from his lecture at the Peacock Theatre for the First Annual Yeats Theatre Festival, repeated his smug charge based on *The Playwright as Thinker* (187–89) that Yeats was "hostile to the idea of an audience. He liked to play to three English ladies in a drawing room." This is both an oversimplification and a misreading of Yeats's dramatic goals.

4. Only David Nowlan of the *Irish Times* expressed a dissenting opinion, and this was offset somewhat by Fintan O'Toole's very positive "Second Opinion" column a few days later (16 September 1989) and by Nowlan's history of dissatisfaction with productions of this type.

5. On a visit to Anne Yeats, a few days before the opening of the 1990 Yeats Theatre Festival, I began to say something about Cathleen emerging from the chorus when she comes into the Gillane house.

"But there's no chorus in *Cathleen ni Houlihan*," she said.

"There is now!" I told her in a not too subtle effort to prepare her for the shock of opening night. Anne Yeats had staged the Abbey's first production of her father's *Purgatory*, and while I explained a few of Flannery's experiments staging that play, too, I do not believe I mentioned that the mother and her groom would appear before the Old Man and the Boy, and of course the entire audience, totally naked.

6. Flannery never came right out and said this, but he certainly is familiar with the "deeps of the mind" approach which Barton R. Friedman applied to the Cuchulain cycle (*Adventures in the Deeps of the Mind: The Cuchulain Cycle of W. B. Yeats*. Princeton: Princeton University Press, 1977), and there is no reason why such a theory could not be applicable to *The Dreaming of the Bones*.

7. See James McGarry's *Place Names in the Writings of William Butler Yeats* (Toronto: Macmillan of Canada, 1976) for an interesting compilation of many such references.

8. See my article "A Most Conscious Craftsman: A Study of Yeats's *Purgatory* as the Culmination of His Expressed Dramatic Theories" (*Eire-Ireland*, Winter 1967) for a closer look at this point.

9. Anne Yeats told me that she had to make do with a hole cut in a simple black backdrop for the window when she created the set for the original production at the Abbey in 1938. When I directed a faculty performance at Bronx Community College of the City University of New York in 1966, we used neither window nor tree but allowed the lines to carry the effect.

WORKS CITED

Bentley, Eric. *The Playwright as Thinker*. New York: Meridian, 1955.

Bushrui, S. B. *Yeats's Verse Plays: The Revisions 1900–1910*. Oxford: Clarendon, 1965.

Cave, Richard Allen. "Time for a Yeatsian Revolution." *Theatre Ireland* 22 (1990): 22–26.

Ellmann, Richard. *Yeats: The Man and the Masks*. New York: E. P. Dutton, 1958.

Finneran, Richard J., ed. *Critical Essays on W. B. Yeats*. Boston: G. K. Hall, 1986.

Flannery, James W. *W. B. Yeats and the Idea of a Theatre: The Early Abbey Theatre in Theory and Practice*. New Haven: Yale University Press, 1976.

Friedman, Barton R. *Adventures in the Deeps of the Mind: The Cuchulain Cycle of W. B. Yeats*. Princeton: Princeton University Press, 1977.

Griffin, Christopher. "Memories and Prophecies." *Theatre Ireland* 20, 21 (1989): 5–11, 14–19.

Hogan, Robert, Richard Burnham, and David Poteet. *The Rise of the Realists 1910–1915. The Modern Irish Drama: A Documentary History IV*. Dublin: Doleman Press, 1979.

Hogan, Robert, and James Kilroy. *Laying the Foundations 1902–1904. The Modern Irish Drama: A Documentary History II*. Dublin: Doleman Press, 1976.

Johnston, Denis. *Selected Plays of Denis Johnston*. Chosen and with an introduction by Joseph Ronsley. *Irish Drama Selections 2*. Gerrards Cross, U.K.: Colin Smythe, 1983.

Lapisardi, Frederick S. "A Most Conscious Craftsman: A Study of Yeats's *Purgatory* as the Culmination of His Expressed Dramatic Theories." *Eire-Ireland* 2.4 (1967): 87–95.

McGarry, James. *Place Names in the Writings of William Butler Yeats*. Toronto: Macmillan of Canada, 1976.

Pine, Richard. "Cuchulain: From Gang Leader to Hero." *Irish Times* 9 Sept. 1989, weekend: 5.

Yeats, William Butler. *Essays and Introductions*. New York: Macmillan, 1961.

———. *The Letters of W. B. Yeats*. Ed. Allen Wade. New York: Macmillan, 1955.

———. *The Poems*. Rev. New York: Macmillan, 1989. Vol. 1 of *The Collected Works of W. B. Yeats*. Ed. Richard J. Finneran and George Mills Harper. 14 vols. 1989– .

———. *Samhain. October 1901–November 1908*. Rpt. Complete in 1 vol. with additional material. Introd. B. C. Bloomfield. London: Frank Cass, 1970.

———. *The Variorum Edition of the Plays of W. B. Yeats*. Ed. Russell K. Alspach. New York: Macmillan, 1966.

———. *The Variorum Edition of the Poems of W. B. Yeats*. Ed. Peter Alt and Russell K. Alspach. New York: Macmillan, 1965.

———. *A Vision and Related Writings*. Comp. and ed. Norman Jeffares. London: Arena, 1990.

3

The Perilous Edge: Strindberg, Madness, and Other Worlds

Peter Malekin

"It is an axiomatic truth that madness is an inherent phenomenon in all profound artistic manifestations." This observation was made by de Chirico, who defined madness, after Schopenhauer, as a loss of memory. Madness in this sense made a break in habitual perception, with its framework of assumed cause and effect, purpose and origin. "That which constitutes the logic of our normal acts and our normal life, is a continuous rosary of recollections of relationships between things and ourselves and vice versa"; madness removed it from us. The mind was thus exposed to the raw shock of a world devoid of its protective covering of explanation. The "reality" dispensed with was a mental set fixed on the mind like inbuilt spectacles by education, upbringing, and social pressure. The reality exposed was "the spectral or metaphysical which can be seen only by rare individuals in moments of clairvoyance or metaphysical abstraction" (Chipp 450). This metaphysical reality might well be multiple—level opening out of level.

Madness in de Chirico's sense is closely related to the fantastic. Both reformulate reality. It is this reformulation that distinguishes the fantastic from mere fantasy, which ultimately leaves the world much as it found it. It was into a fantastic akin to madness that Strindberg was moving in his late plays. In them he is concerned with the metaphysical—that is, the relationship between mind and matter, consciousness and the physical world. This relationship is now commonly regarded as a closed question by our culture and one that must not be reopened, rather like the locked door in *A Dream Play*. Because of the presence of metaphysical issues, the late plays create problems for the critic, lodged as he or she usually is within the predictability of an everyday "reality." To explain the late plays in terms of psychoanalytical theory or to approach them merely as social or political comment is to explain them away. In their immediacy of impact the plays indeed go further than merely dislodging particular conventional assumptions; they call in question the validity of the whole enterprise of explaining human life, whether by rationality or some kind of religious believing.

In this respect, the late plays are akin to the ontological decentering of language insisted upon by Derrida; just as Derrida can be interpreted in very different ways (a Nietzschean interpretation tending toward nihilism, a Midrashic toward a repeated endeavor of inevitably superceded understanding, a Buddhist toward the mind's leaving behind the relativity of language), so the late plays can be interpreted differently by critics and experienced differently in theatrical production. The more interesting responses to the plays have included those of Quigley, Artaud, and Serban (quoted by Goodman).

Austin E. Quigley sees modern theater generally as breaking down the barriers between pluralistic mental worlds. Each world is its own linguistic structure and the crossing of the barriers is an extension of selfhood in the sense of a change or expansion of self-conception. One great virtue of this approach is its explanation of the sense of freedom and growth that ideally forms part of audience response to drama (its limitations are underlying assumptions about the nature of language and the human mind).

One of Quigley's sources of inspiration was Antonin Artaud. Artaud is exhilarated by the anarchic assault potential of total theater, in the sense of the total language of mime, movement, costume, sound and music, lighting, and so on. On the other hand, "Theatre which submits staging and production, that is to say everything about it that is specifically theatrical, to the lines, is mad, crazy, perverted, rhetorical, philistine, antipoetic and Positivist,—that is to say, Western theatre" (*Theatre* 30). He thus favors the "metaphysical inclinations" of Balinese theater to the "psychological inclinations" of western theater, for Balinese theater, with its ritual and its depersonalized characters, seems "to teach us the metaphysical identity of abstract and concrete" (*Theatre* 41). "All creativity stems from the stage in this drama, finding its expression and even its sources in a secret psychic impulse, speech prior to words" (*Theatre* 42). Here Artaud's intuitive experience hovers at the frontier of his theoretical understanding. "Speech prior to words" implies a knowledge of the nonarticulate sources of articulation, an adequate working model of the human mind. The explicit model that Artaud tends to fall back on is the one that was current in surrealism.

The liberty of most surrealism was an oddly licensed liberty, seeking rational respectability despite itself. Breton's first manifesto declares boldly: "Under colour of civilisation, under pretext of progress, all that rightly or wrongly may be regarded as fantasy or superstition has been banished from the mind, all uncustomary searching after truth has been proscribed" (quoted in Gascoyne 60). It then goes on to praise Freud for discovering the strange forces harbored in the depths of the mind. Yet Freud was himself appropriating the irrational in the name of the rational, fixing it into the rationalist framework by reducing much that undermines the validity of the dominant western mode of thinking to a manifestation of the subconscious.

Up to a point Artaud follows Freud, though he also draws on Taoism and eastern thought. He seems to seek through the physical the unity of mind and matter, but he intermittently appears to view mind as an epiphenomenon of matter.

For Strindberg too the physical was never far away, but he often disliked it. Being aware of the psychic, he was also aware of the physical as limiting consciousness and fullness of sensory perception, like Indra's Daughter in *A Dream Play*, who complains of "feeling my sight made weak by an eye, my hearing dulled by an ear, and my thought, my bright aerial thought, bound in the labyrinthine fatty convolutions of the brain" (Act III, original translation). This awareness he shared with Blake (though such awareness tends to be discounted in interpretations fashionably current).

Nonetheless, Artaud finds Strindberg congenial and finds *The Ghost Sonata* appealing: "It gives the feeling of something which is a part of a certain inner reality, without it being either supernatural or inhuman. And that is its attraction. It shows nothing but what is known, although hidden and out of the way" ("Production Plan" 97). His plan for the production of the play envisages a constant shift in the sense of reality, bringing out the play's "constant denaturation in appearances":

voices changing tone arbitrarily, overlapping one another, sudden stiffening of attitudes and gestures, lighting changed, decomposed, unusual importance suddenly given to a small detail, characters *morally* fading away, leaving the noises and music dominant, and being replaced by inert doubles, in the form of dummies, for example, which suddenly take their place. ("Production Plan" 97)

He also notes the rich symbolism and theatrical domination of the old man in Act I and the function of the house as a center of attraction.

Artaud has difficulties, however, with Act III. He dislikes the student and the girl being kept apart by "all the inconveniences of life, all the little household tasks, above all eating and drinking, in short the bodily carcass, the weight of things" so that "Deliverance only comes with death." This "Buddhist thought" is one of the play's "faults," although "the religious sense of the ending may be minimised in production." The ending, however, "may also clarify the play for . . . those who would be frightened by the purely unconscious" ("Production Plan" 99). (His own interpretation could equally be seen as clarifying the play for those who are frightened of the spiritual.) Artaud thus explains away a concern with ultimate questions in *The Ghost Sonata*, since ultimate questions are already answered in his view by the idea of the unconscious. Despite this interpretive decision, however, Artaud has a prodigious sense of the play's force in production terms and does it full justice as potential theatrical experience.

Like Artaud, Andrei Serban also picks up the juxtaposition of realities in the play, though he interprets the juxtaposition within a different frame of reference:

It seems to me that Strindberg, writing this play towards the end of his life, was trying to see through everyday reality to reality of another sort so that, as in Shakespeare's final romances, the real and the unreal, the visible and the invisible are present simultaneously. Here there is a special concern for and inclination towards something spiritual, for music and for art. (Goodman 442)

Here the alternative reality is not *a priori* labeled as the unconscious, and there is a place for the *spiritual*, a term which at least seems to imply something more than the intellectual.

Strindberg's text does indeed articulate a concern with alternative worlds, especially the world after death. His immediate sources are clear. At one remove stands Swedenborg with his interest in the psychic levels intermediate between the gross physical and the spiritual. More immediately, as Strindberg himself noted, is the *kama loka*, or desire world, of the Theosophists, the bardo plane of *The Tibetan Book of the Dead*, the first psychic level entered by the dead on shedding the physical body. There, according to Swedenborg and the Theosophists, the mind begins by recreating its earthly environment or a world akin to its earthly beliefs, but this world is gradually reshaped as the mind faces in a ruthless projected mirror its own hidden desires and memories and aspirations. The process is rendered briefly and very tellingly in "A Theologian in Death," which Borges translated from Swedenborg.

Since, for Theosophists and Swedenborg alike, the factor shaping this immediate postmortem state is the hidden desires of the mind, their views do have affinity within the notion of the unconscious. There is also, however, a difference, for the level entered after death is for them also an alternative reality in its own right, which precedes, succeeds, and underlies physical life. Physical life thus ceases to be the solely real "reality."

Strindberg was not simply illustrating the doctrines of Theosophy, despite the detail as well as major themes drawn from it, and the play is not simply a rendering of *kama loka*. Rather it uses the idea of *kama loka* as one aspect of an interpretative model for our world, producing a metaphor that is also a double correspondence (looking to this world and the psychic level, psychological states here and apparently objective realities there). The effect is achieved by mingling the idea of *kama loka* with the neoplatonic idea of this world as hades, an idea used to reinterpret Christian tradition in Act III: "They say that Jesus Christ descended into hell . . . but that was really His pilgrimage on earth: to this madhouse, this prison, this tomb we call earth. And the inmates killed Him when He tried to set them free, but they let the thief go" (Goodman 471). This theme is worked out much more fully in *A Dream Play*. Its presence changes the nature of the *kama loka* element, making the play world ambiguous, neither the world of the dead nor the world of the living. While not quite of this world, the characters have another world of death and the dead beyond them, and some of them see in it the newly dead Consul and the Milk Maid.

A similar ambiguity and freedom is attained, especially in Act III, through a development out of the theosophical idea of the Buddha and Christ as both members of a lodge of spiritual masters. Neither figure is constrained by the doctrines of the respective religions. Each, in its development, is seen as part of "myth," to be treated as the Greeks treated their religious myths. The myths are adapted and read in new ways. They are not absolute frames of reference, and they are not stories to be placed within some other absolute frame of reference such as psychoanalysis. They are part of a shifting referential complementarity. Hence the audience's mode of apprehending frames of reference is itself shifted. This makes any attempt to extrapolate the "meaning" of the play, except through itself in production, reductive, and usually reductive in the extreme. The element of the fantastic in the play is thus adoctrinal, itself a new and freer mode of apprehending, reaching beyond the limitations of discursive rationality and into the imaginative and creative. Nevertheless, it remains a mode that gives new life to the old metaphysical questions, including questions concerning "established" doctrine.

The established and the establishment are both savaged in *The Ghost Sonata*. There is a constant undermining of personality and role identity. The Colonel, whose personality is his role, turns out not to be a nobleman and not to be a colonel, but an ex-footman. The Baron is a jewel thief, Hummel is a vampire, and so forth. Similarly, the conventional morality is a farcical pretense, a means of manipulation and gaining power. This remains true even of the good and the wronged. The Mummy uses her suffering and repentance to break Hummel's power but forces him into her cupboard to commit suicide, while tasking a moral rise out of him by claiming that she and her companions are superior in that they do not like what they are. As the vampire cook observes: "You suck the marrow from us, and we suck it from you" (Goodman 469). The vampires are human and the humans are vampires, and the characters all live off one another. Conventional moral categories and a conventional moral resolution are replaced by an interlocking nexus of relationships that are so intimately tangled that there is no way out of them. The characters are, as they feel themselves to be, trapped. One consequence of this is again an infringement of the individual, this time as supposed autonomous moral agent. There is a total action with no foreseeable end, and within it individuals periodically swap roles and identities.

Conventional morality is replaced by something different, or the hope of something different, in Act III, though the ambiguities do not disappear. The scene is dominated by the statue of the Buddha, a very peaceful icon, and by the hyacinths that surround the Young Lady. The symbol of the hyacinth is explained at some length in the dialogue and combines the Hindu-Buddhist iconography of the lotus, as used by Eliot in "Burnt Norton," with the Christian temporal expectation of a heaven on earth. The hyacinth is also identified in the opening words of the act as the flower of the Young Lady's soul.

At the opening of the act, the Young Lady's joy in the hyacinths contrasts with the Student's reaction, which is ambiguous. He loves them and explains their symbolism, but at the same time he claims that they hate him, poison him, blind him, deafen him, drive him out of the room, and set his head on fire. To begin with it is the Student who seeks worldly happiness by proposing to the young woman, who disabuses him of his illusions about the aesthetic perfection of life in her room by pointing out its shortcomings and the attendant drudgery of maintaining it in the teeth of sabotage by the housemaid. She also eludicates the activities of the vampire cook, who cannot be got rid of, and she rejects childbearing and rearing in the midst of these imperfections with the question "Is life worth that much trouble?" (Goodman 469). She is intent on getting away from the world of the room, not living in it. To this extent she seeks truth rather than compromise with appearances.

The Student is more uncompromising. Whereas the Young Lady believes in frankness only "within reason," he adheres to the Blakean adage that standing waters breed reptiles of the mind. Once his proposal is rejected, he insists on uttering all that he knows about the shortcomings of those he has been associating with in the course of the play. Berating the world for not living up to the perfection of his imagination, he claims that "Your flowers have poisoned me, and now I am poisoning you," and when he plucks the harp it is silent.

The relationship between the Young Lady and the Student, rooted in thwarted love and idealism, seems to be developing in much the same way as earlier relationships in the play, and indeed it grows out of them and is tainted by them, as the Student points out. There is in the minds of both, however, the possibility of an alternative world, different from the worlds of the living or the newly dead, even though it is not immediately realizable. The Student and the Young Lady are the only characters to invoke the imagination, and the Student is the only character to use it to pursue the truth in the sense of the essence of things and a vision of their alternative functioning.

The ending is ambiguous. The Young Lady is killed by the Student's insistence on speaking the truth. Her death might lead to something better. The Student prays to the Buddha in uncertain hope. He makes a double declaration about his imaginings: "I saw the sun, / And I seemed to see the Hidden One" (Goodman 471). The sun suggests a vision of happiness in this life and his attempt to marry the Young Lady; the Hidden One suggests the ultimate Reality, the Absolute by whatever name (the Void, Brahman, Plotinus's One, the godhead). The happiness of this world turned out to be dogged by imperfections; the greater the proposed happiness, the greater the imperfection. The Hidden One he did not see, but *seemed* to see.

The subsequent moral aphorisms have no support from the earlier dramatic action, which emphasizes nemesis but not its avoidance through right action, though they do gather some symbolic resonance as the harp springs to life and the stage is bathed in white radiance.

Meanwhile, the picture of Böcklin's "Island of the Dead" also appears in the background. The picture was presumably clearly visible in Strindberg's Intimate Theatre, with its audience capacity of 161. The picture is the final ambiguity, since the tall figure on the boat can be seen as looking either toward the island or away from it, and the boat can be interpreted as moving in either direction.

The Ghost Sonata eschews easy answers. Moral categories and categories of reality are undercut, and individual personality is undermined. Feeling and reason are undivorced and contradictory views are encouraged in the awareness of the audience, while sudden shocks lay open its sensibility, as Hummel rides in triumph or slumps in abject terror, or the Mummy emerges from a cupboard to grasp someone from behind (this was before Hollywood had vulgarized the horror potential of the incident). The play lays bare what our culture regards as better hidden and better not asked about. It exposes those aspects of experience that do not fit, that have to be suppressed to make any conventional frame of reference—material, spiritual, or religious—appear adequate.

The probing of appearances and opinions is carried further in *A Dream Play*, which combines a more coherent symbolism with many of the techniques of *The Ghost Sonata*. The symbolism starts with the design of the opening curtain, which shows the constellations of Leo, Virgo, and Libra with the planet Jupiter shining brightly in the midst, and it is continued in the dialogue of the Prelude. The sun is in Libra, or the Scales, a sign associated with the deliberate weighing of alternatives and with forms of partnership, preeminently marriage. Indra's Daughter has just left behind Shukra, a reference to the story in the *Devi Purana* and elsewhere that the great spiritual teacher Shukra was so successful in teaching the *asuras*, or enemies of the gods, that the gods were nearly defeated and the balance of the universe was threatened. To restore it, Indra's daughter Jayanti ("Victorious") served and then married Shukra and prevented him from continuing his tuition, so that the gods were saved. Shukra is also the planet Venus, which presides over the constellation of the Scales, and Venus is both the morning and evening star. Jupiter is the planet of the guru, or spiritual instructor, in Indian astrology. In moving from Shukra as morning star to the Scales presided over by Venus as evening star, the Daughter enters an area of balance between what the Platonists termed the earthly and the heavenly Aphrodite, foreshadowing the tension through the play between her roles as spiritual guide and as earthly woman, mistress, wife, and mother.

The Prelude casts the horoscope of the incarnating Daughter, who descends from the celestial or spiritual world, through the psychic to the third or material world, leaving behind Indra, who is traditionally the cosmic Self, or rather the Self-aware self. From this opening the double structure of the play unfolds. The major characters are, as Strindberg's prefatory note suggests, aspects of one mind (Indra, the divine ground; the Daughter, spiritual intelligence; the Poet, creative imagination; the Lawyer, discursive reason, and so forth). They are also characters in a biography. The Daughter is a young woman in Act I, a wife and mother in Act II, and an older spiritual teacher in Act III; and she mounts her funeral pyre in the Epilogue. In Act I she falls in love with the Officer and attempts to free him. In Act II she marries the Lawyer, and when her marriage collapses, elopes with the Officer, her girlhood sweetheart. In Act III she refuses to return to domesticity, derides approved conventional learning, and retires into solitude to instruct the Poet in ultimate truth. Interspersed are scenes of social comment, which also often give information about the lives of the other major characters, and visionary scenes, such as that in "Indra's Ear" (the end of the universe as the sea of time and space and the beginning of the universe as vibratory subtle sound, an actual level of consciousness).

Within this framework there develops a nexus of interlocking symbols. The rose is traditionally a symbol of Christ's passion and of earthly love, and it transmigrates from the Officer's bouquet, which becomes thorns, to Christ's crown of thorns given to the Lawyer instead of the laurel wreath used in the ceremonial award of doctorates, and to the roses of Victoria (corresponding to Jayanti, "Victorious"), the Officer's unfaithful love, as she goes into the pur- gatorial ovens of the Quarantine Master. The roses are linked to the other flower symbols—the hollyhock (literally "stock-rose" in Swedish), the aconitum ("storm-hat," a cure for fever), the heliotrope longed for by the Daughter during her marriage, the flower of the castle or great house with seven walls, the symbol of incarnated man (recalling the seven human principles of the Theosophists and the flower symbolism used in the hyacinth scene in *The Ghost Sonata*). Claus- trophobia and airlessness recur. The sulphur fumes of the Quarantine Master link with the ineffective sulphurous fumigation of the Lawyer's office. Christ appears and reappears in the passages from the liturgy and the walking on the water described in Act III. The symbols ramify in scene after scene, and they are too numerous to record.

Two sets of symbols, however, recur and dominate the ending of the play. Water and earth are set over against fire and air. Earth recurs as mire or mud, figuring especially in the Poet's mud bath. Water occurs primarily as the sea, with strong overtones of the Platonic sea of time and space, which become explicit in the Song of the Waves with its reference to gestation and generation. The sea is always presented as treacherous, whether to the He and She of golden love in their boat or to the sunk and sinking ships of the last act. Air is often felt by those choking through its lack and figures in the Song of the Winds as the spirit that blows through the material world, experiencing it but untainted and untrammelled by it. Fire is purgatorial in the burning heat of the ovens and the sulphur fumigations but is in itself purifying. It is into the final pyre that the majority of the characters throw the limiting factors that have dogged and nar- rowed their lives, and it is the fire that sets the Daughter free. It is also fire that consumes the great house at the end, as the chrysanthemum flowers on its roof and the myriad faces of shifting human moods go up with it. For a Nordic public the conflagration would carry overtones of the fire that destroys the old order of the universe before the new order and the return of Baldur the Beautiful in Norse myth.

Within this symbolic structure is set the wisdom of earthly experience that is usually the province of realism. The Daughter's marriage and divorce is played out in a page or two of dialogue, which shifts rapidly and sometimes abruptly in tone and nuance, making unaccustomed demands on the skills of the actors. Undercutting irony and sardonic humor abound. Brief remarks such as the Quarantine Master's "So what?" when the Officer discovers that it is *his* Victoria in the boat with another man, carry a world of bitter experience with them. Social comment is balanced: the misery of the coal heavers with an appetite and no dinner is set off against the misery of the rich man who owns the birds of the air, and the fishes of the sea, as well as the forests and human habitations on land but who is blind and has lost his wife and loses his son. The play does not register necessarily the worst forms of misery, or list all forms of misery, but it probes the essence of the human suffering that dogs life even in its joys. This essence is located by the play not in the physical as such but in the cramping of human consciousness when it allows its experience through the physical to cost it the freedom of its own inner nature. Again the thought is Blakean.

Despite the coherence of the symbolism and the way the action sums up worldly experiences, the play is emphatically not a kind of emblematic allegory with a closed system of meaning as its referent. Two factors work against this. The first is the counter-structure of skepticism in the play; the second is the theatrical technique. The Daughter is ambiguously placed as both the victim of all right-thinking people and the official representative of a cosmic order that is supposed to guarantee justice. To a lesser extent, the same is true of the Lawyer. The Lawyer, the tool of justice, is hideously aware of injustice and also of sheer meaninglessness, especially in the inexplicable divorce feudings that start over a bowl of lettuce or some other triviality. Law prevents or hinders awkward questions in thwarting the attempts to open the locked door, bars the coal heavers from going swimming or picking fruit in the heat, and systematizes the hatred and lust for vengeance of the Lawyer's clients. It falls to the Daughter to defend supposed religious justice and the workings of providence. These are arraigned by the Poet's diatribe on Lena in the incident of the return of the prodigal Daughter, by the Poet's list of complaints in the last act, and by a host of minor incidents and the recurring refrain "Mankind is to be pitied." At times, indeed, these elements almost degenerate into whining. Nonetheless, the questions to which they give rise recur in life, and they prove to have no answer of the simple rational kind. The final "explanation" is instead given to the creative imagination of the Poet in the form of myth.

Similarly, the dramatic impact of the play is different from the symbolic structure that can be extracted from it, rather as the experience of moving through a building is different from the structure that props it up. The sharp cuts from scene to scene, the alternations of light and pitch dark, the juxtaposition of realist and symbolic elements, the sudden switching in mood and intensity, the ritualistic recurrences in action and dialogue, the sudden changes in the characters themselves, the mental quality of the physical props and backdrops and their unlike likenesses as they change, together with the Ensor-like juxtaposition of the mask and masklike face of the Quarantine Master and Lawyer with the unmasked faces of the other characters—all produce a constant dislocation of audience sensibility. The madness induced is the madness of de Chirico that removes the habitual frame of reference. With this technique the audience has no symbolic meaning thrust upon it; rather, there is room for an uneasy inkling of a hidden order, no more, and the final conflagration could be experienced as destruction rather than resolution.

In so far as there is any possibility of resolution it is in the opening of the door and in the myth told to the Poet by the Daughter in Act III. The two incidents occur in that order for good reason. As the Deans of the four university faculties point out, there is nothing behind the door. Since the *Nicomachean Ethics*, in which Aristotle rejected Plato's transcendent Good or Absolute, the infinitude beyond the boundaries of subject and object, with the demand ''Show it to me'' (that is, turn it into an object), the general tenor of Western culture and theology has been positivist; it has demanded that ultimate reality appear as an object. The Deans, with their positivist bias, reject the emptiness as meaningless, or a fraudulent response to the question of the nature of reality; they try to turn it into an idea that can be manipulated. The Daughter's view is that seeing, they have not seen; they have failed to understand. The alternative approach to the Absolute is preserved in the west within the Platonic tradition and was summed up by Plotinus when he said that you could know the Absolute as an object, but only by entering a state in which you are your finite self no longer (quoted in Stace 112). In this sense, the nothing behind the door is the Brahman without attributes, the Buddhist Void, or the *Nichts* (Nothing) of Jacob Böhme. It is the failure to know this reality that lays the Deans of the learned disciplines open to satirization for inconcludable wrangling over a learning that is without basis.

The emptiness behind the door leads on to the myth of Maya. The idea of maya is based on direct experience. If infinitude becomes established as the ground state of awareness, yet all other experience is in terms of changing subject-object boundaries, then there is a gap or radical difference between these two modes of consciousness (Maharishi 150–51, 170, 313). The name of that gap is maya. Until the gap is experienced, maya has no real meaning, and it is said that when the relative and Absolute are finally experienced as one, maya is transcended. The Daughter's myth of Maya is therefore an imaginative means of pushing at the limits of human understanding, of opening the mind to new ways of experiencing.

The myth of Maya and Brahma is also told with a western emphasis on sin and death, which relates it to other recurring concerns. Throughout the play to this point, the negative aspects of sexual relationships have been stressed. The male characters have pursued a dream of beauty that has ended in disillusion. The females have found themselves trapped by domesticity, poverty, and child rearing, and in the case of the Daughter have been torn between a vocation and family duties. Nonetheless, they have yearned for sexual love. The fall of Brahma for the purpose of creation symbolically unites the two aspects and gives a mythical base for the vision of cosmic beauty that haunts the love relationships.

Equating the fall and creation, in the manner of Böhme, it also shifts any ensuing blame from humanity to God.

The myth of Maya and Brahma is thus itself twofold and ambiguous. From a structuralist position it could be seen as symbolically reconciling the irreconcilable contradictions in our culture. From a psychoanalytical position it could be seen as pointing towards a resolution of conflicting forces emerging from the unconscious mind. From a metaphysical point of view it could be seen as moving the mind towards an opening into pure consciousness, which is a very different matter from the psychoanalytical unconscious. From all these points of view, however, the play does focus urgent concerns of contemporary living and dying.

Strindberg was himself approaching death when he wrote *The Ghost Sonata* and *A Dream Play*, and he had lived much of his life on the perilous edge of madness. He was also, like Milton's Satan on the perilous edge of battle where it raged, in the front line of a rebellious struggle against what his culture and its standards, internalized in his own nature, had made of God. With three marriages and two divorces behind him, and a third to come, he was not without insight into the difficulties of sexual relationships. He had suffered legal prosecution by the right thinking. He suffered interminably from debt. He was, in an unconventional fashion, immensely learned. He was ferociously, though sometimes guiltily, independent in intellect. He was sensitive, often to the point of paranoia, and all the time he sensed behind the thin wall of matter another dimension to life. His use of the techniques of the fantastic in his later plays had behind it the drive of a lifetime's experience and the thrust of a lifelong quest. In these plays he honestly faced the unfaceable while refusing to blur the issues or opt for the easy answer. To us as readers or audience these considerations may be irrelevant, but the resulting plays brought back into western drama much that had been excluded for centuries. They could not have done so without the techniques of the fantastic, and they did so by using the full technical range of the modern theater. The fantastic thus moved back into the mainstream of modern drama as a powerful weapon. The plays themselves have undiminished force and a range of resonance that has yet to be fully exploited in production. They are indeed becoming contemporary, for we are beginning to catch up with them. To label them expressionist or symbolist is inadequate; only the fantastic now has the explosive power to shatter the restrictive and the erroneous and, potentially at least, to free the mind to rise beyond boundaries to a state of truth.

WORKS CITED

Artaud, Antonin. "Production Plan for Strindberg's *The Ghost Sonata.*" *Collected Works.* Vol. 2. London: Calder, 1971. 97–105. 4 vols.

————. *The Theatre and Its Double.* Trans. Victor Corti. London: Calder, 1970.

Borges, Jorge Luis. "A Theologian in Death." *A Universal History of Infamy.* Trans. Norman Thomas di Giovanni. Harmondsworth, England: Penguin, 1975. 103–105.

Chipp, Herschel B., ed. *Theories of Modern Art: A Source Book by Artists and Critics.* Berkeley: University of California Press. 1968.

Gascoyne, David. *A Short Survey of Surrealism.* 2nd ed. San Francisco: City Lights, 1982.

Goodman, Randolph. *Drama on Stage.* 2nd ed. Fort Worth, Tex.: Holt, 1978.

Maharishi Mahesh Yogi. *On the Bhagavad-Gita.* Harmondsworth, England: Penguin, 1969.

Quigley, Austin E. *The Modern Stage and Other Worlds.* New York: Methuen, 1985.

Stace, W. T. *Mysticism and Philosophy.* London: Macmillan, 1960.

4

Wassily Kandinsky's Stage Composition *Yellow Sound*: The Fantastic and the Symbolic Mode of Communication

Kent W. Hooper

Prominent expressionists productive in more than one medium, such as Wassily Kandinsky, Ernst Barlach, Oskar Kokoschka, Alfred Kubin, and others, are frequently alluded to, although the relations among their works in the varying media are seldom explored. More specifically, scholars rarely consider in detail lesser known literary works by artists generally associated with nonliterary media—for example, Arnold Schönberg's dramas, Paul Klee's poems, Hans Arp's prose and poetry, or Wassily Kandinsky's poems and stage compositions.

Wassily Kandinsky, primarily known for his works in the visual arts, reminisces in 1938 about his volume of poems, *Sounds*, published in 1913 but written in 1908–12—that is, during the same brief period he worked on his stage compositions:

For many years I have written, from time to time, "poems in prose" and even some "poetry."

Which for me means a "change of instrument"—the palette put aside and in its place the typewriter. I use the word "instrument" because the force that prompts me to work always remains the same, that is to say, an "inner pressure." And it is this pressure that often asks me to change instruments.

Oh! I remember very well; when I started "writing poetry" I knew that I would become "suspect" as a painter.

In the past they used to look "askance" at the painter whenever he wrote—even letters. They almost expected him to eat not with a fork, but with a brush.

Those were hard days, filled with strict "divisions" and rather simple in their logic. If the theorist thinks without being able to paint, it is up to the painter to paint without being able to think.

Those were the days of the "analytical" world of specialization, permanently divided from one another, the "boundaries" of which were not to be crossed. (2:817)[1]

Kandinsky conceived his stage composition *Yellow Sound* in 1909;[2] it was first published in 1912, when it was included in *The 'Blaue Reiter' Almanac*, and it was not performed until after the death of the artist.[3] Although the significance of this almanac to the history of modern art has long been acknowledged, *Yellow Sound* was virtually overlooked until the mid–1960s, primarily because it contains so many unconventional—that is, fantastic[4]—compositional elements. Indeed, only in 1975 does one locate the first attempt, by R. W. Sheppard, to interpret systematically this piece.

Early critics of *Yellow Sound*, including Sheppard, are unable to come to terms with the stage composition because they are unaware of the ground rules of Kandinsky's narrative world. And as Eric Rabkin remarks in *The Fantastic in Literature*, "unless one participates sympathetically in the ground rules of a narrative world, no occurrence in that world can make sense" (4). Sergei Eisenstein, for example, feels that the stage composition "evokes obscurely disturbing sensations—but no more than this" (117), adding that he finds a "total absence of content—as well as theme" (115). Although he admits there are scenes where "one eventually senses the presence of some mystic 'seed,' " Eisenstein argues that "it would be very difficult to arrive at any clear definition of [this 'mystic' seed]" (114). Such a reading confirms Rabkin's suspicion that "where there is no frame of reference, no set of perspectives waiting to be fulfilled, assaulted, or reversed, [one] apprehends almost nothing" (14).

On the whole, critics have shied away from interpreting *Yellow Sound*. R. W. Sheppard's explanation for this is that "most writers dealing with Kandinsky are art historians and not literary critics" (165), as if to imply that it is not the business of art historians to consider literary texts, even if done by someone known primarily as a visual artist. Sheppard does note that in 1958 the art historian Will Grohmann, in his book on Kandinsky in which works in all media are considered, is "relatively prolix, devoting several paragraphs to the drama" (165); but Sheppard also remarks that Grohmann too concludes the stage composition defies interpretation. Indeed, Grohmann characterizes *Yellow Sound* as "an unreal dream play, archaic, dark, pointing to the unknown . . . with the action . . . remaining unfathomable" (100).

Literary critics who have considered Kandinsky's stage composition, as Sheppard also appropriately contends, are generally "not much more informative" than the art critics (166). Lothar Schreyer in 1948 attempted to make sense of *Yellow Sound* (166), yet Sheppard quite convincingly argues that Schreyer often "reads his own ideas into *Yellow Sound*" (168). Nonetheless, despite Sheppard's claims to the contrary, Schreyer's main contention that the piece is essentially a utopian work (80) proves valid, as will be demonstrated.

Sheppard shows that Paul Pörtner merely confines himself to lengthy generalities which add up to the conclusion that nothing concrete can be said about the drama (166). Sheppard also feels little is to be gained by consulting Horst Denkler's analysis, although the latter's remarks are praised as being "more extensive than Pörtner's, and more helpful to the extent that they link [*Yellow*

Sound] with Kandinsky's theory of colour'' (166). Sheppard astutely identifies that despite all the background material related to the literary historical epoch and the lengthy descriptions of and quotations from the stage composition he provides, Denkler also is eventually forced to characterize *Yellow Sound* as ''hermetic—impervious to interpretation . . . ; [it is reduced by Denkler to a succession of mere] '*Stimmungskomplexe*' [see Denkler, *Drama* 35]: intuitively but not conceptually graspable'' (166).

Although not mentioned by Sheppard in his review of research on *Yellow Sound*, Christoph Eykman, writing in 1974, fully accepts Denkler's reading of *Yellow Sound*, without contributing further supporting evidence: ''What actually 'happens' . . . cannot be definitively interpreted. This has already been pointed out by Horst Denkler in his careful analysis of the text'' (148).[5]

While Denkler never does arrive at what could be termed an interpretation of *Yellow Sound* (Eykman's contention that Denkler's analysis is ''careful'' is accurate only in relation to the virtually vacuous analyses that preceded it), he at least places the stage composition and some of its compositional elements within a historical context. Denkler mentions similarities between *Yellow Sound* and ''Mimodramas'' (32–33), dramas featuring mime and gesture, and also lists characteristics of *Yellow Sound* that reflect literary trends or concerns of writers at the turn of the century—such as the antipathy toward conventional naturalism in drama and toward the reliance on dialogue and the belief that language was no longer able to convey existential truths (33). Thus, to his credit, Denkler successfully deflates claims that *Yellow Sound* stands out as a truly revolutionary, creative effort, a view propagated by many of Kandinsky's friends and early worshipers—Thomas von Hartmann, for example, who in an unpublished speech in New York in 1950 called *Yellow Sound* ''the greatest venture of stage art to this day'' (Lankheit 42).[6]

Most pertinent to this study, however, is Denkler's assertion that, in part, compositional weaknesses inherent in *Yellow Sound* allow for many elements to be interpreted in a number of different ways (36). And yet, it is not weakness that allows for multiple interpretations; rather the possibility of different and yet equally valid readings demonstrates the presence of the symbolic mode of communication, as will be explained.

Sheppard, noting the inadequacies of previous studies of *Yellow Sound*, advocates a critical reevaluation of the stage composition (168) and yet in the remainder of his essay unfortunately fails himself to arrive at many significant insights. Like Denkler (*Drama* 34–35) and even Schreyer (80), Sheppard does note that color assumes a symbolic or allegorical function in *Yellow Sound* (168). But he does not expand significantly upon this insight and instead merely summarizes (168–70) Kandinsky's well-known color theories, which the artist outlines in his theoretical treatise *On the Spiritual in Art*, primarily in chapter 6, ''The Language of Forms and Colors.'' Furthermore, Sheppard's main contention, based on an unduly cursory analysis of Kandinsky's color theories and on an apparent unfamiliarity with Kandinsky's other theoretical writings and works in the visual arts,[7] that the drama is to be read as a pessimistic statement, is not well supported by textual evidence. In this regard, Susan Stein notes that "save the single dissenting voice of Sheppard, those scholars who have remarked on the meaning of the play have reached similar conclusions regarding an optimistic finale suggestive of a salvation-regeneration theme" ("Ultimate" 26). Sheppard himself concedes that "Kandinsky is not normally associated with pessimism" (174), and his examination of Kandinsky's theoretical treatises and paintings of the year 1909–11 does not support adequately the claim that the drama should be viewed as pessimistic.[8]

Significantly, however, Sheppard is the first scholar to note that the illustrations that accompany *Yellow Sound* appear to offer "an ancillary means of interpretation" (170); yet his interpretation of these illustrations—and Sheppard ventures to interpret only a few of them—as they relate to the stage composition is as flawed as his analysis of Kandinsky's color theories and paintings, as later analysis of many of the same illustrations by Susan Stein demonstrates (see "Ultimate" 103–43).

J. M. Ritchie does not really quarrel with Sheppard's interpretation, remarking that Sheppard "has cracked the [color] code" (49), but in the same breath he expresses certain reservations: "Sheppard's interpretation is fairly convincing but not altogether compelling" (49). Ritchie also finds it difficult to accept Sheppard's notion that the stage composition is pessimistic (49). Yet for Ritchie such questions of meaning or interpretation are not terribly important, and he remarks: "[I]t is possible to appreciate what Kandinsky is attempting to do even without groping for 'the meaning' " (50). Once again, one finds no interpretation of this "important but elusive . . . piece," as it is characterized by Ritchie (47).

The aforementioned critics shy away from interpreting *Yellow Sound* because they can make little sense of the many elements of the stage composition that are so unusual. These critics note, with certain exceptions, that there is no immediately apparent plot; no character in the conventional sense; very little use of language and virtually nothing that could be construed as dialogue; frequent but seemingly random use of colored lighting in every scene; a curious collection of apparently unrelated illustrations which accompany the text in *The 'Blaue Reiter' Almanac*; strange creatures, somewhat reminiscent of birds but with large heads bearing resemblance to human ones; hills that grow and change color on stage; a flower shaped like a large bent cucumber; and, in the final scene, a figure who grows upward until he reaches the height of the full stage at which point he then resembles a cross. In fact, hardly anything in *Yellow Sound* appears to make sense. As a result, expectations of readers and scholars are frustrated when they encounter *Yellow Sound* for the first time.

Semioticians such as C. S. Peirce and, more recently, Umberto Eco lead one to recognize that art works are complex systems of signs. Although Peirce explores in great detail various classes of signs, two basic classes emerge that are relevant to the present study: *symbols*, which signify without motivation, through conventions and rules, there being no immediate or direct bond between symbols and objects; and *icons*, which are based on resemblance between sign and object as well as on a putative sharing of properties (Innis 2). There appear to be problems with Peirce's theory of iconism, indeed with any theory of iconism that supposes signs are to some degree similar to, analogous to, or naturally linked with their object. As Eco points out in "Critique of Iconism" in *A Theory of Semiotics* (191–217), when one speaks of a similarity between a sign and an object, one is actually referring to a relationship between the image and a previously culturalized content (204). Nonetheless, as James A. W. Heffernan astutely comments: "Whether or not resemblance itself is something we are taught to see cannot change the fact that we customarily *do* see it between certain kinds of pictures and what they represent" (173).

In *Yellow Sound*, few elements are used iconically; that is, one seldom identifies elements whose meanings conform to models of reality readily identified and accepted by most readers (most readers can interpret passages where elements are used iconically because portions of the encyclopedia of human experience shared by the readers already host the right frames for interpretation). At best, perceptive readers will identify that in Scene 4, the small child, wearing a white blouse, and the very fat man, dressed entirely in black (279), may be interpreted as allegories of joy and spotless purity and grief and death (see, for example, Eykman 149; Sheppard 168, 173; Stein, "Ultimate" 134–36; and Weiss, "Old Russia" 58). In this respect, Sheppard correctly asserts: "[Scene 4] is fairly easy to decipher on its own terms and by recourse to traditional categories" ("Ultimate" 168).

In most other parts of *Yellow Sound*, however, elements are used symbolically; that is, elements are used whose meanings do not conform to models of reality that a reader can readily identify and accept. In Peircean terms, there is no longer a resemblance between sign and object; rather, signs signify without motivation according to conventions particular to Kandinsky's "philosophy" of expression. Thus symbolic elements are ideolectical because their meanings hold only for the particular environment where they appear. Readers should feel "uneasy" in the presence of so many unusual elements in *Yellow Sound*, primarily because these elements appear to have acquired so much importance. Moreover, almost all of these elements violate expressional maxims. Viewers feel a surplus of signification, since they guess that these maxims have not been violated by chance or mistake. Yet signs as symbols relate to ideas that become evident, if the broader context in which the signs occur is more fully understood.[9] Such a distinction between the iconic and the symbolic appears to correspond to Hume's distinction between mimesis and fantasy:

mimesis [is] felt as the desire to imitate, to describe events, people, situations, and objects with such verisimilitude that others can share your experience; and *fantasy* [is] the desire to change givens and alter reality—out of boredom, play vision, longing for something lacking, or need for metaphoric images that will bypass the audience's verbal defences. (20)

An element of the fantastic, a symbol, is purposefully endowed with vague meanings that cannot be anchored into a preestablished code. This is why so many early critics who have considered *Yellow Sound* shy away from definite interpretation and why some, Denkler for one, conclude that many elements seem to be open to many different interpretations. As Eco notes:

> Faced with uncoded circumstances and complex contexts, the interpreter is obliged to recognize that the message does not rely on previous codes and yet that it must be understandable; if it is so, non-explicit conventions must exist; if not yet in existence, they have to exist (or to be posited). Their apparent absence postulates their necessity. (*Theory* 129)

Or as Peirce would phrase matters: "we find some very curious circumstances which would be explained by the supposition that it was the case of a certain general rule, and thereupon adopt that supposition" (2: 624). In *Yellow Sound*, the elements of the fantastic are the "curious circumstances" and one's interpretation would be an explaining hypothesis (creative abduction) or "general rule" (2: 624).

In the late 1970s and early to mid–1980s, Peg Weiss, Rose-Carol Washton Long, and John Bowlt, like Horst Denkler before them, argued that Kandinsky and his works and theories before World War I must be viewed in the context of the turn-of-the-century artistic, literary, and intellectual communities, primarily in Russia and in Munich, where the artist spent a great deal of time between the late 1890s and the war. As Reinhold Heller notes in his review of Weiss's book *Kandinsky in Munich: The Formative Jugendstil Years*, but which could apply equally well to the efforts of Long and Bowlt, these scholars provide a "massive corrective to decades of scholars who chose to ignore precisely the materials [they] treat so well" (315). For example, these scholars convincingly argue that *Yellow Sound* was intended for, or written with the knowledge of, the Munich Artists' Theater, known for performing experimental drama. They also demonstrate that Kandinsky must have been familiar with a wide variety of material (usually ignored by earlier scholars) when he drafted the stage composition, including the writings of divers Russian, German, and French Symbolists; theosophical and occult treatises by Besant, Steiner, Blavatsky, Schuré, Wolfskehl, and others; efforts (musical and otherwise) of such composers as Scriabin and Schönberg; and the dramatic theories of Georg Fuchs.

Unfortunately, although Bowlt helps one to situate Kandinsky's theoretical writings in historical context, he does not apply his insights to an interpretation of *Yellow Sound* or to the artist's ideas concerning stage composition. Similarly, in the chapter of her work devoted to *Yellow Sound* and where so much background material is uncovered related to the stage composition (92–103), Weiss carefully avoids interpreting the text itself. She writes that "an analysis and interpretation of the symbolism of [*Yellow Sound*] is beyond the limitations of this chapter" (*Kandinsky* 201, n. 47). Long, in her chapter "Experiments with

Stage Composition'' (52–64), seems primarily concerned with demonstrating
that the theme of Kandinsky's stage composition is similar to and was influenced
by Alexander Scriabin's experiments with music and the color keyboard and his
plan for a *Gesamtkunstwerk* (58). She also mentions that the technique of the
stage composition "owes a great deal to . . . Maurice Maeterlinck, to the experimental Russian theatre, to the Munich Artists' Theatre, and to several contemporary musical composers'' (61). Long's discussion of these hypotheses
rarely ventures from general remarks to specific analyses or scene-by-scene
discussions. While I do not find fault with the hypotheses, they do not lead to
what one could term a critical discussion of the play itself.

Nonetheless, Weiss, Long, and Bowlt, by situating Kandinsky, his artistic
theories, and *Yellow Sound* in context, suggest that the stage composition, or a
substantial portion of it, can be interpreted. This represents a radical version of
previous opinion. I would like to build on this premise, drawing on contextual
information provided by Weiss, Long, and Bowlt and on the artist's own theoretical treatises to demonstrate that *Yellow Sound* contains veiled themes and
ideas sometimes peculiar to Kandinsky, sometimes characteristic of the era during
which he lived.

Some ground rules can be identified in Kandinsky's artistic and narrative
worlds, ground rules readers must participate sympathetically in, if they are to
make sense of occurrences (symbols) in *Yellow Sound* (see Rabkin 4). Sometimes, as Kandinsky writes in *On the Spiritual in Art*, "understanding entails
the spectator's familiarity with the standpoint of the artist'' (1: 131). Kandinsky
also writes:

The artist's task is to understand, i.e., to know, which means of expression at his disposal
can attain the long-desired inner meaning, and to a lesser extent this is also the critic's
task. But it is certainly not the public's. So often we hear the public say those rather
embarrassed and modest words, "I don't understand anything in art." As if, on being
served some dish or other, I should refuse it and in embarrassment, say "But I don't
understand anything about the culinary art." In this instance, unless you want to stay
hungry, you need not understand—you simply open your mouth and eat. Art is spiritual
bread. The chef-artist has to "understand it," but the "elite" should bare their souls to
it and apprehend it. (''Whither'' 1: 102–103)[10]

On the one hand, Kandinsky expects viewers of an artwork to be touched immediately by what they see (assuming the artwork has been produced according
to the principle of internal necessity, as will be discussed); on the other hand,
he holds they will never arrive at this stage unless they have some idea about
what the artist intends. Kandinsky generally maintains "[J]ust as the body is
strengthened and developed through exercise, so too is the spirit'' (OSA 1: 177).
The complaint from people who cannot understand what they see "arises from
the lack of a properly developed sensibility'' (F 1: 243). In this respect, Kandinsky's theoretical writings provide a useful way to develop one's sensibilities.

In many of his theoretical writings published before World War I, Kandinsky claims humankind is at a spiritual turning point, entering the "epoch of the great spiritual" (OSA 1: 219; cf., for example, *Reminiscences* 1: 377; C/F 1: 88, 90; and "Whither" 1: 102) after a nightmarishly long period he labels materialism: "Our souls . . . are only now beginning to awaken after the long reign of materialism. . . . The whole nightmare of the materialistic attitude, which has turned the life of the universe into an evil, purposeless game, is not yet over. . . . Only a weak light glimmers, like a tiny point in an enormous circle of blackness" (OSA 1: 128). In the first few pages of chapter 3 (1: 139–43), "Spiritual Turning-Point," in *On the Spiritual in Art*, and in the essay "Whither the 'New' Art?" Kandinsky discusses the groups of people he terms materialists—positivists "recognizing only what can be weighed and measured" (OSA 1: 140), realist artists, socialists, and so on. He dismisses "this era of the deification of matter" ("Whither" 1: 98)—that is, most of the nineteenth century: "At such blind, dumb times men place exclusive value upon outward success, concern themselves only with material goods, and hail technical progress . . . as a great achievement" (1: 135). Elsewhere, Kandinsky refers to the nineteenth century as "soulless" (F 1: 256), as a period "in which the existence of the spirit is denied" (F 1: 235), and as a time "far removed from inner creation" (SC 1: 259).

For Kandinsky, the spiritual life of mankind is represented in terms of a large acute triangle, divided into unequal parts, with the most acute and smallest division at the top.

The whole triangle moves slowly, barely perceptibly, forward and upward, so that where the highest point is "today," the next division is "tomorrow", i.e., what is today comprehensible only to the topmost segment of the triangle and to the rest of the triangle is gibberish, becomes tomorrow the sensible and emotional content of the life of the second segment. At the apex of the topmost division there stands sometimes only a single man. (OSA 1: 133)[11]

The age of materialism, the nineteenth century for Kandinsky, represents a period of decline in the movement of the spiritual triangle: "The great epoch of the Spiritual which is already beginning, or, in embryonic form, began already yesterday amidst the apparent victory of materialism. . . . In every realm of the spirit, values are reviewed as if in preparation for one of the greatest battles against materialism" (OSA 1: 88). He predicts the end of materialism ("[O]ur epoch is a time of tragic collision between matter and spirit and of the downfall of the purely material worldview" ["Whither" 1: 103]) and everything materialism represents: "[E]verything that once appeared to stand so eternally, so steadfastly, that seemed to contain eternal, true knowledge, suddenly turns out to have been crushed (and in places smashed to pieces) by the merciless and salutory question, 'Is that really so?' . . . What had stood firm was displaced— as if a great earthquake had erupted in the soul" ("Whither" 1: 103). Even the world of science, upon which Kandinsky feels much of materialist doctrine is based, is entering a new era, due to the further division of the atom: "The collapse of the atom was equated, in my soul, with the collapse of the whole world. Suddenly, the stoutest walls crumbled. Everything became uncertain, precarious and insubstantial. . . . Science seemed destroyed: its most important basis was only an illusion, an error of the learned" (*Reminiscences* 1: 364; cf. OSA 1: 142).

It is the task of visionaries—Nietzsche, Beethoven, Cézanne, Matisse, Maeterlinck, Blavatsky, and many others—to help "the forward movement of the obstinate cartload of humanity" (OSA 1: 134). One reads: "And then, without fail, there appears among us a man like the rest of us in every way, but who conceals within himself the secret, inborn power of 'vision.' He sees and points" (OSA 1: 131). In this respect, art, as a direct function of spirit, serves a positive and prophetic role: "Art . . . is not a mere purposeless creating of things that dissipate themselves in a void, but a power that has a purpose and must serve the development and refinement of the human soul" (OSA 1: 212); that is, "Art must march at the head of spiritual evolution" (C/F 1: 89), "Art is the seer of the future and is a leader" ("Whither" 1: 100). Kandinsky calls on the artist, as an exalted quintessential intermediary, the epitome of the "New Man" of expressionism, to advance civilization by educating the seemingly intransigent masses through art; "Invisible, Moses comes down from the mountain, sees the dance around the golden calf. Yet he brings with him new wisdom for men. His voice, inaudible to the masses, is heard first by the artist" (OSA 1: 137).

The true artist, as mediator, must create works based on the principle of "internal necessity" (SC 1: 263) in order to "provide the expression of the Epoch of the Great Spiritual" (C/F 1: 90). Such art works will purposefully touch a viewer's soul, which will lead to development and refinement of his spirit. That is, "the harmony of colors [and forms (cf. OSA 1: 165)] can only be based upon the principle of purposefully touching the human soul. This basic tenet we shall call the principle of internal necessity" (OSA 1: 160, 165).

The principle of internal necessity and the related principle of inner sound are mentioned in many of Kandinsky's theoretical treatises (most prominently in *On the Spiritual in Art*, chapter 6, "The Language of Forms and Colors" [161–95]) and have been much discussed by scholars—for example, by Fuhr in chapter 2 of his dissertation (primarily 102–45). A summary of the most salient features of these principles is provided by Fuhr:

[Internal] necessity and inner sound displace realism. In[ternal] necessity refers to the artist's right and his duty to his art, to reconstruct and to re-define objective reality according to his private perceptions. Inner sound is the living, inner, vital essence of any given thing whether it is an object, a form, a shape or a color. It is the in[ternal] necessity of the artist which compels him to see into objects and other phenomena to reach, absorb and translate their inner souls into art. (11)

Kandinsky theorizes that a drama based on the principle of internal necessity would differ radically from a typical nineteenth-century drama, which he terms "external," "a castrated art," and which therefore has "no future potentialities" (OSA 1: 131). Kandinsky explains further: "it is not the 'formal' element . . . that matters, but an inner impulse (= content) that peremptorily determines form" (*Reminiscences* 1: 373). In "On the Question of Form," he writes: "of prime importance in the question of form is whether or not form has arisen out of internal necessity" (1: 238). Kandinsky claims that his *Yellow Sound* is "an attempt to draw upon this source [of internal necessity]" (SC 1: 264).

He further describes the drama of the late nineteenth century as "the description of external life, where the spiritual life of man is involved only insofar as it has to do with his external life. The cosmic element is completely lacking" (SC 1: 260). It is expression of a cosmic, or spiritual, element that characterizes a great historical era ("the greater the epoch, . . . the greater the strivings toward the spiritual" [F 1: 239]). This cosmic element is present, apparently, in *Yellow Sound*. For a cosmic element to be expressed, it must be done through material representation—"Form is the external expression of inner content" (F 1: 237)—that is, "the spiritual value seeks its materialization" (F 1: 235).

Kandinsky strives to remove what he perceives to be the superfluous. In this respect, Susan Stein, tracing the evolution of *Yellow Sound* by analyzing earlier drafts, points out that by the time the stage composition was published in 1912, Kandinsky had "taken out his blue pencil when it came to props and setting"— in all cases revamping away from the naturalistic "in favor of more symbolic forms" ("Kandinsky" 63). In *Yellow Sound* Kandinsky clearly rejects three of the most important tenets of nineteenth-century drama that allow for expression of a message: character, plot, and dialogue.

First, the "Participants"—five giants, indistinct beings, tenor and chorus (behind the stage), a child, a man, people in flowing garb, and people in tights— are not conventional characters but rather material representations that emerge "out of internal necessity." Kandinsky writes about the use of human figures in his paintings, but his writing also provides some insight into the artist's choice of participants in his stage composition:

[O]ne asks oneself the question: Are the human figures essential to the composition, or could they be replaced by other organic forms that would avoid disturbing the basic inner sound of the composition? . . . . [O]ne should either find another object more compatible with the inner sound . . . , or else choose to let the whole form remain purely abstract. . . . [T]he choice of object . . . must be based only upon the principle of the purposeful touching of the human soul. . . . The more freely abstract the form becomes, the purer, and also the more primitive it sounds. Therefore, in a composition in which corporeal elements are more or less superfluous, they can be more or less omitted and replaced by purely abstract forms, or by corporeal forms that have been completely abstracted. In every instance of this kind of transposition, or composition using purely abstract forms, the only judge, guide, and arbitrator should be one's feelings. Moreover, the more the artist utilizes these abstracted or abstract forms, the more at home he becomes in this sphere, and the deeper he is able to penetrate it. The spectator too, guided by the artist,

likewise increases his knowledge of this abstract language and finally masters it. (OSA
1: 168–69)

Second, there is no plot in the conventional sense. One finds an "Introduction"
and six "Scenes" which are related through a fairly consistently adhered to
scheme of color symbolism outlined in *On the Spiritual in Art*. As Fuhr already
pointed out:

Most of the pictures end in chaos: the song from the Prelude, the anxious glances, the
blood-filled flowers of [Scene 2], the terrified shrieks in [Scene 3], the inverted inner
sounds of [Scene 4] ending in "Silence!" as well as the orchestral tumult in [Scene 5].
Each scene ending in these ways tends to launch us into the next picture. This propulsion
from one picture to the next replaces any conventional plot structure. . . . [W]e are being
carried along to Picture Six, to the finale of *Yellow Sound*. (221–22)

Furthermore, there is nothing that suggests conventional dialogue. The fragmentary lines spoken by the chorus, for example, represent Kandinsky's use of
language to give form to his preoccupation with the principle of the juxtaposition
of opposites or counterpoint, which he feels has a tremendous effect on the
soul—whether in the visual arts or in literature (OSA 1: 171, 173, C/F 1:90;
Reminiscences 1: 366; "Composition 4" 1: 383–84) and which has been much
discussed (cf., for example, Stein, "Kandinsky" 62—"Kandinsky was sensitive
to the dramatic potential inherent in dissonance"). Contradictory images are
enjoined in the "Introduction":

First, deep voices:
    "Dreams hard as stones . . . And speaking rocks . . .
    Earth with riddles of fulfilling questions . . .
    The motion of the heavens . . . And melting . . . of stones . . .
    Invisible rampart . . . growing upward . . . "
High voices:
    "Tears and laughter . . . Prayers while cursing . . .
    The joy of union and the blackest battles."
All voices:
    "Dark light on the . . . sunniest . . . day
        (vanishing fast and suddenly).
    Blindingly bright shadow in darkest night!!" (210–11)

These opposing elements symbolize the dualistic nature attributed by Kandinsky
in all his works, theoretical and creative, to existence: between the material and
the spiritual, superficial and profound, outer and inner, death and life. In Kandinsky's theories of color, antithetical combinations such as black and white or
yellow and blue create tension but are generally resolved in some sort of formal
or thematic dialectic progression. The antithetical elements in the "Introduction," however, are not immediately resolved. Since Kandinsky concludes that

art, as a direct function of spirit, is positive and prophetic, some synthesis of the opposing forces should eventually appear in *Yellow Sound*.

One also encounters nonsensical words shouted at the conclusion of Scene 3: "one hears from behind the stage a shrill tenor voice, filled with fear, shouting entirely indistinguishable words very quickly (one hears frequently [the letter] *a*: e.g., 'Kalasimunafakola!')" (278). In conjunction with reference to works by Maeterlinck, "one of the first of the artistic sages and clairvoyants" (1: 146), in *On the Spiritual in Art*, Kandinsky writes the following about words:

Words are inner sounds. . . . Skillful use of a word (according to poetic feeling)—an internally necessary repetition of the same word twice, three times, many times—can lead not only to the growth of the inner sound, but also bring to light still other, unrealized spiritual qualities of the word. Eventually, manifold repetition of a word . . . makes it lose its external sense as a name. In this way, even the sense of the word as an abstract indication of [an] object is forgotten, and only the pure sound of the word remains. . . . [T]his pure sound comes to the fore and exercises a direct influence upon the soul. The soul experiences a nonobjective vibration that is more complex—I would say more "supersensible"—than the effect on the soul produced by a bell, a vibrating string, a falling board, etc. Here, great possibilities open up for the literature of the future (1: 147; cf. similar remarks on 191 and in "Whither" 1: 100–101)

In "On Stage Composition," which immediately precedes *Yellow Sound* in *The 'Blaue Reiter' Almanac*, and which the artist calls "a preface to *Yellow Sound*" in a letter in 1912 to Arnold Schönberg (in Hahl-Koch 57; cf. "Self-Characterization" 1: 432, published in *Das Kunstblatt*, 1919), one finds more specific comments relating to the use of words in the stage composition: "Words as such, or linked together in sentences, have been used to create a particular 'mood,' which prepares the ground of the soul and makes it receptive. The sound of the human voice has also been used purely, i.e., without being obscured by words, by the sense of the words" (264).

Kandinsky constructs a stage composition that indicates a rejection of those tenets that characterize naturalistic and realistic works of art, generally, and naturalistic drama of the late nineteenth century, specifically. It remains to be seen how messages are conveyed in *Yellow Sound*, if not through character, plot, and dialogue. At the conclusion of his "On Stage Composition," Kandinsky emphasizes: "The reader is asked not to ascribe to the principle the weaknesses of the following short composition, *Yellow Sound*, but to attribute them to the author" (265). That is, the artist has well-outlined principles regarding composition. The question remains whether they can be implemented by Kandinsky.

The illustrations that accompany *Yellow Sound* echo Kandinsky's theoretical comments and serve as visual portrayals of themes or ideas found in the stage composition. Kenneth Lindsay and Peter Vergo, in *Kandinsky: Complete Writings on Art*, note: "We have included the illustrations . . . because recent scholarship[12] has shown that they were not decorative devices but instead played an explicatory role" (2: 881). Lindsay and Vergo credit R. W. Sheppard for having initiated this line of thinking and Susan Stein in her thesis for having pursued it further. Fuhr also arrives independently at this conclusion (albeit phrased quite tentatively) in his dissertation from 1982, as he too contends that "a loose alignment between these images and the text is possible, and may have been intended" (220). He feels "it is more than coincidence that the text is accompanied by three [sic] Christian images" (220).[13] In an interesting note, Lindsay, one of Stein's thesis advisors at SUNY/Binghamton, points out that Lankheit, who edited the documentary version of The 'Blaue Reiter' Almanac in 1965 (the English version appeared in 1974), did not always respect the placement of these illustrations (2: 881), which could lead one to misinterpret the relationship of an illustration to the text. This oversight appears to have been corrected in the second edition of the German version which appeared in 1979.

Sheppard and Stein conclude that the illustrations accompanying Yellow Sound play an explicatory role by relating them to certain themes that appear in the stage composition. This conclusion would be further supported if it could be demonstrated that the illustrations in other parts of the The 'Blaue Reiter' Almanac have been carefully arranged. Kandinsky and Franz Marc are listed as joint editors of The 'Blaue Reiter' Almanac, and yet Kandinsky is widely acknowledged to have been the driving force behind the almanac. One realizes that the illustrations are carefully chosen and are not arranged haphazardly, if one considers the illustrations that accompany Kandinsky's theoretical essay "On the Question of Form"—by far the longest contribution in the almanac and arguably the most developed and thought provoking. Here, Kandinsky, demonstrating the identity of abstraction and realism, refers to Henri Rousseau's works (see 252–53). Seven illustrations of Rousseau's paintings accompany the text and do not appear elsewhere in the almanac. The Rousseau illustrations express, in visual terms, ideas in "On the Question of Form." Illustrations of works by other artists discussed in this essay—for example, Matisse, Marc, Münter, and Le Fauconnier—appear in the essay but also elsewhere in the almanac (see the discussion on 255–56 and the corresponding illustrations on 106, 107, 143, 159, 171, and 181). Reinhold Heller is not sure whether the illustrations were chosen by Marc or Kandinsky, or even the publisher Piper, and seems to indicate they might be due more to chance than to choice: "Among the illustrations for the play Yellow Sound, a woodcut for the apocalyptic Whore of Babylon . . . is included, but whether it was Kandinsky, or Marc, or even someone else who selected it for inclusion is not certain" ("Kandinsky" 21). Heller mentions in an endnote: "This print is identical to ill. 30 of Wilhelm Worringer. Die alt-deutsche Buchillustration. Munich: [Piper], 1912, so that the possibility that the publisher, Reinhard Piper, was instrumental in its selection for inclusion in the Blaue Reiter Almanac cannot be rejected" ("Kandinsky" 26). Kandinsky himself writes in "On the Question of Form": "If the reader . . . leafs through the book, passing from a votive picture to Delaunay, from Cézanne, to a Russian folk-print, from a mask to Picasso, from a glass picture to Kubin, etc., etc., then his soul will experience a multitude of vibrations and enter into the realm

of art. Then he . . . will arrive spiritually not at a minus, but at a plus'' (256).
I would contend that, whereas Piper may have put illustrations at Kandinsky's
disposal, it was certainly Kandinsky who was instrumental in their selection.

The illustrations accompanying *Yellow Sound* may be grouped into five categories: (1) Circe and Odysseus; (2) the nineteenth-century French lithograph;
(3) the "Primitives"; (4) the horse, rider, and slaying of the opponent; and (5)
the portrayals of various biblical passages, primarily apocalyptical in nature.

A depiction of Odysseus, the voyager, and Circe adorns the title page of the
stage composition. The reader is in the position of a voyager into the realm of
the spiritual. The idea of one embarking on a spiritual voyage is often touched
on in *On the Spiritual in Art* ("the struggle toward the nonnaturalistic, the
abstract, toward inner nature" [1: 153]), but nowhere more explicitly than in
the following passage, which is part of a discussion of Kandinsky's conception
of Monumental Art, or stage composition:

The reader should merely apply the corresponding principles laid down for painting, and
of its own accord the happy dream of the theater of the future will rise up before his
spiritual eyes. Upon the tortuous paths of this new kingdom—which lie through dark
jungles and over immeasurable chasms, to icy heights and to the edge of the heady abyss,
like an endless maze stretching out in front of the explorer—the same guide will lead
him with unfailing hand: the principle of internal necessity. (1: 207)

The picture and the suggestion that the reader should be prepared for a voyage
into the realm of the spiritual reinforce the symbolic nature of the color blue as
it appears in the "Introduction." Immediately after the curtain is lifted at the
beginning of *Yellow Sound*, the stage is immersed in a "dark-blue twilight,
which at first has a pale tinge and later becomes a more intense dark blue"
(269). Kandinsky in all of his writings associates profound meaning with blue
and contends that "The deeper the blue becomes, the more strongly it calls man
toward the infinite, awakening in him a desire for the pure and, finally, for the
supernatural" (OSA 1: 182). Blue, "the typically heavenly color" (1: 182),
represents the spiritual when it appears in *Yellow Sound* or, for that matter, in
any number of his poems—in "See" (1: 297–98), "Unaltered" (1: 308–09),
"Some Things" (1: 313), "Water" (1: 318–19), "Hymn" (1: 326), and
"Springtime" (1: 330), for example.

Preceding Scene 2, one finds a nineteenth-century lithograph of a man, un-
shaven, shabbily dressed, with a vacant stare. One's outer state often mirrors
one's inner state; outer decay corresponds directly to inner or spiritual decay.
As has been discussed, Kandinsky considers the nineteenth century to have been
a period during which "the transubstantiated bread remained inaccessible, [a]
period of decline in the spiritual world" (OSA 1: 135). The presence of the
beggar in *Yellow Sound* does not appear to be due to chance: one of Kandinsky's
other early stage compositions, *Green Sound* (which is designated by Stein as
Bühnenkomposition I, and which was written at the same time *Yellow Sound*

Exhibit 4.1. *Instruction in Zoology* from *Hortus sanitatis* (Mainz, 1491), as reproduced in Worringer, ill. 36.

Exhibit 4.2. Nineteenth century lithograph from an album formerly owned by Franz Marc. Probably not French, but it is from Scholz, Mainz.

Exhibit 4.3. Figure from Egyptian Shadow Play, *Der Islam* 2 (1911), 160, fig. 47.

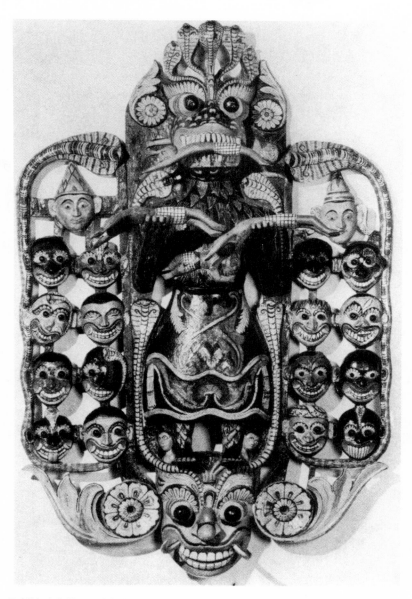

Exhibit 4.4. Dance Mask. Mask of the demon of disease, Maha-cola-sanni-yaksaya, Ceylon; height 47¼ ″. Munich, Staatliches Museum für Völkerkunde, Inv. No. B. 3454. Photo in *The 'Blaue Reiter' Almanac* provided by the Staatliches Museum für Völkerkunde, Munich.

Exhibit 4.5. Bavarian glass painting. The Infant Jesus with torture instruments of the Passion; Seehausen, Upper Bavaria, second to third quarter of the nineteenth century; painting on glass 7″ × 9½″. The caption, deleted for the reproduction in the almanac, reads: "Here I am lying as a child: soon as a judge I will punish all sin."

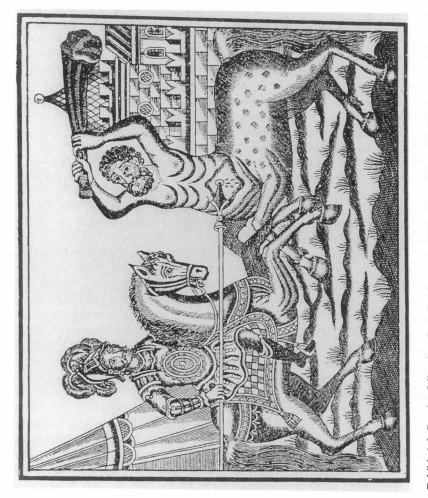

Exhibit 4.6. Russian folk print. One of eight prints exhibited in the Second Exhibition of the Editors of the *Blaue Reiter*, Nos. 258-65.

was conceived), concludes with the voice of a beggar. Stein remarks in this regard: "The beggar's presence offers a poignant commentary on the human condition in the present materialistic age" ("Kandinsky" 65; cf. similar remarks in "Ultimate" 1: 103–04 and 144, n. 3). In the poem "Song," one encounters a similar figure: "There sits a man / In the narrow circle, / In the narrow circle / Of frugality. / He is satisfied. / He has no ear. / His eyes are missing. / Of the red sound / Of the sun's globe / He can perceive no trace . . . " (1: 333). I agree with Fuhr's assessment of this poem: "Song" is "a song of lifelessness. . . . Kandinsky sings of a man content with death in life, caught in complacent inertia. He is figuratively deaf, and figuratively blind, deaf and blind to inner sound, to the heart and source of life—the red sound of the strong form of the sun" (111–12). Such an image can also be found in *On the Spiritual in Art*: "in this town live deaf people, deafened by unfamiliar wisdom, who cannot hear the collapse, blind people also—for unfamiliar wisdom has blinded them, and they say, 'Our sun gets brighter and brighter—soon we shall see the last spots disappear.' But these people too will hear and see" (1: 142). The collapse to which Kandinsky refers concerns the "massive walls" of materialism which now lie in ruin.

No positive developments result in the realms of art or the spirit when the concentration of a society lies in the material, the outer. The spirit, on whose strength depends the advancement of civilization, is weakened. The abstract spirit must be allowed to develop and must be heard. Kandinsky writes: "The power that impels the human spirit forward . . . is the abstract spirit. . . . Thus one sees that it is not in the form (materialism) that the absolute is to be sought. . . . Form is the external expression of inner content" (F 1: 236–37). *Yellow Sound* deals with the expression of the abstract spirit, with "inner sounds."

Kandinsky identifies a similarity between artists of so-called primitive cultures and artists of the age of spirituality which he thought to be dawning: "Just like us, those pure artists wanted to capture in their works the inner essence of things, which of itself brought about a rejection of the external . . . " (OSA 1: 128; cf. OSA 1: 173). This belief is also expressed in *The 'Blaue Reiter' Almanac*, in articles by Franz Marc ("Two Pictures"), David Burliuk ("The 'Savages' of Russia"), and especially August Macke ("Masks"); the belief also results in the inclusion of the illustrations of many examples of so-called primitive art in the almanac. The "primitive" Egyptian shadow plays that accompany *Yellow Sound* literally represent the reduction of an object from a three-dimensional portrayal—the superficial material aspect of an object as it appears in space—to a two-dimensional portrayal. Objects are thus effectively dematerialized. These Egyptian "profile paintings" are referred to by Burliuk in "The 'Savages' of Russia" as examples of a "rediscovered tradition [which is] the sword that smashed the chains of conventional academicism and freed art. . . . [This tradition] is the revelation of new truths and new means" (*The 'Blaue Reiter' Almanac* 79).

Dematerialization or simplification is an important idea in *Yellow Sound*, if one considers the props and setting, as well as, for example, the list of characters, or "Participants." Humans are not used as characters unless they are necessary, unless they serve as material representations of ideas. The flower in Scene 2, grotesque and distorted, represents what Kandinsky thinks of the results of the creative processes characteristic of the nineteenth century. The aim of art is not to imitate nature; that is, the aim of art is not to be mimetic, not to strive to employ signs that function as icons. As Kandinsky notes in *Reminiscences*: "the aims (and hence the resources too) of nature and of art [are] fundamentally, organically, and by the very nature of the world different" (1: 360; cf. 1: 373). In *On the Spiritual in Art*, Kandinsky asserts that "art is above nature" (1: 208) and valorizes the artist "who sees that the imitation of natural appearances, however artistic, is not for him—the kind of creative artist who wants to, and has to, express his own inner world . . . " (1: 154). In support of the idea that art is above nature, Kandinsky quotes similar remarks made by Goethe ("The artist with his free spirit takes precedence over nature, and can adapt her according to his higher aims"), Oscar Wilde ("Art only begins where imitation ends"), and Delacroix ("One should define realism as the antithesis of art") (all quotes OSA 1: 208). Elsewhere, Kandinsky comments on the works of Rodin: "Rodin does not lay his art at the feet of man and material, but subordinates them to the aims of his art—sculpture. Via man he seeks to express the movement, distribution and consonance, etc., of lines and form. For him, organic form is merely a convenient pretext for creating plastic forms. The material serves the abstract" ("Whither" 1: 101).

Beauty for Kandinsky depends entirely on whether form is an adequate expression of inner sound—that is, whether form has arisen according to the principle of internal necessity. If this is the case, then a work of art might not be what one could call beautiful in a conventional case. Indeed it might result in a work being termed either primitive or downright ugly by the public. For Kandinsky, "Beauty of color and form (despite the assertions of pure aesthetes or naturalists, whose principal aim is 'beauty') is not a sufficient aim of art" (OSA 1: 197). When discussing the music of the modernist composers Scriabin and Schönberg, Kandinsky notes: "inner beauty is achieved by renouncing customary beauty, and is occasioned by the demands of internal necessity. This inner beauty naturally appears ugly to those not accustomed to it, since man in general inclines toward the external, and does not willingly recognize internal necessity" (OSA 149). Kandinsky later asserts, programmatically:

The artist should be blind to "accepted" or "unaccepted" form, deaf to the precepts and demands of his time.

His eyes should be always directed toward his own inner life, and his ears turned to the voice of internal necessity.

Then he will seize upon all permitted means, and just as easily upon all forbidden means.

This is the only way of giving expression to mystical necessity.

All means are moral if they are internally necessary.
All means are sinful if they did not spring from the source of internal necessity. (OSA 1: 175–76)

Three illustrations relate to the motif of St. George and the dragon: knight slaying dragon, horse and rider killing centaur, horse and rider shooting opponent. These illustrations symbolize the conquest of the material by the spiritual or the liberation of modern art from the oppressing, stifling burden of the nineteenth-century materialistic doctrines. The importance of this motif in Kandinsky's paintings, and which even graces the cover of The 'Blaue Reiter' Almanac, has been much discussed by scholars, especially Weiss and Long.

The conquest of the spiritual over the material is also symbolized by the rejection of the flowers, which represent the creative process of the nineteenth century, by the characters of Scene 2.

> The flowers cover all, cover all, cover all.
> Close your eyes! Close your eyes!
> We look. We look.
> Cover conception with innocence.
> Open your eyes! Open your eyes!
> Gone. Gone. (276)

The material—that is, the superficial—dominates art. One should close one's eyes to the outer and look within. The inner feeling, the inner inspiration should be allowed to conceive its own products. Open the spiritual eyes. Penetrate the superficial, allow the inner spirit to express itself, and the trivial world of the material will be superseded. "At last [the figures] throw away the flowers as if they were filled with blood, and wrenching themselves free from their rigidity, run together toward the front of the stage" (277).

Related to the St. George motif are the apocalyptic images in Kandinsky's artistic works completed between 1910 and 1914 (for example, Horsemen of the Apocalypse, Deluge, All Saints' Day, and Last Judgment). Long notes and attributes these images, in part, to the influence of the writings of H. P. Blavatsky, founder of the Theosophical Society,[14] and her follower, until the winter of 1912–13, Rudolf Steiner. Blavatsky lived near Kandinsky in Munich, and her works are mentioned in On the Spiritual in Art (145) and preserved in the artist's library.[15] On the Spiritual in Art reveals Kandinsky's esteem for and interest in theosophy:

[The Theosophical Society] consists of brotherhoods of those who attempt to approach more closely the problems of the spirit by the path of *inner* consciousness. . . . The theosophical theory that serves as the basis for the movement has been set out by Blavatsky. . . . Theosophy, according to Blavatsky, can be equated with *eternal truth* [see Blavatsky 304]. "A new emissary of truth will find the human race prepared for his message through the Theosophical Society: there will exist a form of expression in which he will be able to clothe the new truths, an organization which, in a certain sense, expects his coming, and exists for the purpose of clearing away material hindrances and difficulties from his path'' [a rephrasing of Blavatsky 307: "the new torch-bearer of Truth . . . will find the minds of men prepared for his message . . . (and) an organization awaiting his arrival, which will remove the merely mechanical, material obstacles and difficulties from his path"]. (1: 143–45)

The apocalypse is a destruction of the ruling powers of evil, the destruction of obsolete forms followed by renewal, regeneration, a messianic kingdom, for theosophists, in the Bible, and for Nietzsche to whom Kandinsky refers:

When religion, science and morality are shaken (the last by the mighty hand of Nietzsche), when the outer supports threaten to collapse, then man's gaze turns away from the external toward himself. . . . [Men] turn away from the soulless content of modern life, toward materials and environments that give a free hand to the nonmaterial strivings and searchings of the thirsty soul. (OSA 1: 146)

Elsewhere, Kandinsky writes: "The old picture of the new spring is our time. The time of awakening, resolution, regeneration, and the hurricane, the time of glowing vigor and wondrous power . . . , a time of sweeping upheaval . . . , of the great liberation" ("On the Artist" 409–10). And the apocalyptic images in Kandinsky's paintings must be understood in the context of his, at the time, generally positive outlook for the future of humankind.

Five illustrations in *Yellow Sound* reflect this preoccupation with apocalyptic visions. The picture that follows that of Odysseus and Circe is entitled "Instruction in Zoology." It is striking to note, however, that the only animals presented are birds and a snake. Such a scene is reminiscent of the Bible: "Babylon the great is fallen, is fallen, and is become the habitation of devils, and the hold of every foul spirit, and a cage of every unclean and hateful bird" (*Revelation* 18:2). The snake, which Klaus Brisch notes appears in a number of Kandinsky's paintings—in *Improvisation 27*, for example—(1: 219–20) can be viewed, aside from its obvious connection with the devil and evil, as a reference to "the dragon of materialism; who blocks the attainment of the utopian paradise," as Long has already identified ("Kandinsky" 55). Stein also, in relation to this particular illustration, remarks, "the struggle of bird and snake in the foreground [is] an emblem for Christ's struggle with Satan and the forces of light against darkness" ("Ultimate" 104).

The next illustration one encounters is "The Jews with the Ark of the Covenant at the Walls of Jericho." Although this episode is not one that occurs in *Revelation*, it is nonetheless a type of apocalyptic image. The destruction of Jericho is symbolic of the destruction of the old realm—characterized by the worship of physical deities or idols—by the new, spiritual age of Christianity. Kandinsky frequently employs an image of crumbling walls when referring to the struggle to end the age of materialism—in *On the Spiritual in Art*, for example: "part of the massive wall lies fallen like a house of cards. There, an enormous tower that once reached to the sky, built of many slender, and yet 'immortal' spiritual pinnacles, lies in ruins'' (1: 142). Visionaries, those who herald the dawning of the new age of spirituality, are sometimes compared to warriors or "soldiers, sacrificing themselves for others at the desperate storming of some beleaguered fortress. But 'there is no fortress so strong that it cannot be taken' '' (OSA 1: 142). These warriors, in Kandinsky's utopian treatises and works, will triumph, even as "an evil, invisible hand casts new obstacles in the way" (OSA 1: 131).

Before Scene 1, one encounters an illustration that visually depicts various apocalyptic scenes in *Revelation* 14: 14–16 ("Thrust in thy sickle, and reap") and *Revelation* 17: 3–8 (Whore of Babylon). Similarly, the Bavarian painting on glass of a Christ-child at the end of Scene 2 may be viewed as a depiction of the Last Judgment in *Revelation*. The inscription that accompanies this piece, unfortunately not included by Lindsay and Vergo (277), reads in translation: "Here I lie as a child, until I return as judge to punish the sinners."

Yellow Sound symbolizes the "turning away from the soulless content of modern life, toward materials and environments that give a free hand to the nonmaterial strivings and searchings of the thirsty soul," an idea expressed in *On the Spiritual in Art*. Scene 6 is preceded by an illustration of a six-winged seraph, a messenger who harkens the dawning of the new age of spirituality (what may be perceived as seraphs have already appeared in Scene 1 as the red flying creatures, as Stein correctly perceives in "Ultimate" 1: 109). The scene itself represents the culmination of the apocalyptic imagery:

In the middle of the stage, a bright yellow giant, with an indistinct, white face and large, round, black eyes. . . .
He slowly lifts both arms parallel with his body (palms downward), and, in doing so, grows upward.
At the moment he reaches the full height of the stage, and his figure resembles a cross, it becomes suddenly dark. The music is expressive, resembling the action on stage. (283)

This fantastic image symbolizes a physical manifestation of the cosmic or spiritual element and serves to predict the transcendence of values characteristic of the nineteenth century. Scene 6, the climax of *Yellow Sound*, is not to be viewed as a pessimistic statement; rather, this scene demonstrates Kandinsky's hopes for the future of humanity.

This essay has attempted to provide the reader with some indication that *Yellow Sound* is more than a confusing jumble of bits and pieces hastily thrown together by Kandinsky. Detailed analysis of the use of colored lights based on Kandinsky's theories of color symbolism is possible. There are similarities between images that appear in the stage composition and those that appear in the artist's paintings (yellow giants, crooked yellow flowers, crucifixes, seraphs, fortresses, hills, and so forth). Similar principles of construction appear to have been used in both *Yellow Sound* and Kandinsky's volume of poems, *Sounds*, from the same period and which appears just as strange to most critics as the stage composition. In short, it is hoped that future scholars of literature will not be so quick to dismiss the experimental literary efforts of those artists generally not associated with literature.

NOTES

A Martin Nelson Junior Sabbatical Fellowship awarded by the University of Puget Sound allowed the author the time to conduct research for and write the original draft of this chapter.

1. Unless otherwise noted, quotations from works by Kandinsky are from *Kandinsky: Complete Writings on Art*, edited by Kenneth C. Lindsay and Peter Vergo, in two volumes.

2. In "Kandinsky and Abstract Stage Composition: Practice and Theory," Susan Alyson Stein outlines in considerable detail the origin and evolution of *Yellow Sound*, relating it to handwritten drafts of Kandinsky's stage compositions (as yet unpublished) included in Notebook GMS 415 at the Städtische Galerie im Lenbachhaus, Munich— *Riesen (Giants)*, *Bühnenkomposition I (Stage Composition I)*, later titled *Green Sound*, and *Bühnenkomposition III—Schwarz und Weiss (Stage Composition III—Black and White)*. In addition, Weiss, in 1983, notes: "Jelena Hahl [-Koch] is currently preparing the publication of all of Kandinsky's color operas . . . and notes in one volume . . . " (12– 13). As of this writing, the volume to which Weiss refers, most probably volume 2 of Kandinsky's *Gesammelte Schriften*, edited by Hahl-Koch and H. K. Röthel, has yet to appear (volume 1 appeared in 1980). Scholars writing before Stein have noted that *Yellow Sound* was written in 1909; Stein conclusively demonstrates that although the stage composition was conceived in 1909, and bears resemblance to *Giants*, a date of 1911 or 1912 for the completion of *Yellow Sound* seems more congenial (64). Jelena Hahl-Koch adds: "First rough draft, with the title *Giants*, c. 1909, written in German in Thomas von Hartmann's handwriting [who composed the music to *Yellow Sound*, which, except for a fragment, has since been lost]—probably from Kandinsky's dictation [Notebook GMS 415 at the Städtische Galerie im Lenbachhaus, Munich]. Second, more detailed version, written in Russian in Kandinsky's handwriting, dated 'March 1909'; the title *Riesen* is changed to *Der gelbe Klang* (Nina Kandinsky Archive, Paris)" (1984 117).

3. In 1976 Ritchie boldly declares: "it immediately becomes clear that [*Yellow Sound*] is not capable of legitimate production" (48). Nonetheless, *Yellow Sound* premiered in 1982 at the Marymount Manhattan Theater, in the Guggenheim Museum, as part of the exhibit "Kandinsky in Munich, 1896–1914." Although it probably would not contribute significantly to one's understanding of the stage composition, an accurate history of attempts to stage *Yellow Sound* would at least serve to clear up conflicting or differing accounts provided by scholars. Tassel, in an article in the *New York Times*, notes that "three abortive attempts" were made to stage *Yellow Sound*: "two in Paris, in 1956 and in 1976, the other at the Guggenheim in 1972" (4). Grohmann relates: "Not until 1956 was [*Yellow Sound*] prepared for production by Jacques Polieri, the stage director, and Jean Barraque, the composer" (56). Weiss writes that *Yellow Sound* was "produced for the first time in May 1972, at the Guggenheim Museum. . . . Unfortunately, the production neither adhered to Kandinsky's original instructions . . . nor revealed any familiarity with the theatrical (or musical) possibilities available to Kandinsky at the time of composition" (*Kandinsky* 197). And Jelena Hahl-Koch comments: "In the most recent times there have been three performances; in New York (1972), in Baume, southern France (1975) and

in Paris (1976). None of these three stagings, however, held even approximately to Kandinsky's directions; they were free, relatively inadequate renderings'' (159). In a note (200, n. 112), Hahl-Koch mentions: "About these performances, as also about Kandinsky's work for the theater in general, a detailed discussion will appear within the framework of his *Gesammelte Schriften*, ed. H. K. Röthel and J. Hahl-Koch.'' Only volume 1 of this series has appeared, in 1980; whether volume 2 appears, remains to be seen. It is hoped that Hahl-Koch is able to set the record straight regarding the performance history of *Yellow Sound*. I am not terribly optimistic that Hahl-Koch's discussion of Kandinsky's work for the theater in general will prove terribly useful, since what she has already written about *Yellow Sound* is not terrifically insightful:

In the context of his striving towards abstraction, [Kandinsky] gives up all claim to a plot in the usual sense, and attains—although it still includes human figures, hints of landscape and recognizable objects—what is basically already a random play of color, movement and noise. It may have excited him to add to the elements of color and form, which were familiar from painting, the temporal element of music and noise, as well as the likewise temporal element of movement and lighting, both of which could modify form and color,—in order, so to speak, to transform his pictures into movement. (1984 160–61).

4. For a very brief review of how the fantastic is defined in recent monographs on the fantastic available in English—such as those by Todorov, Rabkin, Jackson, and Schlobin—the reader is referred to Olsen (14–22). Recent literature on the fantastic written in German, not often enough consulted by Anglo-American scholars, would include the essays in Thomsen and Fischer, as well as works by Rottenstein, Fischer, Marzin, Lenk, Wörtche and, of course, the many theoretical essays in *Phaïcon*.

5. Quoted passages from works by Eykman and Denkler have been translated by the author.

6. The manuscript of this lecture is "in possession of the composer's widow, Olga von Hartmann (New York)'' (Hahl-Koch, 1984 200, n. 109).

7. Unlike his analyses of secondary literature on Kandinsky which are quite insightful at times, Sheppard's views on Kandinsky's works, not only in "Kandinsky's Abstract Drama 'Der gelbe Klang': An Interpretation'' but also in other essays, are often so far out of the mainstream that I find them difficult to consider seriously. It is almost as if Sheppard is not aware of efforts by Weiss or Long or many others that provide evidence that directly undermines his own theories regarding Kandinsky's works.

8. Stein remarks that Sheppard's article was brought to her attention while she was completing the final draft of her Master's thesis. Nonetheless, she too feels that Sheppard's reading of the stage composition is "as problematic as his interpretation of Kandinsky's paintings during the years 1909–1910'' ("Ultimate'' 18–19).

9. The reader is referred to Umberto Eco's *Semiotics and the Philosophy of Language*, chapter 4, for a discussion of the symbolic mode of communication.

10. Abbreviations of work by Kandinsky: OSA = *On the Spiritual in Art*; SC = "On Stage Composition''; F = "On the Question of Form''; "Whither'' = "Whither the 'New' Art?''; C/F = "Content and Form''; all in Lindsay and Vergo.

11. Lindsay and Vergo (2: 875, n. 21; 2: 869, n. 4) astutely refer the reader to similarities between Kandinsky's views on progress of spiritual life in *On the Spiritual* and those found in Tolstoy's "What Is Art?'' which Kandinsky pans in his essay "Critique of Critics'' (36), published in Moscow in 1901. Lindsay and Vergo could have provided

the reader with the passage to which they refer, since differences then between Kandinsky's theories and Tolstoy's would become immediately evident. Tolstoy writes:

Humanity unceasingly moves forward from a lower, more partial, and obscure understanding of life, to one more general and more lucid. And in this, as in every movement, there are leaders—those who have understood the meaning if life more clearly than others,—and of these advanced men there is always one who has . . . expressed this meaning more clearly, accessibly, and strongly than others. This man's expression of the meaning of life, together with those superstitions, traditions, and ceremonies which usually form themselves round the memory of such a man, is what is called a religion. Religions are the exponents of the highest comprehension of life accessible to the best and foremost men at a given time in a given society; a comprehension towards which, inevitably and irresistibly, all the rest of that society must advance. (389–90)

12. Peter Jelavich curiously does not consider the illustrations when he writes on *Yellow Sound* (217–35). Most unfortunate was Denkler's decision not to include the illustrations with *Yellow Sound* in the anthology *Einakter und kleine Dramen des Expressionismus*—the edition, because of cost and availability, where most students and scholars of literature will encounter the stage composition for the first and perhaps only time.

13. I also arrived at this conclusion, spurred on by Sheppard's hypothesis, as an undergraduate at Northwestern University. A paper entitled "Understanding Wassily Kandinsky's *Der gelbe Klang*," written in spring 1980, delivered in shortened form at the Second Midwest Comparative Literature Graduate Student Conference held at the University of Minnesota, April 10–11, 1981, and subsequently published unrevised in the proceedings *C.L.A.M. Chowder* in 1983 (75–83), contains the identical breakdown of illustrations into five categories (cf. 78–80) that I employ in the current study and also brief analyses of numerous illustrations. In large measure, the conclusions I draw regarding individual illustrations are similar to those drawn by Stein in her Master's thesis (with certain exceptions), although her analyses are much more detailed and better supported than mine, much to her credit.

14. Kandinsky refers to passages from the German version of Blavatsky's *Key to Theosophy* (1889), published by Max Altmann in Leipzig in 1907. As Long notes:

For centuries the word 'theosophist' had been used as a synonym for those interested in uncovering 'secret doctrines' and uniting or illuminating all religions. But by the time of the publication of *The Key to Theosophy*, the term 'Theosophist' began to be specifically applied to those who followed in Blavatsky's attempt to blend the hidden secrets of Eastern and Western religions and to explore such esoteric or occult practices as seances and mesmerism. By 1889 a number of branches of Blavatsky's Theosophical movement had been established across Europe and they united to form the International Theosophical Society. . . . Because of increasing differences with the International Theosophical Society, Steiner founded his own group, which he called Anthroposophical, in the Winter of 1912–13. (1984 58, n. 19–20; for more detail, cf. 1980 13–41)

15. Lindsay and Vergo refer the reader to the appendix of Ringbom's "Art in the Epoch of the Great Spiritual" for a list of the theosophical and other literature preserved in Kandinsky's library (2: 876, n. 28). Ringbom presents Kandinsky's annotations of some of Steiner's articles appearing in the theosophical journal *Luzifer-Gnosis* between 1904 and 1908 in "Die Steiner Annotationen Kandinskys." For a detailed discussion of the theosophical influence on Kandinsky's ideas, the reader should consider Ringbom's *The Sounding Cosmos: A Study in the Spiritualism of Kandinsky and the Genesis of Abstract Art* (1970). Following Ringbom's lead, but also at times critical of his conclu-

sions, are Heller ("Kandinsky"), Lindsay and Vergo, Long (*Kandinsky* and "Occultism"), Weiss (*Kandinsky*), and Bowlt. As Heller notes: "[Ringbom's] conclusion . . . has come under attack as too excessive and too ready in its zeal to deny non-Theosophical associations" ("Kandinsky" 19). Therefore, the reader is referred to the writings of the other aforementioned scholars to obtain a more rounded view of the issue of Kandinsky and theosophy.

WORKS CITED

'Blaue Reiter' Almanac, The. Ed. Wassily Kandinsky and Franz Marc. New Documentary Edition. Ed. Klaus Lankheit. New York: Viking, 1974. *Der Blaue Reiter*. Documentary Ed. Munich and Zurich: R. Piper, 1965. 2nd ed. 1979.

Blavatsky, H. P. *The Key to Theosophy*. 1889. Rpt. Pasadena, Calif.: Theosophical University Press, 1972.

Bowlt, John E. "Vasilii Kandinsky: The Russian Connection." *The Life of Vasilii Kandinsky in Russian Art: A Study of "On the Spiritual in Art."* 2nd ed. Ed. John E. Bowlt and Rose-Carol Washton Long. Newtonville, Mass.: Oriental Research Partners, 1984. 1–41.

Brisch, Klaus. "Untersuchungen zur Entstehung der gegenstandslosen Malerei an seinem Werk von 1900–1921." Diss. Bonn University, 1955.

Denkler, Horst. *Drama des Expressionismus: Program, Spieltext, Theater*. Munich: Wilhelm Fink, 1967.

———, ed. *Einakter und kleine Dramen des Expressionismus*. Stuttgart: Philipp Reclam, 1968.

Eco, Umberto. *Semiotics and the Philosophy of Language*. Bloomington: Indiana University Press, 1984.

———. *A Theory of Semiotics*. Bloomington: Indiana University Press, 1976.

Eisenstein, Sergei M. *The Film Sense*. Trans. and ed. Jay Leyda. New York: Harcourt, 1947.

Eykman, Christoph. *Denk- und Stilformen des Expressionismus*. Munich: A. Franke, 1974.

Fischer, Jens Malte. "Science Fiction—Phantastik—Fantasy: Ein Vorshlag zu ihrer Abrenzung." *Neugier oder Flucht? Zu Poetik, Ideologie und Wirkung der Science Fiction*. Ed. Karl Ermert. Stuttgart: Ernst Klett, 1980. 8–17.

Fuhr, James Robert. " 'Klänge': The Poems of Wassily Kandinsky." Diss. Indiana University, 1982.

Grohmann, Will. *Wassily Kandinsky: Life and Work*. Trans. Norbert Guterman. New York: Abrams, [1958].

Hahl-Koch, Jelena, ed. *Arnold Schönberg-Wassily Kandinsky: Briefe, Bilder und Dokumenter einer aussergewöhnlichen Begegnung*. Salzburg: Residenz, 1980. *Arnold Schoenberge-Wassily Kandinsky: Letters, Pictures and Documents*. Trans. John C. Crawford. Boston: Faber, 1984.

Heffernan, James A. W. "Resemblance, Signification, and Metaphor in the Visual Arts." *Journal of Aesthetics and Art Criticism* 44 (1985): 167–80.

Heller, Reinhold. "Kandinsky and Traditions Apocalyptic." *Art Journal* 43 (1983): 19–26.

———. Review. *Art Journal* 39 (1980): 313–29.

Hooper, Kent. "Understanding Wassily Kandinsky's *Der gelbe Klang*." *C.L.A.M. Chow-*

der: Proceedings of the Second Midwest Comparative Literature Graduate Student Conference. Ed. Brady Axelrod et al. Minneapolis: Comparative Literature Association of Minnesota, 1983. 75–83.

Hume, Kathryn. *Fantasy and Mimesis: Responses to Reality in Western Literature*. New York: Methuen, 1984.

Innis, Robert. *Semiotics: An Introductory Anthology*. Bloomington: Indiana University Press, 1985.

Jackson, Rosemary. *Fantasy, the Literature of Subversion*. London: Methuen, 1981.

Jelavich, Peter. *Munich and Theatrical Modernism: Politics, Playwriting, and Performance, 1890–1914*. Cambridge: Harvard University Press, 1985.

Lankheit, Klaus. "A History of the Almanac." *The 'Blaue Reiter' Almanac*. Ed. Wassily Kandinsky and Franz Marc. New Documentary Edition. Ed. Lankheit. New York: Viking, 1974. 11–48.

Lenk, Elisabeth. *Kritische Phantasie: Gesammelte Essays*. Munich: Mattes and Seitz, 1986.

Lindsay, Kenneth C., and Peter Vergo, eds. *Kandinsky: Complete Writings on Art*. 2 vols. Boston: G. K. Hall, 1982.

Long, Rose-Carol Washton. "Kandinsky and Abstraction: The Role of the Hidden Image." *Artforum* 10.10 (1972): 42–49.

———. "Kandinsky's Vision." *The Life of Vasilii Kandinsky in Russian Art: A Study of "On the Spiritual in Art."* 2nd ed. Ed. John E. Bowlt and Rose-Carol Washton Long. Newtonville, Mass.: Oriental Research Partners, 1985. 43–61.

———. "Kandinsky's Vision of Utopia as a Garden of Love." *Art Journal* 43 (1983): 50–59.

———. *Kandinsky: The Development of an Abstract Style*. Oxford: Clarendon, 1980.

———. "Occultism, Anarchism, and Abstraction: Kandinsky's Art of the Future." *Art Journal* 46 (1987): 38–45.

———. "Vasily Kandinsky, 1909–1913: Painting and Theory." Diss. Yale University, 1968.

Marzin, Florian F. *Die phantastiche Literatur: Eine Gattungsstudie*. Frankfurt and Bern: Peter Lang, 1982.

Olsen, Lance. *Ellipse of Uncertainty: An Introduction to Postmodern Fantasy*. Westport, Conn.: Greenwood Press, 1987.

Peirce, Charles Sanders. *Collected Papers*. 8 vols. Ed. Charles Hartshorne, Paul Weiss, and Arthur Burks. Cambridge: Harvard University Press, 1935–1938.

Phaïcon: Almanach der phantastischen Literatur. Ed. Rein a Zondergeld. 6 vols. to date. Frankfurt: Insel, 1974–.

Pörtner, Paul. "Expressionismus und Theater." *Expressionismus als Literatur: Gesammelte Studien*. Ed. Wolfgang Rothe. Bern and Munich: Francke, 1969. 194–211.

Rabkin, Eric S. *The Fantastic in Literature*. Princeton: Princeton University Press, 1976.

Ringbom, Sixten. "Art in the Epoch of the Great Spiritual." *Journal of the Warburg and Courtauld Institutes* 29 (1966): 386–18.

———. "Die Steiner-Annotationen Kandinskys." *Kandinsky und Munchen: Begegnungen und Wandlungen 1896–1914*. Ed. Armin Zweite. Exh. cat. Städt. Galerie im Lenbachhaus München, 18 Aug.–17 Oct. 1982. Munich: Pestel, 1982. 102–05.

———. *The Sounding Cosmos: A Study in the Spiritualism of Kandinsky and the Geneses of Abstract Art*. Acta Academiae Aboensis, A, 38:2. Abo, Finland: 1970.

Ritchie, J. M. *German Expressionist Drama*. Boston: Twayne, 1976.

Röthel, H. K., and Jelena Hahl-Koch, eds. *Wassily Kandinskys Gesammelte Schriften*. Vol. 1. Berne: Bentelli, 1980.

Rottenstein, Franz. "Vorwort: Zweifel und Gewiß heit. Zu Traditionen, Definitionen und einigen notwendigen Abrenzungen in der phantastiche Literatur." *Die dunkle Seit der Wirklichkeit. Aufsatze zur Phantastik*. Ed. Rottenstein. Frankfurt: Suhrkamp, 1987.

Schlobin, Roger, ed. *The Aesthetics of Fantasy Literature and Art*. Notre Dame, Ind.: Notre Dame University Press, 1982.

Schreyer, Lothar. *Expressionistisches Theater: Aus meninen Erinnerungen*. Hamburg: J. P. Toth, 1948.

Sheppard, R. W. "Kandinsky's Abstract Drama 'Der gelbe Klang': An Interpretation." *Forum for Modern Language Studies* [St. Andrews, Scotland] 11 (1975): 165–77.

―――. "Kandinsky's Early Aesthetic Theory: Some Examples of Its Influence and Some Implication for the Theory and Practice of Abstract Poetry." *Journal of European Studies* 5 (1975): 19–40.

―――. "Kandinsky's *Klänge*: An Interpretation." *German Life and Letters* NS 33 (1980): 135–46.

Stein, Susan Alyson. "Kandinsky and Abstract Stage Composition: Practice and Theory, 1909–12." *Art Journal* 43 (1983): 61–66.

―――. "The Ultimate Synthesis: An Interpretation of the Meaning and Significance of Wassily Kandinsky's 'Der Gelbe Klang.' " M. A. Thesis. State University of New York at Binghamton, 1980.

Tassel, Janet. "Staging a Kandinsky Dream." *New York Times* 7 Feb. 1982: 4.

Thomsen, Christian, and Jens Malte Fischer, eds. *Phantastik in Literatur and Kunst*. Darmstadt: Wissenschaftliche Buchgesellschaft, 1980. 2nd ed. 1985.

Todorov, Tzvetan. *Introduction à la littérature fantastique*. Paris: Editions du Seuil, 1970. *The Fantastic: A Structural Approach to a Literary Genre*. Trans. Richard Howard. Cleveland, Ohio: Case Western University Press, 1973. Ithaca, N.Y.: Cornell University Press, 1975.

Tolstoy, Leo. "What Is Art?" [Trans. Aylmer Maude]. *The Novels and Other Works of Lyof N. Tolstoï: The Kingdom of God Is within You. What Is Art?* Ed. Nathan Haskell Dole. 22 vols. New York: Charles Scribner's Sons, 1899–1902. vol. 19: 337–47.

Weiss, Peg. "Editor's Statement: Are We Ready to Memorialize Kandinsky?" *Art Journal* 43 (1983): 9–13.

―――. "Kandinsky and 'Old Russia': An Ethnographic Exploration." *Syracuse Scholar* Spring 1986: 43–62.

―――. "Kandinsky and the Symbolist Heritage." *Art Journal* 44 (1985): 137–45.

―――. *Kandinsky in Munich: The Formative Jugendstil Years*. Princeton: Princeton University Press, 1979.

Wörtche, Thomas. *Phantastik und Unschlüssigkeit: Zum Strukturellen Kriterium eines Genres. Untersuchungen an Texten von Hanns Heinz Ewers und Gustav Meyrink*. Meitingen: Wimmer, 1987.

5

Ionesco and *L'insolite*

Elizabeth C. Hesson and Ian M. Hesson

The "absurd" nature of Eugène Ionesco's theater has presented many difficulties over the past 40 years to spectators, to actors, and, most particularly, to directors. Directors are faced with the problem of translating into the concrete terms of the stage a universe that is essentially a rejection of the basic points of reference of everyday reality. In this universe, which is a strange mixture of the commonplace and the oneiric, one finds characters who are both invisible and inaudible, but nevertheless "present"; others who turn into rhinoceroses; a corpse that grows across the stage as the play progresses before becoming a banner that carries the principal character off heavenwards; a man who can fly; and a general undermining of the concepts of identity, time, and space. Nor is the director's position made any more comfortable by Ionesco's attitude. "I have always been at odds with my producers," he writes in *Notes and Counter Notes*, "My text is not just dialogue, but also 'stage directions.' These should be respected as much as the text, they are essential, they are also sufficient" (208). Typical of his disagreement with his directors was the argument he had with Jean-Marie Serreau who wished to reduce the gigantic proportions of the corpse's feet in *Amédée or How to Get Rid of It*. Ionesco's response was the same as that to the director of *The Chairs* who wanted to keep the number of empty chairs within the bounds of reason: "Do not minimize its effects . . . everything should be exaggerated, excessive, painful, childish, a caricature, without finesse" (*Notes* 187). The directors may have wished to retain some semblance of realism because they thought that what was needed was symbolism or allegory, but for Ionesco the aim was to dislocate reality: "We need to be virtually bludgeoned into detachment from our daily lives, our habits and mental laziness, which conceal from us the strangeness of the world" (*Notes* 26).

The intrinsic strangeness of the world for Ionesco forms the basis of his theater, for which he is less inclined to use the reason-based term *absurd* than the perception-oriented *insolite*, which he defines as the "unusual . . . or feeling of the unusual" (*Entre la vie* 123). He adds that "what is unusual is first and foremost what exists, reality" (*Entre la vie* 136), confirming that his plays are less the product of a wild imagination or an intellectual rejection of causality than the expression of a particular perception of reality. While Ionesco's "unusual" does not correspond exactly to any of the categories of the fantastic, it does contain many of the elements and themes of the genre—the weakening of the barrier between the mental and the physical and the disappearance of the distinction between subject and object. These elements, which Todorov relates to the fantastic (116–17), correspond to Ionesco's externalization of his inner world—or the inverse—and produce themes such as flight, metamorphosis, acceleration, and proliferation. Todorov's connection of these aspects of the fantastic with the perception of the small child is also apposite, for Ionesco too points to childhood, albeit a slightly later one, as a source of inspiration. The childhood paradise that he continually tries to recreate was characterized by a sense of being the center of the universe—that is, with no distinction between self and external reality and in a time that was an eternal present. He was ejected from this paradise at "the age of reason"—about seven years—when he became aware of the passage of time and the existence of death. His attempts to regain it were both conscious, through the use of alcohol and other stimulants—to which Todorov also refers (118)—and unconscious, in episodes during his adolescence which he terms "Illuminations" and in which he experienced the sense of plenitude for a brief time. These "Illuminations" were characterized by bright light and a feeling of lightness, and they became less frequent with the passage of time. The link between the fantastic themes in Ionesco's theater and his quest to rediscover his childhood paradise, viewed in the light of Jung's theories on the relationship between personality and perception, not only suggests an alternative to the "absurdist" explanation of his "unusual" but also illuminates from a new perspective the developments in his theater in the course of his career.

In "A Psychological Theory of Types," Jung suggests that the individual's perception of reality is conditioned by the interplay of two fundamental attitudes, introversion and extraversion, which manifest themselves through four psychic functions: thinking, feeling, sensing, and intuition. Ionesco's diaries suggest that he has many of the characteristics that Jung ascribes to the introverted feeling type. The selective vision that colors his polemics, allowing him, for example, to see only the similarities between Fascism and Marxism and not the differences, suggests the introvert's tendency to subordinate external reality to his own, often inflexible, perception of it. At the same time, his hostility to progress reflects the equally typical distrust of anything new. He shares the introvert's suspicion of outside reality in general, and his battle with the leftist critics of Paris in the 1950s and 1960s is symptomatic of what Jung calls "the psychology of the underdog" which leads the introvert to see others as oppressors against whom he must continually defend his private, inner identity (cf. Coe 150). His attitude to reality is equally colored by the feeling function: "I'm more affective than cerebral," he tells Bonnefoy (*Conversations* 41), and this is confirmed by his description of the "Illuminations" in which his perception of reality undergoes a drastic change into a form of euphoria, into "this profound, total, organic intuition which, surging up from my deepest self, might well have inundated everything, both my other self and others" (*Present Past* 151). This overwhelming of the conscious, which is involved with others, by the euphoric and intensely self-centered intuition rising out of the unconscious corresponds to Jung's description of what happens to the introverted feeling type when excessive egocentricity distorts his perception: "The intensification of egocentric feeling only leads to inane transports of feeling for their own sake. This is the mystical, ecstatic stage which opens the way for the extraverted functions that feeling has repressed" (Jung 388). It also points up the destruction of the distinction between self and others brought about by the change in perception, which parallels the erasure of the subject/object dichotomy suggested by Todorov as a possible source of the fantastic.

The conflict between the consciousness dominated by affective involvement with his fellow men and the unconscious characterized by withdrawal from all emotional attachment, whether to himself or to others, plays a determining role at different stages of Ionesco's career. At first, the theater offers him a means of withdrawing from an external reality with which he cannot come to terms, just as the "Illuminations" of his adolescence had acted as a defense against the stress of social living. "The great surprise and joy of literature lay in that astonished discovery of oneself . . . of a self which was suddenly no longer outrageous, a scandal, but an integrated being, enveloped in a context, that is to say justified by that rich, immense and universal context" (*Découvertes* 91–92). Here we see the poor self-image and sense of incompatibility with external reality, which Jung ascribes to the introvert (378–79), being replaced by a new feeling of worth and, above all, of integration. This conforms exactly to Jung's belief that "to the introverted type the universe does not appear beautiful and desirable, but disquieting and even dangerous; he entrenches himself in his inner fastness, securing himself by the invention of regular geometrical figures full of repose, whose primitive, magical power assures him of domination over the surrounding world. 'The urge to abstraction is the origin of all art', says Worringer" (505–06). Like the geometrical figures, Ionesco's early theater mediates between his internal and external worlds: "So I really created my theatre in order to speak, to surround myself with a world, to speak to the world from this world, from this world on a stage" (*Découvertes* 91).

Ionesco's early theater creates this bridge by providing a universe that is controllable and, therefore, nonthreatening and undemanding of emotional response. It appeared at a time when he was clearly overwhelmed by the pressures of social living and no doubt served as a defense mechanism against them. The theater is for him a means of withdrawal in which the "unusual" is a function of emotional detachment, for where there is no affective involvement, the introverted feeling type necessarily experiences a reduced sense of reality: "Then the universe seems to be infinitely strange and foreign. At such a moment I gaze upon it with a mixture of anguish and euphoria; separate from the universe, as though placed at a certain distance outside it" (*Notes* 136). In this state his perception of the world is completely transformed. It is no longer something in which he participates; it is rather a spectacle in which he dispassionately watches the meaningless antics of his fellow men.

Ionesco's first plays exemplify the working of this psychological defense mechanism. His description of the moment of inspiration in the creation of *The Bald Soprano* makes this clear. While copying sentences from an English language conversation manual, he says, "I had felt genuinely uneasy, sick and dizzy. Every now and then I had to stop working and, wondering what the devil could be forcing me on to write, I would go and lie down on the sofa, afraid I might see it sinking into the abyss; and myself with it" (*Notes* 179). *The Bald Soprano* is the product of this panic attack which corresponds both to Ionesco's "Illuminations" and to Jung's description of the ecstatic stage in the change in the introverted feeling type's perception. The play is concerned primarily with communication, and the accelerating proliferation of words and sounds that gradually slip from sense to meaninglessness is the first example of the connection between the fantastic and Ionesco's withdrawal into the purely contemplative state.

Proliferation is less a device than an expression of Ionesco's reduced sense of reality. It is particularly prevalent in his first plays where it forms part of the general breakdown of the accepted temporal, spatial, and causal basis of existence. In the derisive universe of these first plays, proliferation is always accompanied by a loss of individual identity or the threat thereof. In *The Bald Soprano* the Smiths replace the Martins at the end of the play and begin again with exactly the same dialogue as at the beginning, while a plethora of Bobby Watsons is discussed with no differentiation between male and female, young and old, or even living and dead. In *The Lesson* it is the pupil victims of the Professor who proliferate—41 in a day—as Ionesco's view of society's use of education to destroy the individuality of its young is expressed by the process that culminates in the symbolic rape-murder of each pupil.

In these first plays, the fantastic reflects Ionesco's contemplative view of humankind, and they are peopled by characters with whom he does not identify and who make no emotional demands on him. One must have an individual identity in order to elicit sympathy, and this is totally lacking in the interchangeable Smiths and Martins, in the proliferating Bobby Watsons, and in the nameless pupil and teacher of *The Lesson*. Ionesco links these characters, whom he calls "characters without character. Puppets. Faceless creatures" (*Notes* 181), specifically to his own peculiar and fragile perception of reality: "The absurd is conceived as being in some way an intrinsic part of existence. Now for me, intrinsically, everything that exists is logical, there is nothing absurd about it. It is the consciousness of being and existing that is astonishing. . . . And I believe I am a comic writer thanks to this faculty, not only for observation, but for detachment, for being able to stand outside myself'' (*Notes* 121). It is not difficult to see in this statement the potential both for sudden changes in perception and for the disappearance of the distinction between subject and object that favors the fantastic.

The "tragic farces" of the mid–1950s—*The Chairs*, *Victims of Duty*, and *Amédée or How to Get Rid of It*—reveal a change both in his perception of reality and in the nature of the fantastic in his plays. In *The Chairs*, external reality seems to be just as much undermined as in the earlier plays, for the guests invited into the old couple's tower home are both invisible and inaudible. Their arrival also follows the pattern of accelerating proliferation established in the first plays. There is, however, one important difference which Ionesco himself points out when he talks of *The Chairs*: "I myself would find it difficult to say whether some of the characters exist or not, whether the real is truer than the unreal or the reverse" (*Notes* 136). This comes remarkably close to Todorov's definition of the fantastic as the moment of hesitation between belief and disbelief and is closely related to the growing tension between the internal and the external, between withdrawal and involvement. Ionesco himself distinguishes between the two groups of plays by pointing out that the tragic farces mark the first appearance of the feeling function in his theater: "Let us say that they are different in that there is in them emotional involvement on my part" (Marcabru 3).

At the same time, *The Chairs* might well be seen as a classic case study of the introvert, for the island tower which is the old couple's home corresponds closely to Jung's suggestion that the ideal of the introvert is "a lonely island where nothing moves except what he permits to move" (380). Similarly, the visitors' loss of physical presence on entering the tower reflects the introvert's characteristic tendency to subordinate external reality to his subjective perception of it. The guests, on being invited into the tower, enter an internal domain where their reality falls prey to the controlling central consciousness and is replaced by mental images that it creates. There is also a clear parallel with the function of art as described by Jung and Worringer, that of allowing the introvert to meet external reality on his own terms by replacing it with his own interpretation of it. Indeed, *The Chairs* might also be seen as a commentary on this function of Ionesco's first plays, which were the product of the psychological defense mechanism and its subsequent contemplative stance. The Old Man's message, delivered by the deaf and dumb Orator, is meaningless, and when the old couple throw themselves out of the windows they land in water, which in Ionesco's theater is a symbol of social involvement. One inference that can be drawn is that Ionesco is beginning to realize that the withdrawal represented by his first plays is an ephemeral and no longer wholly satisfying episode.

The Chairs provides an excellent example of how the tension between the internal and external universes of the introverted feeling type is expressed through the fantastic. It is the first of Ionesco's plays in which the conflict between involvement and withdrawal becomes a theme rather than a source. He defines the new emotional involvement evident in *The Chairs* as "the projection on to the stage of my own internal conflicts" (Marcabru 3), and this awareness of the growing struggle within him becomes a constant and determining factor in his theater from this point on. It is no coincidence that it is also at this time that certain fantastic elements make their appearance, for they translate the two conflicting forces within him into dramatic terms.

In all three tragic farces the temptation to withdraw is presented through the related images of light, lightness, ascension, and flight. In *The Chairs* the Old Man tells the Emperor how his attempts to escape the woes of the world have been frustrated by his fellows: "In order to forget, Majesty, I tried to take up sport . . . mountaineering . . . my feet were pulled from under me" (*Plays* 1: 76). In *Victims of Duty*, the principal character, Choubert, actually takes flight in his search for Mallot, who may represent his authentic self: "I can fly. . . . I'm bathing in the light. (*Total darkness on the stage.*) The light is seeping through me. I'm so surprised to be. . . . I am light! I'm flying!" (*Plays* 2: 301–02). The attempts by his wife, Madeleine, and the Detective to bring him back to earth underline the connection between the fantastic theme of flight and withdrawal: "Have pity, pity!" Madeleine cries, while the Detective calls, "Remember the solidarity of the human race" (*Plays* 2: 299). Again, there seems to be a commentary on Ionesco's withdrawal in his first plays, for when Choubert's flight ends, and the stage is lit again, he is found sprawling in a large wastepaper basket. In *Amédée* the theme is taken one stage further, for Amédée succeeds in flying off and escaping from two policemen. This flight promises no more than the earlier ones, for there is a part of him that rejects withdrawal: "I didn't want to run away from my responsibilities. . . . I didn't do it on purpose, not of my own free will!" (*Plays* 2: 237–38).

The force opposing flight is involvement through guilt, and it too is expressed through the fantastic. In *The Chairs*, the old couple's leap into the water surrounding the tower to escape the proliferation of disembodied guests may be seen as the death of the egocentric, contemplative perception of reality and the return of the consciousness to affective involvement with the world around it. In *Victims*, it is coffee cups, a more obvious symbol of social intercourse, that proliferate as Madeleine brings them at an increasing rate, significantly while the Detective is forcing the dry bread of involvement down Choubert's throat. Similarly, in *Amédée*, not only does the corpse grow incredibly but also Amédée's apartment is invaded by a profusion of mushrooms which, with their connotations of dark and damp, also suggest involvement in society.

Further examples of the fantastic tendency to blur the frontier between the mental and the physical emphasize the role of guilt in the individual's involvement in the affairs of his fellows. The old couple's outward behavior changes constantly in an exaggerated way to reflect their changing inner thoughts and attitudes. In *Victims*, Madeleine and the Detective suddenly age 20 years with a change of clothes, become Choubert's parents, and reenact the scene between Ionesco's parents which he witnessed as a small child and which he claims implanted the original seed of guilt in him. It was an argument that ended in his mother's attempted suicide. Whereas Ionesco's father stopped her from drinking the poison, in the play the Detective does not: "*The Detective goes to Madeleine and takes her by the arm to prevent her swallowing the poison; then, suddenly, as the expression on his face changes, it is he who forces her to drink*" (*Plays* 2: 284). Here too the transition from mind to matter is made literal, and when Choubert then tells the Detective/Father figure, "I take after you . . . I've all the same faults as you," the reference to Ionesco's assumption of his father's guilt is clear (*Plays* 2: 286). Finally, when the Detective forces the dry bread of everyday living down Choubert's throat, the role of his sense of guilt in Ionesco's gradual involvement with his fellow humans is given vivid dramatic expression.

The theme of guilt reaches its climax and finds its most fantastic expression in *Amédée*. "It is a drama about guilt," Ionesco says, in a program note written in 1970, "Amédée and Madeleine . . . could be Adam and Eve; so the corpse would be the concrete symbol of the original sin, which they don't remember." Madeleine confirms this: "If he'd forgiven us, he'd have stopped growing" (*Plays* 2: 169). Theirs is a generalized sense of guilt, not connected with any specific event. Thus the identity of the corpse is variously given as Madeleine's lover, Amédée's father, a neighbor's baby, and a woman whom Amédée had left to drown. It is a vague guilt which has the effect of anchoring Amédée in the morass of everyday living and, at the same time, of preventing him from writing his play. The corpse, with all its connotations of guilt and responsibility for others, continues to grow until Amédée can stand it no longer and decides to remove it. When it then turns into a gigantic banner and carries him off toward the Milky Way, it is not difficult to recognize the parallel with the psychological mechanism of the drive toward detachment and the contemplative view, too long and too completely subordinated to its opposite, bursting the repressive barriers all the more violently for having been so effectively suppressed. Confirmation that this is indeed the purport of the fantastic episode can be found in Ionesco's description to Bonnefoy of how washing on a line was transformed into "banners" by a similar change of perception brought about by one of his adolescent "Illuminations" (*Conversations* 32).

The tragic farces of the mid–1950s helped establish the terms of the conflict within Ionesco but also led to a hiatus in his dramatic production, which he ascribes to the realization that his theater could no longer be the spontaneous exercise it had once been: "It's annoying, before it used to be a game, unwholesome, perhaps, and equivocal, but nevertheless a game. Now it's a job! That's why I've hardly produced anything for two years'" (Mègret). The very success of his early plays had led to a notoriety and to expectations that precluded further creations of the same type. Nor were his efforts to rediscover the pristine state of his beginnings helped by the clamor of the left-wing critics of Paris who, when he did not propose a leftist social model to replace the bourgeois one that he had so successfully discredited, attacked him for having betrayed the revolution in both art and politics. The result of these intrusions of the world into Ionesco's artistic Garden of Eden was not a banner to sweep him heavenwards but a period of stocktaking that ended with the creation of *The Killer*, which was both the result and the transcription of his meditations on the question of involvement and detachment.

In the first act of *The Killer*, Ionesco looks back to one of his adolescent "Illuminations." The "radiant city" that Bérenger visits is, according to Ionesco, a dramatic depiction of the state of "astonishment at being," of withdrawal, which he sets in opposition to involvement in the mundane affairs of social living: "There he [Bérenger] is acting out the fundamental attitude. . . . This attitude is almost indescribable; and if we were simply to stop at it, then obviously everyday existence, history, all kinds of problems would simply not exist. We don't always live on the same level of consciousness" (Bonnefoy 125–26). It is a science fiction, man-made paradise which elicits in Bérenger the euphoria of Ionesco's "Illuminations" and which is significantly marked by the absence of human beings: "Not a man in the street, not a cat, not a sound, there was only me. . . . And yet I didn't suffer from being alone, I didn't feel lonely" (*Plays* 3: 23). Here, in the contemplative state, there is no tension between involvement and detachment, for others no longer exist; once again the detached paradise is linked to the theme of flight: "I'm sure I could have flown away. . . . I was lighter than the blue sky I was breathing" (*Plays* 3: 24). When the first signs of a human presence appear, the radiant city's illusion of perfection is destroyed, and Bérenger is exiled from his paradise because he recognizes the existence of evil in the world, in the form of people's aggressive instinct, which is embodied by the uncanny killer who is known by all but who cannot be stopped. "I can't remain indifferent," Bérenger replies to the Architect's "If we thought about all the misfortunes of mankind we could never go on living" (*Plays* 3: 36). Brightness changes to drabness as a sense of responsibility and guilt replaces his former childlike, innocent enjoyment of the world. "Familiarity is a grey cover beneath which we hide the world's virginity; that's what original sin is about. . . . It's also the introduction of an evil into the world," Ionesco tells Bonnefoy (*Conversations* 31).

The change from the simplicity and egoism of the child's outlook to the adult's awareness of the sufferings of others is the reverse of the metamorphosis of the corpse in *Amédée*, and it too is accompanied by an element of the fantastic: a *dédoublement* in Bérenger as he meets Edouard on his return home. Edouard is without doubt meant to be Bérenger's alter ego: both have keys to the apartment, although Bérenger does not recall having given any to Edouard, and neither has been seen entering or leaving the apartment, although the Concierge has been on duty all day. The implication is that Bérenger has not in fact left the apartment to visit the radiant city and that he and Edouard represent two aspects of the same individual consciousness, as perhaps the old couple of *The Chairs* and Choubert and Madeleine of *Victims* also do. If Bérenger is the Ionesco who has returned from the flawed paradise with the intention of alleviating the suffering

of humankind, Edouard, skulking in the darkness, appears to represent the Ionesco who, trapped in the everyday, seeks to withdraw from human solidarity,
if not to the detachment of the contemplative state, at least to the relative security
of his art which serves as a pretext for noninvolvement. Bérenger attacks Edouard
for living in an ivory tower—"You're always wrapped up in your own little
world. You never know anything" (*Plays* 3: 62)—and for having no feelings
for his fellows—"Your indifference makes me sick!" (*Plays* 3: 64). Indeed,
when the proliferation of items in Edouard's briefcase is revealed to include all
the information required to apprehend the Killer, he excuses his inaction on the
grounds that the material was acquired for purely literary purposes: "The criminal
sent me his private diary, his notes and index cards a very long time ago, asking
me to publish them in a literary journal. . . . I'm sorry I didn't . . . see the connection between these documents and what's been happening" (*Plays* 3: 71).
Bérenger, on the other hand, has left the detached universe of art, and become,
as Edouard points out, "quite a man of action" (*Plays* 3: 72).

It is typical of Ionesco, torn as he is between involvement and detachment,
that Bérenger, the regenerated man of action, does not prove to be a hero who
has found the key to the salvation of humanity. He is, Ionesco tells Sarraute,
just as much a paradoxical product of *dédoublement* as his creator: "A nice boy
. . . full of the finer feelings. He has the chivalry of Don Quixote and the courage
of Sancho Panza. And it's easy to foresee what a Sancho Quixote can do to
counter this evil and tackle the killer" (12). Indeed, when Bérenger leaves Mother
Peep and her goose-stepping cohorts behind, he embarks on a Kafkaesque journey
through a weird landscape toward the police headquarters which, with its promise
of salvation, constantly retreats before him, leaving him alone and fearful.

The final confrontation between the now reluctant hero and the Killer combines
the real and the unreal. The Killer, who has shown a superhuman ability to avoid
capture, and who has an uncanny influence over human beings, is revealed to
be not an impressive personification of the devil but a pitiful wreck of a man:
"*He is very small and puny, ill-shaven, with a torn hat on his head and a shabby
old gaberdine; he has only one eye . . . his toes are peeping out of the holes in
his old shoes*" (*Plays* 3: 97–98). Although Bérenger is physically stronger than
the Killer, marshalls a whole litany of rational arguments, and finally raises a
pair of pistols against the Killer's knife, he eventually gives in to what he calls
"the resistance of an infinitely stubborn will" (*Plays* 3: 108). The Killer never
speaks and, indeed, according to the stage direction, need never appear on stage,
so that it is clear that this is a debate taking place in Bérenger's mind.

Ionesco has a much greater emotional investment in Bérenger than in any
previous character, no doubt because he represents more accurately the ambivalence of his creator toward attempts to improve the lot of his fellow humans,
but at the same time he does not restrain his derision for Bérenger's efforts:
"Bérenger should be pathetic and naive, rather ridiculous; his behaviour should
seem sincere and grotesque at the same time, both pathetic and absurd" (*Plays*
3: 99). In answer to the critics who called for a positive alternative to the

bourgeoisie which he had discredited in his first plays, Ionesco produces Bérenger whose final address to the Killer contains a variety of ideas proposed throughout history in attempts to improve the human condition; at the same time, the address reveals the futility of these ideas. "In *The Killer*," Ionesco tells Schechner, "Bérenger destroys his own clichés as he speaks. . . . After all to have no answer is better than to have a false one" (164).

The Killer introduces a new phase in Ionesco's development, one in which the *point de départ* is his recognition of the fact that he is involved, like it or not, in the fate of his fellows. The other plays of the Bérenger cycle represent attempts to come to terms with this realization, and the resultant increase in tension is expressed in further examples of the fantastic. It is a fantastic, however, that is less spontaneous than that of his earlier plays. "It was partly a nightmare," he says of *Rhinoceros*, "A distant, assimilated nightmare. Which means it wasn't really a nightmare any more, it was something I had thought about quite coolly. . . . I was doing it in a completely lucid way, yet basing it upon my nightmare image. But I was no longer inside the nightmare, whereas when I was writing *Victims of Duty* or *How to Get Rid of It*, I was in a nightmare state or at least in a state of astonishment" (Bonnefoy 70–71).

The principal fantastic element in *Rhinoceros* is the metamorphosis of the inhabitants of a small town into the animals for which the play is named. The nightmare on which it is based is that of the rise of Fascism which Ionesco witnessed in prewar Romania. The development of the fantastic follows the classic pattern described by Todorov. As in the majority of Ionesco's works, the play opens with a very ordinary scene, and even when the first rhinoceros appears in the street, several reasonable explanations are suggested for its presence—escape from a zoo or from a traveling circus. All of these are refuted by other characters, but a rational explanation still seems possible up to the moment when one of Bérenger's co-workers suddenly arrives at the office changed into a rhinoceros and causes much noise and destruction before thundering off with his wife on his back. From this point on, the audience shares Bérenger's growing anguish as first his friend Jean becomes a rhinoceros in an equally fantastic scene, and then the other inhabitants of the town suffer the same metamorphosis in increasing numbers until Bérenger is the sole survivor of the human race. This acceleration and proliferation form the same pattern as found in the early plays, and they express the same panic reaction to the threat of the individual's being drowned in a sea of social involvement, for the totalitarian state, to which "rhinoceritis" leads, is the most suffocating form of social structure.

For Ionesco, the rhinoceros is the focal point of the play, for it transcribes an experience he had in Romania when one of his friends began to show signs of accepting Fascist thinking. A 1940 diary entry describing the incident seems to make this clear: "I spoke to him. He was still a man. Suddenly, beneath my very eyes, I saw his skin get hard and thicken in a terrifying way. His gloves, his shoes, became hoofs; his hands became paws, a horn began to grow out of his forehead, he became ferocious, he attacked furiously. He was no longer intelligent, he could no longer talk. He had become a rhinoceros. I would like very much to follow his example. But I can't'' (*Present Past* 80). A second look, however, suggests that the crucial change in the fantastic image is less in the friend than in Ionesco's perception of him. Jean's metamorphosis is similar to that which robbed the old couple's visitors of their reality, in that it reflects the crumbling of the barrier between mind and matter, and is symptomatic of a spontaneous movement of withdrawal in which mental images replace external reality. This withdrawal, however, does not produce euphoria: both the diary entry and the play end with a sense of isolation and bad conscience. Bérenger's first reaction on being left alone is the introvert's characteristic withdrawal and suspicion of both change and the outside world: ''You won't get me!'' he shouts, carefully closing the door and windows, ''I'm not joining you. . . . I'm staying as I am.'' This is followed by a feeling of responsibility for Daisy's metamorphosis: ''It's my fault she's gone. . . . That's one more person on my conscience'' (*Play* 4: 105). From this it is but a short step to acceptance of the rhinoceroses' standards: ''Now I'm a monster, just a monster. Now I'll never become a rhinoceros. . . . I want to, I really do, but I can't'' (*Plays* 4: 107). This bad conscience contrasts sharply with the feeling of self-worth that his first plays afforded him and shows clearly the extent to which he had become involved in the affairs of his fellow humans.

This same outlook is revealed in *A Stroll in the Air*, the third play in the Bérenger cycle. Like *Rhinoceros*, this play begins in a very ordinary setting before gradually slipping into the fantastic. Against a background of English families out for a Sunday walk in the sunshine, Bérenger, a famous dramatist, is interviewed in his country retreat by a journalist who wants to know when he will write a new play. The answer appears to be ''never,'' because he feels that his art can no longer be a spontaneous, gratuitous game but should lead to something beyond. He goes on to admit that he has produced a theater with a message, although it is not an expected or acceptable one. Shortly afterward, Bérenger's cottage is destroyed by bombs from what he claims to be a German bomber that has been left over from World War II. Gradually the ordinariness of the scene is undermined. Bérenger remains miraculously unhurt, one of the little English girls is revealed to be ''the little bald soprano,'' and the Visitor from the Anti-World appears, an old-fashioned gentleman who smokes an upside-down pipe from which the smoke falls instead of rising. He is seen only by Bérenger and his daughter, Marthe. Bérenger explains that the Visitor must have slipped through a crack in his Anti-World into a no-man's-land between the two worlds. He says that there is an infinite number of anti-worlds: ''The Anti-World. . . . There's no proof that it exists, but when you think about it, you can find it in your own thoughts. . . . These worlds interlink and interlock, without touching one another, for they can all co-exist in the same space'' (*Plays* 6: 27–28). What better definition could there be of the concept of solipsism, of reality's changing according to the consciousness perceiving it—or of the blurring of the distinction between internal and external worlds that Todorov sees as a source of the fantastic? And what is more understandable than that such a description be put forward by an introvert?

At this point the movement begins that leads to Bérenger's flight. His happiness begins to translate into a feeling of weightlessness, and the fact that it is due to a change in perception is made clear: "It's as though I was seeing everything for the first time. As though I'd just been born" (*Plays* 6: 36). What he feels is a sort of "divine intoxication" in which he has no anxiety: "My head is reeling with conviction" (*Plays* 6: 37). Clearly, he is describing the onset of a psychological crisis and a change in the mode of perception that corresponds to Jung's description of the introverted feeling type's "mystical, ecstatic stage." Bérenger takes flight, but from the beginning it is clear that this is not the flight to the contemplative stance of the first plays. A circus bicycle is thrown to him from the wings, circus bleachers appear on the stage, and Bérenger demonstrates the art of flight as he rides the bicycle in circles above the spectators' heads. After this devaluation of the fantastic image, it is not surprising that, shortly after Bérenger's true flight begins, he suddenly shows signs of distress and then disappears.

The reasons for Bérenger's failure to achieve the euphoric state during this flight are suggested by the scenes that follow his disappearance. These depict the various demands for emotional involvement that Ionesco perceives in his own world. In the first scene, the journalist argues for replacing the effete emotion of love with the energy of hatred, which recalls Jean's views as he becomes a rhinoceros. There follows a nightmare scene in which a guard captures and apparently executes two children who are climbing a wall. Interspersed with these scenes is the greatest deterrent to flight from involvement: scenes that reflect his sense of guilt at having abandoned his wife, Joséphine, to the vagaries of life. In the first, she finds herself in court, before a 20-foot-tall judge. She protests her innocence—of what we do not know, but in this Kafkaesque court this seems to have little importance. Before a verdict can be handed down, however, the court suddenly disappears. Shortly after, the court and judge are replaced by an equally gigantic Man in White accompanied by an executioner and gallows in another scene straight from a nightmare. The Man in White tries to persuade Joséphine to avail herself of the gallows, and when she refuses, he points out that she cannot stave off the inevitable forever.

In the meantime, Bérenger is being assailed by further appeals for solidarity with the human race. "I can see, I'm afraid I can see everything! And there's no more hope," he says in despair (*Plays* 6: 70). What his flight reveals to him is an apocalyptic view of all of the horrors, human-made and natural, which make up the lot of humankind, and to which people blind themselves by burying their heads in the sand of everyday living. He reports having seen men with heads of geese, a clear reference to Mother Peep's goose-stepping totalitarian legions in *The Killer*; columns of guillotined men marching along without heads; giant grasshoppers; fallen angels; and "whole continents of Paradise all in flames. And all the Blessed were being burned alive" (*Plays* 6: 75). He has also witnessed natural disasters like earthquakes and landslides with oceans of mud and blood. This vision, a mixture of Hieronymus Bosch and Franz Kafka, is far removed from the irrational eruption of the subconscious which led to previous flights. Ionesco states unequivocally that it is the consciously inspired part of the play: "My starting point was both a dream and a conscious thought. The dream part was the man flying. The conscious part was what he sees as a result of this flight" (Bonnefoy 65).

A Stroll in the Air introduces a new dimension to the question of perception in Ionesco's theater. Until now there have been only two mutually exclusive modes of perception: the involved and the detached. Now he redefines them in terms of three alternatives. "There's daytime consciousness and night-time consciousness; daytime unconsciousness is a sort of oblivion," he tells Bonnefoy (*Conversations* 70). The diurnal consciousness, characterized by sunlight, is the joyous, heightened awareness of being which is found in Ionesco's "Illuminations" and which gradually builds up in Bérenger until he flies off. Its nocturnal counterpart, bathed in moonlight, exposes the human condition in all its misery: "This black brightness brings me, with a certainty beyond question, the revelation of disaster, of catastrophe, of failure irremediable and absolute" (*Fragments* 40). This is the vision that appears to Bérenger as the detached lucidity of the contemplative state changes to anguish instead of euphoria and that is discounted by the English families who represent the third mode of perception: the diurnal, unmindful state of mind blinded to the actual and potential horrors of human existence by the trivia of social life.

The replacement of diurnal consciousness by nocturnal lucidity during Bérenger's flight is indicative of the changes that have taken place in Ionesco's outlook since the early plays, and indeed most of the fantastic elements in the play might be seen as a commentary on his career. Thus the idyllic scene bathed in sunlight at the beginning of the play, with Bérenger safely ensconced in his country retreat, reflects Ionesco's state of mind in the early 1950s, when his theater offered him a means of withdrawal from the external world. With the appearance of the journalist, whose request to "Give us a message" recalls the left-wing critics of the mid–1950s, Bérenger's comfortable isolation, like Ionesco's, is disturbed. The arrival of the World War II bomber and its destruction of Bérenger's haven suggest a further reason for Ionesco's renewed involvement: the guilt that he felt for having cynically avoided active involvement in the struggle against Nazism, not only because he believed that all causes were invalidated by the absurdity of existence but also for the very practical reason of self-protection. The increasingly brief and rare appearances of the Visitor from the Anti-World anticipate Bérenger's gradual loss of the contemplative view and recall Ionesco's similar increased involvement. All of these hints are made explicit when Bérenger, shortly before he flies off, states that he wishes to be both "a pedestrian and a pedestrian in the air" (*Plays* 6: 50). It is no longer a question of one or other of the two initial modes of perception dominating to the exclusion of the other; it is a question of his search for a means of reconciling them in one outlook. This is the key that explains both the catastrophic results of the flight and Ionesco's experience in the Bérenger cycle of plays where unconscious inspiration is mingled with—at one point he would have said, diluted by—conscious intent.

The conclusion to be drawn from Ionesco's reflection on the development of his theater—and it is one that he drew himself—is that he has once more been drawn out of his contemplative detachment by his affective attachment to his fellow beings and by the need he feels to warn them of the dangers menacing them in their carefree fool's paradise. The result for him is the loss of the pure joy of the spontaneous creation of his first plays and frustration at his inability to bring about greater lucidity in his contemporaries. It is perhaps a combination of these two factors that led to the gradual decrease in his dramatic output and eventually to a complete halt in the late 1960s when, for a four-year period, he abandoned the theater and devoted himself to editing and publishing his diaries which could be more explicit.

Macbett (1972) seems to combine aspects of both the early plays and the Bérenger cycle, for it manages to purvey an apocalyptical view of human existence, deal with contemporary politics, and still maintain a highly derisive tone. "What one must not do in my plays," Ionesco tells Bonnefoy, "is to replace the unusual with pathos. One must avoid pathos; derision and irony must predominate. Even if one has an apocalyptic view of history, behind it there is also this idea that the world is nothing but a joke" (*Entre la vie* 162). This was the advice that he failed to follow in the Bérenger plays, which were essentially inward- rather than outward-looking, and it pinpoints the fundamental change in attitude that the new beginning sought to establish. It is a black humor like that of the early plays which represents not an escape from awareness but a heightened lucidity accompanied by and dependent on a release from emotional response: "It's as if I was dancing on tens of thousands of corpses, and on whole countries destroyed by floods or flames. . . . Happy in my misery, happy in the misery of others. And I don't feel guilty" ("Jamais je n'ai écrit" 5). *Macbett* is not, however, a return to the spontaneous expression of the psychological defense mechanism found in his first plays; it is a consciously crafted interpretation of an external inspiration: "*Macbett* is a satirical attack on politics and indeed on action, and the position I take is a completely conscious one in which the subconscious has no part" (Coleman 815). *Macbett* thus constitutes one more effort to reconcile the two conflicting tendencies, involvement and detachment, but, as the rejection of action suggests, with a bias toward the latter. The examples of the fantastic in the play reflect this.

In *Macbett*, the fantastic takes many forms. Doubles, ghosts, and witches abound, and the themes of proliferation and of flight also make their appearance. There is a considerable amount of *dédoublement* in the play, but not all of a fantastic nature. Macbett and Banco are presented as "extremely alike. Same costume, same beard" (*Plays* 9: 23). They also pronounce more or less the same speeches in response to the same situations. In addition, as a pair, they closely resemble Candor and Glamiss whom they replace as comspirators against Duncan, repeating much of the dialogue in which the first duo build up a rationalization justifying their attack on the king. They are not, however, true doubles; they are portrayed as similar in order to point up the universality of the influence of ambition and power on men throughout the ages. Macbett's confusion of the portrait of Duncan for his own in the banquet scene is more akin to the fantastic. It may be the expression of Macbett's guilty conscience, and it certainly reflects Ionesco's belief that even rebels with the purest of motives quickly come to resemble the tyrants they have overthrown. The appearance of Duncan's ghost immediately afterward, however, places the event firmly in the realm of the marvelous. Banco's ghost and Macol's parentage are further forms of the fantastic that are of greater importance for the action of the play. Born to Banco and a gazelle that had been turned into a woman by a witch, Macol is not affected by the witches' assurance that no man born of woman can strike Macbett down.

The fantastic theme of proliferation and acceleration also makes its appearance in *Macbett*. After the revolt led by Glamiss and Candor has been put down, the insurgents are executed by guillotine—not just the leaders, but the whole army of 130,000 men. The accelerating cadence reflects Ionesco's growing horror at the atrocities committed in the name of political ideologies. In a similar vein, there is the scene in which Duncan cures the halt and the sick at an increasing rate. This scene ends in Duncan's assassination and suggests both Ionesco's view that a return to a relatively benevolent monarchy might not be the worst fate that could befall France and his belief that regimes tend to become less repressive with the passage of time and that it is this mellowing that allows revolutions to take place. This idea is reinforced by the proliferation of guillotines that accompanies Macol's accession to power and promise of greater evils to come.

The most complex and significant example of the fantastic in *Macbett* centers on the role of the two witches, around whom there forms a constellation of themes such as flight, doubles, metamorphosis, and the satanic. The witches have both metaphysical and psychological connotations and are central to Ionesco's efforts to identify the reasons for people's susceptibility to the corrupting influence of power.

The maleficent forces that tempt humans along the road to disaster appear at first to belong to the metaphysical realm, for they are presented in terms of good and evil, and there are references to a satanic influence behind the witches. Macbett is vaguely aware of this: "As soon as I glimpse the shadow of this woman or hear her address herself to me, then my hair stands on end. The stench of sulphur seems to pervade the air, and if I place my hand on my sword, it's because it is more than a weapon, it's a cross as well" (*Plays* 9: 52). Elsewhere he calls the witches "daughters of Satan" (*Plays* 9: 55), and the First Witch's behavior suggests that they are servants of the Devil. She is burned by the cross on the necklace she wears in her guise as Lady Macbett, the Host that she took during the wedding ceremony "was like thorn or burning ember" in her throat, she almost fainted at the sight of ikons, and as she rids herself of the trappings of the now unnecessary beauty, she emphasizes the metaphysical aspects of her role: "The two forces of good and evil are now locked in combat in that cross. Which will prove stronger? Such a puny battlefield! Yet it contains a universal war!" (*Plays* 9: 88). The cross to which she refers is the one on the necklace, but the reference is even more significant when applied to the cross-shaped dagger with which she tempts Macbett into the path of crime. Her parting words suggest the permanence of evil. "The boss will be happy," she says as they prepare to fly off, having set in motion the diabolical chain of events; "He's got another mission for us" (*Plays* 9: 89).

If there is a satanic power at work, it is exercised, as in Cocteau's *The Infernal Machine*, through human nature, for the witches also represent a force that derives from a zone deep within the human psyche. The scene in which they take control of Macbett in a form of magic ritual reveals that the external political change from loyal subject to usurper is in fact what Ionesco has always considered to be the only effective change: a change in mentality. It begins with the Second Witch dancing around the First Witch "as though for some act of magic," and the change in Macbett is initiated by the command "Alter ego surge" (*Plays* 9: 58). When his other, normally repressed self comes forth, the change is reflected externally, as the distinction between spiritual and physical disappears. What has been considered an abhorrent crime now becomes attractive, and the witches gradually metamorphose into the beautiful Lady Duncan and her servant. The First Witch's change into Lady Duncan introduces the principal psychological theme: that of the *libido dominandi*. Erotic love is linked to the quest for power. "It would hardly surprise me if Macbett was after my wife, too," Duncan says, when he first suspects Macbett (*Plays* 9: 65). The theme is introduced most clearly, however, in the scene of Macbett's entrancement by the witches. The Second Witch's dance around the First Witch recalls the Teacher's dance around the Pupil in *The Lesson*, and the scene is charged with erotic connotations— from the phallic symbol of the dagger which the First Witch offers to Macbett with the exhortation "Take it, if you want it, if you want *me*" (*Plays* 9: 61), to the ultimate in metamorphosis-cum-striptease. In this, the First Witch removes not only her filthy, ragged clothes but also her pointed nose, hooked chin, and hunched back to reveal the beautiful Lady Duncan who continues the striptease until left in a dazzling bikini, with a black and red cape over her shoulders and holding the dagger which is both instrument of death and phallic symbol. Ambition and lust combine in an infernal and irresistible siren-song: "This is the tool with which to further *your* ambition, *our* advancement. . . . Help yourself and Hell will help you. See how desire rises within you, how ambition stands revealed and ignites your purpose" (*Plays* 9: 61, emphasis in original).

The witches stand in a no-man's-land between the sexual and the political, between the psychological and the metaphysical. The play also stands on a frontier between involvement and detachment. Ionesco states that *Macbett* is a conscious attack on political activity in general and on revolution in particular, which places it firmly in the domain of involvement. His treatment of the political theme, however, counters the bias in the content in two ways: first, by universalizing it into what might be termed a Freudian study with metaphysical overtones introduced by the veiled references to the Devil; second, and more important, by consciously increasing the derisive treatment, which can be seen particularly with respect to the fantastic elements. The departure of the two witches is indicative of this. They fly off, not on the traditional broomstick but astride a giant suitcase, symbolic of the subconscious. This flight has none of the pristine fantasy of Amédée's or Bérenger's, for Ionesco goes out of his way to devalue the fantastic by offering a pseudorational, derisive explanation: "The First Witch is in front, looking as if she were turning a steering wheel—the motor is noisy. The Second Witch extends her arms on either side to imitate wings" (*Plays* 9: 89–90). Similarly, when Macol reveals his strange parentage, the fantastic circumstances are undermined by being "spoken or sung in a Wagnerian style" (*Plays* 9: 101). Other examples of this are to be found in the witches' reference to the Devil as "the boss," in the ironic deflating of the *dédoublement* of the portrait scene by the suggestion that myopia tends to accompany accession to power, and in the Birnham Wood scene where Macbett's one-word expletive on seeing the advancing forest completely defuses everything, including the fantastic effect. This new approach to the fantastic lends weight to the belief that Ionesco is no longer capable of flight to the detachment of the contemplative state and that his only recourse is to a consciously crafted cynical and derisive treatment of the apocalyptic, themes that would once have triggered the psychological defense mechanism.

The realization that he is caught in a trap, torn between his hunger for human warmth and his thirst for the detachment of the absolute, may be the reason for the dramatic shift in emphasis and direction that is obvious in Ionesco's last two major plays to date, *The Man with the Luggage* (1975) and *Journeys among the Dead* (1981). Whereas the plays of the early 1970s showed both a greater, more desperate involvement in contemporary affairs and a conscious, counterbalancing intensification of the derisive treatment of the themes, these last two plays reveal an equally deliberate rejection of external reality in favor of an exploration of his inner world through the medium of dreams. They constitute a further attempt to recreate the oneiric universe of his first plays with its uninvolved, contemplative stance, for they are, he claims, the most direct and objective descriptions possible of his dreams.

The Man with the Luggage comprises 19 scenes that present a series of unrelated, nightmarish images of Ionesco's life in France and Romania in the 1930s and 1940s. According to Ionesco, the First Man's suitcases, referred to in the title, represent the subconscious, are frequently noted to be very heavy, and contain different things at different times. Like his character, Ionesco carries a great deal of ballast in his subconscious, but he is able to unburden himself by writing the play. The resulting oneiric universe lacks most of the solid points of reference on which we depend in everyday life. Time is distorted, with a young woman being presented as an old woman's mother, and death itself being a reversible condition. Equally, space does not conform to the laws of normal or even theatrical reality, with the scene shifting without the slightest warning from Paris to a nameless totalitarian state which resembles the Romania of the years before and during World War II. Identity also suffers the destabilizing effects of the dream, with characters sharing or exchanging identities, and the First Man so unsure of who he is that he feels obliged to telephone Paris to find out what his real name is. In the course of the First Man's journey, which appears part Kafka and part Lewis Carroll, many elements typical of the nightmare occur: missed trains, inability to remember names and places, court scenes that reflect guilt, a Sphinx with its riddle, the permanent sense of being lost without documentary justification of his existence, and the inability to communicate, presented here through the vagaries of the public telephone system.

Reaction to *The Man with the Luggage* has suggested to Ionesco that he has succeeded, as in *Rhinoceros*, in portraying the essence of the totalitarian experience through the presentation of his individual experience. "It is a case of personal experience being transformed into mythology," he tells Bonnefoy, "But it is an experience which is also that of many others, and thus it becomes a collective experience. Many people who came originally from totalitarian countries, or who are living there at present, have asked me: How did you know what happened to me?" (*Entre la vie* 173–74). There can be little doubt that the fantastic, with its universalizing effect, plays an important part in the creation of this mythology. Although most of the play appears to be a direct transposition of personal experiences that haunt his dreams, he admits to Bonnefoy that some of the scenes have a conscious purpose: "Even if *The Man with the Luggage* is to a large extent made up of dreams, not everything in it stems from dreams. The hospital scene is not a dream scene. It has sometimes been taken to be an attack on psychiatric clinics. In fact, it is a criticism of euthanasia" (*Entre la vie* 172).

It is perhaps the intrusion of the last vestiges of conscious intent into the fantastic dream world of retrospection and introspection that leads to what Ionesco considers his failure to come to terms with his past in *The Man with the Luggage* (see "Why Do I Write," *Plays* 11: 121). Certainly, in *Journeys among the Dead* he abandons even more completely the external world of conscious rationality in order to explore more intensively the internal reality revealed by dreams: "In my latest play *Journeys among the Dead* there is no longer any clear explanation; there is destruction of the language, destruction of all meaning, and at the same time it is a subconscious autobiography, an oneiric play. . . . It is, I believe, my best play because it is completely free of all ideology" ("L'insolite" 67). Ionesco's description of the positive aspects of the latest play reveals by implication the weaknesses he sees in *The Man with the Luggage* and shows how much he wishes to renew contact with the pristine inspiration of his first plays. There is the same destruction of language and meaning as in *The Bald Soprano*; there is confusion of identity and *dédoublement*, as when Jean watches himself dealing with his father; and there is the theme of light which is followed closely by apocalyptic lucidity—all presented in a nihilistic series of dream scenes without the slightest semblance of a rational organizing principle other than the presence of Jean in each. In these dreams Jean confronts friends and relations who have caused him suffering or whom he believes he has wronged at various times in his life. His main concern seems to be to exorcise the regrets and remorse that stem from his past, and in this sense the play represents a withdrawal from contemporary involvement. This is confirmed in the play, for when Jean asks why he keeps returning to his father in his dreams, the latter replies, "It's because you're not interested in the world any more." And Jean agrees: "I get worse and worse at contending with the sound and the fury. I pretend to be interested in it, but I'm fed up with the whole business" (*Plays* 12: 16).

Elsewhere, the nihilism in which external values dissolve is found in the scene where Jean takes stock of the works that have brought him fame and finds that they have literally turned to dust. "Everything has to be begun again," he says, "But I shall continue to defend the Occident" (*Plays* 12: 27). The reference is clear both to Ionesco's disillusionment on looking back over his life's work and to his 25-year struggle to make the West aware of the threat to its civilization which he sees approaching from the marxist East. The futility of both the artistic and the political efforts is emphasized as his defiant words, which recall Bérenger's final stance in *Rhinoceros*, crumble into a series of sense and sound associations reminiscent of *The Bald Soprano*, leaving him in a state of physical collapse: "The defence of the Occident, the dance of the stimulant, the defence of the Occident, the Occident of defence, the March on Rome, the Invasion of Tuscany, the tusks of the elephant, his tusks are his defence, the tusker's defence, the defence of the Occident, the defence of the occiput . . . (*He collapses*.)" (*Plays* 12: 27). The pointlessness suggested here of any attempt to understand the human condition is also the final impression left by the play. Jean's closing monologue, which significantly is given on a brightly lit stage, begins and ends with the words "I don't know" and is almost Beckettian in character, as Ionesco, through deconstruction of language and free association of sounds and ideas, expresses his sense of the impotence of human reason in the face of existence and rejects action in favor of the contemplative stance.

It should come as no surprise to find a strong element of the fantastic in Ionesco's theater. For the introvert, the boundary between the internal and the external, between subject and object, between the mental and the physical is at most a fragile barrier; with Ionesco there is a clear predisposition to the intermingling of the two which leads to the fantastic. *The Chairs* perhaps offers the clearest description of this tendency in Ionesco's theater.

The fantastic appears in two distinct forms and serves two functions that correspond to two modes of perception. Ionesco's earliest plays show the collapse of the barriers most clearly, for in them the unusual is the product of a process in which external reality is completely internalized and stripped of its meaning. "It was by plunging into banality," he says of *The Bald Soprano*, "that I tried to render the strangeness that seems to pervade our whole existence" (*Notes*

28). The distinction between subject and object disappears, as he is unaware of himself as an entity separate from his surroundings. This corresponds both to Todorov's connection of the fantastic with the child's perception of reality and to the experience of Ionesco's own childhood paradise as he describes it to Bonnefoy: "Time was a wheel that was spinning round me, while I remained immovable and eternal. I was the centre of the world" (*Conversations* 13). His sense of being the center of the world, rather than merely *at* the center, is the key to both the childhood and the artistic paradises, for it represents an absolute integration that rids him of feelings of guilt and responsibility.

The appearance of the fantastic theme of flight, with its connotations of liberation from involvement, paradoxically marks the end of the age of innocence for Ionesco the dramatist. It is a reaction to a renewed awareness of himself in relation to others, and the fantastic in his theater takes on a new aspect, becoming a means of expressing the tension between the opposing tendencies within him. The decisive factor in this change in perception and in the fantastic is his recognition of the presence of evil and of the suffering it causes: "Evil astounds me, as much as light does. But it weighs much heavier. . . . That is what I feel as an artist. I could accept the enigma of existence, but not the mystery of evil" ("Why Do I Write?" *Plays* 11: 123). The conflict between these two elements is presented through the themes of light and flight which contrast with those of darkness, dampness, and proliferation; although the images remain within the domain of the fantastic, their use becomes increasingly conscious until they border on symbolism and allegory.

This conscious factor is the main reason for Ionesco's inability to recreate the satisfying universe of his early plays, for where there is consciousness, for the introverted feeling type there is also affective involvement. His last two plays illustrate the point. They turn away from contemporary reality but still represent an emotional involvement that is the opposite of the perception on which his first plays are based. The dreams that they present feature the author as the principal character and deal with human relations, with regret and remorse, while the fantastic takes the form of oneiric symbolism rather than the derisive view of external reality of the early plays. This turning inward may attract the introvert, but it fails to be wholly satisfying, because it is a conscious substitute for the spontaneous psychological defense mechanism that alone can offer integration and that is the sole source of Ionesco's own detached form of the fantastic. Ionesco's *insolite* is a function of perception, as is the fantastic, according to Todorov (120), and it also suggests that the absurd can represent an emotional reaction to existence as much as an intellectual one.

WORKS CITED

Bonnefoy, Claude. *Conversations with Eugène Ionesco.* Trans. Jan Dawson. London: Faber, 1970.
Coe, Richard N. *Ionesco: A Study of His Plays.* London: Methuen, 1971.

Coleman, Ingrid H. "Conscious and Unconscious Intent in the Creative Process: A Letter from Eugène Ionesco." *French Review* 54 (1981): 810–15.

Ionesco, Eugène. *Découvertes*. Geneva: Skira, 1969.

———. *Entre la vie et la rêve: entretiens avec Claude Bonnefoy*. Paris: Belfond, 1977.

———. *Fragments of a Journal*. Trans. Jean Stewart. London: Faber, 1968.

———. "L'insolite du language." *Spirales* Mar.–Apr. 1984: 67–69.

———. "Jamais je n'ai écrit avec autant de plaisir sur des thèmes aussi sinistres." *Figaro littéraire* 7 Jan. 1972: 1+.

———. *Notes and Counter Notes*. Trans. Donald Watson. New York: Grove, 1964.

———. *Plays*. Trans. Donald Watson, Derek Prouse, and Barbara Wright. 12 vols. London: Calder, 1958–85.

———. *Present Past Past Present*. Trans. Helen R. Lane. New York: Grove, 1971.

Jung, C. G. "A Psychological Theory of Types." *The Collected Works of C. G. Jung*. Trans. H. G. Baynes. Rev. R.F.C. Hall. Ed. H. Read et al. Bollingen Series 20. Vol. 6. Princeton: Princeton University Press, 1971. 524–41. 19 vols.

Marcabru, Pierre. "Notre théâtre est une expérience pour demain." *Arts* 15 Feb. 1956: 3.

Mègret, Christian. "Eugène Ionesco ou le dramaturge malgré lui." *Carrefour* 6 Mar. 1957: 15.

Sarraute, Claude. "Eugène Ionesco: '*tueur sans gages* s'inscrit dans la ligne faussement classique des pièces faussement policières.' " *Le Monde* 13 Feb. 1959: 12.

Schechner, Richard. "An Interview with Ionesco." *Tulane Drama Review* 7.3 (1963): 163–68.

Todorov, Tzvetan. *The Fantastic: A Structural Approach to a Literary Genre*. Trans. Richard Howard. Cleveland, Ohio: Case Western University Press, 1973.

6

Ambiguity and the Supernatural in Cocteau's *La machine infernale*

Ralph Yarrow

The first act of *La machine infernale* is centered on a "Shakespearean" ghost; the second is centered on the Sphinx and a mixture of Egyptian and Greek mythology; the third is full of dreams, portents, and drunkards; and the fourth, dominated by the seer Tirésias, has another kind of ghost and achieves the sacralization of Oedipe. All four acts treat their material in unusual and disturbing ways, so that the supernatural is by turns grotesque, comic, tender, awesome, inscrutable, threatening, uncomfortably familiar, and horribly predictable. In a program note, I wrote (as producer):

Dans ce théâtre aigu nous sommes toujours mal à l'aise, car le ton qui domine est celui de l'équivoque: par rapport au genre—psychodrame, comedie satirique ou tragédie? au langage—quotidien, melodramatique, stylisation idiosyncratique? aux personnages—Jocaste et Oedipe seraient-ils bêtes ou criminels, Tirésias pédant ou voyant? La renommée d'Oedipe et de Jocaste serait-elle finalement à peu pres celle de Cocteau, c'est-à-dire la mythologisation de l'ambigu?

I want now to add an account of the way the play achieves this sense of ambiguity precisely by its "play" with all these equivocal possibilities; in so doing it not only keeps us alert to the ghosts, monsters, half-acknowledged intuitions, and subterfuges of our own awareness but also demonstrates that "performance" for Cocteau is essentially geared to this end of the mythologizing of ambiguity. Play is a way of producing the ambiguity, the living-on-the-edge, which comes from the juxtaposition of dream and daytime reality, of myth and social form, of the repressed and the admitted; as an oscillation between styles, as a set of parallel but discontinuous acts, as a confusion and a hierarchy of blindness and understanding; ultimately, as a confrontation across all the borders we erect around knowing ourselves. Play is a ritual initiation into the "poetry of theater." Cocteau's *La machine infernale* is a paradigm for this initiation, a form of total catharsis, for the transformations of fantasy, and for the embodiment of a collective response which may be another form of the "supernatural."

The play is written in four acts, as follows:

ACT I.   *THE GHOST*

On the ramparts of Thebes, the guards, nerves on edge discuss the possible appearance of the ghost of Laius and are interrogated by their Captain. Jocaste, widow of Laius, wants to find out what is going on; although the ghost appears, its desperate attempts to communicate a dire warning fail to be perceived by Jocaste and her escort, the chief priest, Tirésias.

ACT II.   *THE MEETING OF OEDIPE AND THE SPHINX*

At the same time, Oedipe encounters the dreaded Sphinx on the outskirts of the city. But the Sphinx is weary of killing and would rather let its mortal and feminine form succumb to the desire for love. Oedipe's cocksure arrogance fails to sense either the chance of love or the threat of death presented by the Sphinx, and he believes his victory to be all his own doing.

ACT III.   *THE WEDDING NIGHT*

Oedipe has claimed his reward and married Jocaste. Their wedding night is interrupted by dreams, omens, thunder, and an embarrassing drunkard; Tirésias warns Oedipe that his alliance is ill-fated. Fatigue, the lure of the marriage bed, and deception about the past combine to compound the blindness of the royal pair to their situation.

ACT IV.   *OEDIPUS REX*

Blow by blow the truth of patricide and incest is revealed, and the tragic denouement takes its course after 17 years of living a lie. But Oedipe and Jocaste may at last achieve a status which, though too late for mortal ends, will establish them as symbols of their human plight.

Ghosts and mythological monsters, like gods in various traditions, are representations of aspects of our psychic reality or of a relationship with our environment that we have not fully acknowledged or find too powerful to understand comfortably and that we therefore externalize in disturbing form. Traditionally, ghosts and monsters represent chthonic forces, powerful instinctual feelings like revenge or jealousy which fester and take on even more bizarre and threatening form if not dealt with. They are frightening to face, although they may be less so in reality than in anticipation. In a sense, all ghosts are benign in that, at least, they are trying to issue warnings. The ghost of Laius in *La machine* is particularly benign, because he is rather pathetic and ineffectual and symbolically constrained to appear only above the sewers. Jocaste's nose tells her that something is wrong, but she is unable to see or hear the desperate signals of the ghost since she evidently cannot identify the source of the trouble. The simple soldiers, on the other hand, both get the message and, once they have overcome their initial superstitious shivers built up by popular horror rumors, find the poor old thing rather touching. But they sensibly decide it is not their business to meddle in the affairs of royalty, thus presenting a neat analogy of another way in which information from the lower depths frequently fails to get through to the upper echelons of consciousness.

These heights are indeed dizzy and isolated, to judge by Oedipe and Jocaste. They are both cut off in their own worlds, quite out of contact with what goes on in other parts of themselves or on more mundane levels. Jocaste flits round the ramparts dreaming of muscled youths and trying to recapture her own past, but she is affected by a disturbing tendency to trip herself up or get strangled by her own scarf; Oedipe strides out into the desert to confront monsters but only wants to play with those who are ready to be slain by his own St. George fantasy. When the ghost has to be sought in the cold night air in the face of frustration and discomfort, and when the dragon turns out to be a rather uncomfortably direct young girl, the protagonists pass on as rapidly as possible with one hand firmly clasped to eye or nose in case anything untoward should penetrate. In other words, they choose fantasy-as-escape (Oedipe the Sphinx slayer, Jocaste the femme fatale) when they need to choose fantasy-as-confrontation. In so doing, they "block off the access and passage to remorse," and cut themselves adrift from contact with the feelings and needs they and the real world might have; this inevitably causes a tragedy.

They want to go on playing king and queen, but on their own terms: nothing unsettling must come too close. They are happy to accept the privileges (pleasure and sexual domination for Jocaste, power and glory for Oedipe) without realizing the fatally significant nature of the attraction these things hold in regard to their own personal inadequacies and without coming to terms with or accepting the responsibility for themselves or others. Jocaste cannot see the ghost and treats the soldiers, who can, as "innocents" and Tirésias, who has powers of insight in spite of his blindness, as an impotent old fool (she calls him Zizi, which is the equivalent of "willy"). Oedipe thinks he has defeated the Sphinx but defeats himself by ignoring the self-knowledge the oracle represents. Both of them are blind and deaf to all warnings about the limitations of their own vision.

Oedipe runs away from manhood (the pivotal state of the answer to the Sphinx's riddle and the condition of being fully responsible both sexually and humanly). Jocaste runs away from old age and death (the ultimate end of human life); Laius's ghost would remind her of both. In both cases, Oedipe and Jocaste shun the repressed, the unknown, the potentially disruptive. They fear a change of state, mental and physical, and want to stay just as they are—as their own protective and protected image of eternal youth and macho strength. Instead, because they fear to change, they trap themselves in an outdated external mold and neglect any internal qualities. For Jocaste, love is feeling soldiers' biceps; for Oepide, it is a swollen sense of self-importance. They determinedly ignore all the promptings of dream, subconscious, fantasy, and supernatural: all manifestations of the internal energies, which they are blocking and which cause them to live a kind of straitjacketed life of adequate efficiency (the 10 years' rule of Thebes), are built upon a lie. This blocked energy then erupts (externalized as plague, a typically Artaudian example) and forces them finally to face what they had been so resolutely avoiding. When they do so, they achieve a far greater stature: they become a man, a woman, parents, lovers, mother, and son all together; they escape from their self-imposed exile, but too late to reap the benefits.

In Act II, the Sphinx is both young girl and monster, both the chance of salvation (through a kind of love) and the alternative of death. Like the Act I ghost, she is benign if dealt with openly but deadly if ignored. The bumptious Oedipe, unlike his original model who could mediate supernatural wisdom, cannot deal with what is most immediate. He ducks her frank sexuality and direct invitation: it would force him to be a man, not a power-crazed youth. She poses problems that would make him acknowledge the personal. Instead he avoids it, or naively believes he has "defeated" it. He stalks off with the Sphinx's pantomime monster skin slung over his shoulder, like a colonial hunter—another emblem of the class and culture trap as metaphor for his lack of awareness. By using a feminine Sphinx, Cocteau underlines precisely the kind of consciousness the braggart male overlooks. In fact the Sphinx returns, immediately, to trap him: the Sphinx's power derives from the whole world of insight and feeling that Oedipe has overlooked, and it gives him a reminder of its influence which in his jaunty fashion he shrugs off. He is enmeshed in a web of words, woven in metaphor and incantatory rhythm by the Sphinx: an enactment of the trap of self-deceit which he and Jocaste are rushing toward, as they entangle themselves in the threads of their own fate.

In Act III, the refusal of responsibility becomes even more urgent, amid an atmosphere of increasing claustrophobia and impending doom. The protagonists are plagued by perceptive drunkards (singing about mothers and sons), threatening thunderstorms and the eruption of a furious Tirésias, who spells out all the indications Jocaste and Oedipe refuse to see. Instead, they take refuge in each other's arms, though the intimacy is heavily maternal, rather than adult sexuality, in exhausted dream-ridden sleep. Oedipe cries out, "Mummy," and the presence of his cradle is another sign clear to everyone except the bizarre lovers, whose exhaustion is a psychic mark of the lack of energy to pursue painful or difficult situations. They opt for the familiar (Jocaste nurses Oedipe and treats him like a child) without examining its awful implications and turn aside from any opening into the exploration of the "past" (or of what motivates their present actions). They grope along on the surface of consciousness in a kind of self-willed fog.

In the first three acts, then, fantastic and supernatural elements are used as messages that Oedipe and Jocaste ignore at their peril. The supernatural keeps knocking on the door, but they shut their ears. (The poor ghost waves his arms and shouts "Jocaste" to no avail; the seductive Sphinx steps briefly aside to offer Oedipe a glimpse of the avenging Anubis behind her; guards, watchmen, and drunkards convey hints; and Tirésias finally bursts in with his prescience and intuition sharpened by anger at continually being dismissed.) Extended forms of knowing are thus available, from the poetry and prophecy of Tirésias to the direct perception of the soldiers. Jocaste and Oedipe ignore all information from higher and lower centers alike and close themselves off increasingly behind the walls of Thebes and their royal games, fostering their own illusions of control. They refuse ambiguity and knowledge in favor of confirmation of their own image, and in so doing they trap themselves in ever narrower limits—Act III is stiflingly confined—and evade any chance of learning. They merely repeat themselves, and thus even their children, who in normal circumstances might represent a fuller admission of feeling and response, only tighten further the incestuous knot that will destroy them.

In this process, Jocaste and Oedipe discount and devalue their own full stature, living instead a clichéd and facile version. They refuse to be full human beings, responsible to themselves as private worlds, and so they fail to exercise genuine responsibility for the public world too, which they claim as image and role (Genet-style) but not as reality. They are not in command of themselves, and so they have no loyalty to offer to others. They fail to confront and work out in themselves the desires that govern their behavior, and thus they continually fall prey to them. They are ruled, not ruling. In particular, they are unable to cope adequately with power drives, with sexuality, and with guilt. As a result, these energies manifest themselves as monsters (Sphinx, Anubis), ghosts, and theatrical dreams, in ways frequently found in fantasy and dream.

The play is thus able to make clear to the audience what the characters cannot see. It presents physically everything they try to shut out, and it demonstrates those kinds of consciousness or seeing that, if heeded, could provide insight and a basis for growth. The play plays, in the sense of offering a spectacle of the roles Jocaste and Oedipe elect to adopt and a catalog of those they suppress. It plays in another sense in creating a space where play can occur, where the possibilities of being can be explored, and where movement and action are possible. It demonstrates the increasing lack of space that Oedipe and Jocaste allow themselves, moving from the open air of ramparts and desert to the stuffy interior of the bedroom. Act IV is confined by the formality of palace and public duty, by the rigid determinism of the unfolding tragedy, and by the restricted room for maneuver which finally leads the protagonists to suicide and blinding. In another way, Cocteau ironically points to the sphere from which Oedipe and Jocaste exclude themselves, for only in the pain and dignity of the final moments do they become fully human. By then, the relative freedom of the first three acts, which they use merely as irresponsible license, has served as a noose— for them human responsibility is only realized as anguish. The truth of their psychic and existential situation dawns too late to be anything other than a symbol. Their freedom is located not in their own lives but in their transformation into archetypes. Their darkness becomes a warning beacon for others.

The audience may benefit from this not just by being able to sit back and contemplate the protagonists with a sigh of relief but by being given a chance to live through the sequence that they avoid. *They* push the uncomfortable away; *we* are increasingly drawn into it and forced to confront it in various ways. Right from the beginning our expectations are upset. We might expect the well-known story, and indeed the introductory synopsis by the "Voice" appears to confirm this; but immediately we are plunged into a world very different from the traditional idea of classical Greece. Act I is virtually slapstick, with a queen who is the epitome of a good-time girl. There are deliberate shocks of style, period, and tone. The linguistic register is colloquial and anachronistic; there are frequent suggestions of disrupted or inverted status in the queen's behavior and in the way she treats Tirésias. The callous Oedipe of Act II confirms this sense of oddness, together with the mixture of Greek myth and Egyptian gods.

The unease that we feel is essentially that of border situations, of being on the verge of knowledge that may split the configuration of the world apart. Theater itself is a space and performance that enacts that situation, as conscious or unconscious legacy of rituals by which communal knowing may be enhanced. It is in a way the archetypal experience of fantasy. Cocteau's is an art that delights in and multiplies examples of this ambiguity—in general terms in his operation of many genres (film, theater, novel, visual art) and in his own sexual and artistic reputation, and in his preoccupation with myth and the explanation of key transformatory situations in the psyche (ritual passages from death to life or the reverse in the Orpheus legend, sexuality in *Beauty and the Beast*, adolescence and generation conflict in novels about parents and children). All this is given in the form of fantastic reversals, doubles emerging from mirrors, atmospheres that enact hesitation, transformation, and death in life.

La machine infernale is no exception to this. The borderline and the alternative kinds of knowledge that might be available from beyond it are clearly present in characters and manifestations like the ghost, the Sphinx, Tirésias, and the drunkard; in the key metaphor of blindness and seeing, which dominates every act; in the concealed metaphor of love as a kind of more complete knowledge— concealed because only the Sphinx and perhaps some aspects of Jocaste's maternal tenderness express it openly and because most of the time love is viewed only as a way to sexual or social power; in the changes of mood, tone, and language; and in the shifts between and among the four acts. The acts taken together suggest knowledge as a complex process of interchange. This complex process is present, too, in the way the intimate confusion of Act III is cruelly exposed in the public clarity of Act IV. Each of the borderline visitations has been a chance offered to and refused by Oedipe and Jocaste; but in the 17-year gap between Acts III and IV the self-deception has multiplied to such an extent that it cannot but express itself publicly, because it now threatens the integrity of the whole state of humanity.

By setting most of the play prior to this gap (Act IV is the shortest), Cocteau puts the emphasis on the motivation rather than on the final events, on the

psychological substructure that leads to the revelation. He opts for active presentation rather than retrospective narration. This approach avoids the risks of
static declamation inherent in classical and neoclassical drama; it involves the
audience in a developmental process, rather than explaining it to them via the
end result. Language, spectacle, myth, and character open up changing perspectives; Cocteau's theater is a place of continual transformation, not a comfortable confirmation of accepted values.

Some critics, such as Bettina Knapp, have argued that Oedipe and Jocaste are
not "characters" in the full sense. They are not full human beings, but that is
not the same thing, precisely because we are shown the chances they miss. They
do not accept the risks of knowing themselves, so they cannot become whole
human beings. But "character" becomes in the play a kind of absence, a residue
of possibility that the protagonists avoid. They stick with the roles they know,
and they get fatally stuck in them. "Plot" likewise is exposed as an arbitrary
construction by Cocteau's cheeky inventions and juxtapositions of the first three
acts. At any time, Oedipe and Jocaste could write an alternative sequence, but
all they do is seal their own fate. They create their own character and weave
their own plot; we as audience can be perfectly clear that the versions they opt
for are by no means inevitable. We are allowed the "play" of all the possibilities,
from commoners to kings, from ghosts to monsters, from birth to death, from
the ridiculous to the sublime. Shutting some of them out makes the protagonists
less than fully human and for Cocteau makes a play less than "poésie du théâtre":
the arousal of the ambiguity, that conjunction of openings into other worlds
which seems to fulfill Artaud's demand that theater equate to poetry in providing
a kind of borderline anguish of knowing and not knowing, "cette angoisse
ineffable qui est le propre de la poésie" (Artaud 94).

It is this hovering on the brink of knowledge about the range of self that
Oedipe and Jocaste cannot cope with and that the play provides as experience.
"Character" and "plot" (private world and its incorporation in action and
relationship) are exposed as fearful and finite traps for the protagonists but at
the same time are offered as material for play to the audience. We learn as we
go along, because we are always being presented with images of what is not yet
(but could be) known. The Delphic oracle's script (know thyself) is the impetus
for the Sphinx's riddle (answer equals man); it is the movement of the play, the
way the play discovers and discloses itself. Like Borges' sacred books, it can
be known by anyone's mind or by the whole universe, and the method is a kind
of voluntary dreaming. We are invited to participate, and the "text" becomes
a play, a process, a way of knowing, a continuous moving from one possibility
to another. That is theater for Cocteau. We only know one act at a time, but
what we do not know draws us on. So in Act IV Oedipe and Jocaste are vital
because they open other spheres of human and superhuman being in their final
acceptance of a monstrous knowledge and in the way it transforms them into
eternal symbols of their own defeat.

"Lumiere est faite" is the device of the final act; it is the light of full consciousness that draws us on, as it did the classical Oedipe. If Acts I and II have been a process of initiation, Act IV is the culminating ritual, a communal assumption of theater-as-revelation. In the final moments, Tirésias explains to Creon that Oedipe and Jocaste now belong not to the pragmatic world of justice but to poets and the pure in heart. They represent the full awareness that they have hitherto blocked. If we have allowed ourselves to live the ambiguity and unease of the workings of the infernal machine, we may be able to recognize our destiny in the protagonists' final stature and derive a sense of theater as wholeness, where each individual partakes in the playing out of the full range of human experience.

WORKS CITED

Artaud, Antonin. *Le théâtre et son double*. Paris: Gallimard, 1964.
Cocteau, Jean. *La machine infernale: piece en 4 actes*. Paris: B. Grasset, 1934.
Knapp, Bettina L. *French Theatre 1918–1939*. London: Macmillan, 1985.

7

Beckett and the Horrific
Lance Olsen

Samuel Beckett's postmodern project has produced a critical industry that tells us Beckett's pieces are both Christian in nature, obsessed as they are by humanity's relationship with God; and humanist in nature, believing the world devoid of all meaning save that which humanity gives it. Beckett's writing is deeply Freudian and antipsychological. It is firmly set in Ireland and France and abstractly set outside political and geographical reality. It is comic and tragic. It is absurdist, existentialist, stoic, nihilist—somehow all at once.

After the performance of his first play, *Le Kid*, a 1931 juvenile parody of Corneille's *Cid* and nod to Charlie Chaplin's *The Kid* that Beckett wrote with Georges Pelerson, the Trinity College newspaper lampooned the production saying, "[W]e have a theory it was the work of Guy de Maupassant—his very last work, if not, indeed, posthumous" (Fletcher and Spurling 120). But the lampoon also added a revealing, if grumpy, criticism: "I wish he would explain his explanations" (Cohn viii)—"revealing" because such a phrase indicates a typical reader/viewer response to Beckett's work, a certain irritated bewilderment, that will stalk the writer the rest of his career.

As a defense against that irritation and bewilderment, Beckett's audience has continually attempted imposing explanations on works that themselves seek to subvert explanation. Godot, for example, has become "God, a diminutive god, Love, Death, Silence, Hope, De Gaulle, a Balzac character, a bicycle racer, Time Future, and a Paris street for call girls" (Cohn 64)—all in spite of or perhaps *because* of the fact that Beckett himself stated that all his "work is a matter of fundamental sounds . . . and I accept responsibility for nothing else. If people want to have headaches among the overtones, let them. And provide their own aspirin" (Bair 470). That is, Beckett forced the readers of his fiction and viewers of his play from an act of criticism-as-explication to one of

criticism-as-spiritual-autobiography. He transformed interpretation into a study
of reader responses. His texts exist in order to be interpreted forever, and they
form a set from which an infinite number of subsets can be generated.

What I shall do here is add another optic, or myopia, through which to view
his project. I shall concentrate on his drama—though virtually all my points
apply as well to his fiction—and use as my launching pad a comment made in
a 1973 review of *Endgame* by Harold Hobson, who wrote, "[W]e are driven to
persuade ourselves that [Beckett's] plays are not really filled with terror and
horror, but are, at bottom, jolly good fun. Well, they are not jolly good fun.
They are amongst the most frightening prophecies of, and longing for, doom
ever written." The assumption here, which Hobson does not flesh out, is that
it is somewhat naive and certainly highly optimistic to accentuate the comic in
Beckett's plays, which has much more to do with Kafka's ghastly visions than
with Keatonesque whimsy, since at the plays' hearts beat a deep sense of universal
terror. Moreover, at the margins of his comment ("frightening prophecies,"
"doom"), Hobson suggests a new reading of Beckett's output—as a complex
of fantasy and as a particular subset of that complex, the horrific. This is where
I should like to begin my own spiritual autobiography, first by drawing up a
working definition of *the horrific*; next by showing how a number of Beckett's
plays function within the horror tradition in drama; and, finally, by indicating
the cultural implications of Beckett's postmodern manifestation of this tradition.

In "On Fairy Stories," his Andrew Lang lecture in 1939, J.R.R. Tolkien
argues that fantasy ultimately offers its readers consolation through its use of an
inspiring ending. He calls this type of ending *eucatastrophe*. Roger Schlobin
takes this observation further by opposing Tolkien's sense of fantasy, which
Schlobin sees as "a literature of affirmation" that "assumes nature is essentially
a generative force . . . [and that sees] growth, maturation, and change as positive
tools that are in harmony with natural order" (2262). Schlobin sees texts of
horror as "the literature of negation," which "assumes [that] nightmare rather
than the visionary part of consciousness is the one that merits or draws attention
. . . [and that] creation is a dark force, and its twisted spawn are a seminal part
of the universe" (2263). Texts of horror end in what Schlobin calls *dyscatas-
trophe*, the death of joy.

Howard Phillips Lovecraft, in his seminal 1927 essay *Supernatural Horror
in Literature*, states that "the oldest and strongest emotion of mankind is fear,
and the oldest and strongest kind of fear is fear of the unknown" (12). Uncertainty
is always associated with danger, he continues, and so it is no wonder that any
unknown world is one of potential terror. For horror to exist, unknown forces
must be present and there must be "a suspension or defeat of those fixed laws
of Nature which are our only safeguard against the assaults of chaos and the
daemons of unplumbed space" (15). In other words, the reader's sense of normality must be threatened from within or without. The reader's position of
coherence must be subverted in such a way that he at least momentarily expe-

riences the literary equivalent of insanity. Hence, as Edward Lowry indicates, horror must involve an element of sadomasochism, for the reader is both fascinated by the brutal universe in which the protagonists about whom he is reading find themselves, while at the same time he empathizes with the protagonists because they appear so frighteningly similar to himself (16).

Much has been made of Beckett as an innovator and of postmodernism as a radically avant-garde movement, but it is just as true that the horrific impulse in both is an extension of the tradition that follows a hypothetical trajectory back to some of the first texts produced by Western culture. In the case of Beckett's drama, the trajectory goes at least as far back as the fifth century B.C. and the seven surviving plays by Aeschylus, among which is the *Oresteia* trilogy recounting the series of bloody retributive murders affecting the house of Atreus, as well as the plays by Sophocles and Euripides, the latter of whose drama greatly influenced a first-century A.D. Stoic, Seneca, who wrote his nine surviving tragedies of blood to be recited rather than acted. It is Seneca whose work was translated and imitated in Renaissance Italy, France, and England, whose playwrights mistakenly thought his plays were intended for the stage. In defiance of Horace's dictum that good taste demands leaving the horrific for offstage actions, Senecan tragedy—Kyd's *Spanish Tragedy*, Shakespeare's *Titus Andronicus*, and Ford's *'Tis Pity She's a Whore*, for instance—often placed murders and other terrors on stage, employing along the way much use of dark introspection and soliloquy as well as sensational themes such as adultery, incest, and infanticide. The contemporary echo of this tradition sounds in what has come to be called the Theater of Cruelty—defined in the 1930s by Antonin Artaud and carried on by Jean Genet, Peter Weiss, and others—and in modern horror films such as Alfred Hitchcock's *Psycho*, Tobe Hooper's *The Texas Chainsaw Massacre*, and Ridley Scott's *Alien*.

Beckett's drama is a postmodern extension of this tradition, and it is an extension that transforms physical into metaphysical horror. Its objective is to challenge radically humanist assumptions about the nature of art, normality, and experience. As early as 1930, when he wrote his study of Proust in Paris, Beckett argued that one must smash the idea of conventional perception and rupture the physically and metaphysically normal in order truly to see and feel, for "the creation of the world did not take place once and for all time, but takes place every day." Only when one explores "the perilous zones in the life of the individual, dangerous, precarious, painful, mysterious and fertile" can one for a moment replace "the boredom of living . . . by the suffering of being" (*Proust* 8).

His characters find themselves eternally in the perilous and mysterious zones of being. Often they are sick. Often they cannot move. In their purest form they resemble Belacqua Shuah, the protagonist of Beckett's short story collection, *More Pricks than Kicks* (1934), whose name Beckett found in Dante's *Purgatorio* (iv, 97–135). Belaquah, as Dante tells us, "shows himself more indolent than if sloth were his sister." Notorious for his laziness and apathy, he must wait in the shadow of a rock until as many years have passed as he lived on earth. In Beckett's narrative, all is waiting, sluggishness, and apathy in an ante-purgatorial shadowland. His characters must repeat themselves again and again, with slight variations, almost forever.

The two-part structure of many of his plays points toward his near-eternal recurrence. But it is *only* near-eternal, since the indications are that his characters inhabit a universe that exhibits a Pynchonesque belief in the second law of thermodynamics—nature will eventually reach a state of maximum disorganization and minimum available energy at which time all change will cease. "From bad to worsen," explains the narrator of *Worstward Ho* (1983). "Try worsen. From merely bad. Add—. Add? Never" (23). In *Waiting for Godot* Pozzo can still go blind in the second act; Lucky can still go dumb. In *Happy Days* Winnie can still lose the use of her hands and neck. In the trilogy the reader discovers that something else can always be taken away from the human; Molloy and Moran can become crippled, Malone cannot even crawl, Mahood is just head and torso, Worm is barely that, and the Unnamable is simply a voice drifting in the void. What the reader or audience faces, then, is the literary equivalent of Mark Rothko's stained canvases—a longing for simplification, decomposition, minimalism. But it would be incorrect to assume because of this that one Beckettian piece is much like another. Rather—again like Rothko's paintings—the closer and longer one examines Beckett's works, the more subtle differences are revealed.

Waiting for Godot, which Beckett wrote between October 1948 and January 1949 as a means of relaxation, a method of getting away for a while from what he considered the more serious pursuit of his prose, is without a doubt Beckett's most well-known play. In fact, it has given rise to more books, dissertations, and articles than any other drama in this century. And there is great irony in that, since Beckett always felt it essentially a "bad play" and often refused to talk about it with scholars (Bair 383). It was first performed on January 3, 1953, at the Theatre de Babylone in Paris and took about two and a half hours to get through.

Originally, Beckett had wanted to call it *En Attendant* which would have even more forcefully underscored it as a play concerned with something that will not show itself, unfulfilled desire, deferredness of meaning, jammed completion, frustrated longing, unknown ends, and (im)possibility. In the 120 pages of text, there are an amazing 485 question marks, an emblem of the inability to know that lies at the play's heart. Indeed, Godot at the epistemological stratum signals a textural center, a stability of meaning, which is absent. As Estragon early on admits, "I wouldn't even know [Godot] if I saw him" (16), and later he realizes that in this dreamscape "nothing is certain" (35). And nothing is. An inability to name, to identify and fix, pervades the play. Vladimir, for instance, cannot figure out if the man accompanying Lucky is called Pozzo or Bozzo (15), and the man for whom the two tramps wait may be called Godot, but also perhaps

Godin or Godet (24). This sense of garbled meaning seeps into other pockets of textual language. Pozzo has trouble understanding Vladimir when he slurs "You want to get rid of him?" into "You waagerrim?" (21), Estragon perverts French when he tells Pozzo he is doing "tray bong, tray tray tray bong" (25), and the only discernable refrain in Lucky's aberration of academic discourse is "for reasons unknown" (28). These examples are indicative of a larger epistemological uncertainty that pulses here. Estragon believes he and the other characters are in hell (47), but they might just as easily be in some postnuclear wasteland, or be the Borgesian product of someone's hallucination. The only certainty is that strange people beat Estragon in a ditch every night for no reason; that "time has stopped" (24) or, worse, simply slowed down; and that there are no more carrots (14), no more laughter (8), only the "impression" they exist at all (44). Both Vladimir and Estragon have swollen feet, and Lucky, who has a running sore on his neck because of the rope chafes, is continually terrorized by Pozzo. This is an unstable universe of "private nightmares" (11) where, as the stage directions inform us about Vladimir and Estragon when Pozzo and Lucky arrive, the characters huddle "together, shoulders hunched, cringing away from the menace" (15).

In that very human gesture there is something positive, some sense of redemption. If all around them the world is crazy, at least these Laurel and Hardy characters have each other to hug in the face of it. But *Godot* is the last play in Beckett's project where people can huddle together and cringe away from the menace. His next play, and the one he has called his favorite, *Endgame*, shows us legless Nell and Nagg who live in ashbins, unable to touch each other, barely able to hear each other, and Hamm and Clov who will neither embrace nor leave each other. Their relationship before the menace—and Beckett has said the tenor of this piece should be one of "extreme anxiety" (Bair 468)—is one of "nec tecum nec sine te" (Bair 470). If *Godot* is a play about waiting for someone to arrive, *Endgame* is a play about waiting for someone—Clov—to leave. But he does not leave, and, again like *Godot*, all we are left with is absence, that which fails to show itself.

Endgame, written in 1956 and first presented in 1957, has been performed in a number of bizarre settings—a chicken-wire cage, a playpen, a boxing ring, among others—and has been translated into an opera and a modern dance. But Beckett's stage directions call only for gray light, two small windows in the upper left and right corners of the stage, a picture turned to the wall, two ashbins, and a door. This may well suggest the skullspace of Geulincx's universe. Geulincx, whom Beckett studied in 1930, was a Flemish follower of Descartes who believed that the body and mind were not connected, that at best they were only partially congruent. Hence for Geulincx there existed a mental world that was divorced from the physical one. This set is perhaps, as Hamm believes, a "shelter" (3), a bombshelter, some time after the third world war, and "outside of here it's death" (9). In any case, it contains a hellish universe where there are no more painkillers, no more bicycles, no more navigators, no more coffins, and "no more nature" (11), and where all outside this small room is "zero . . . zero . . . and zero" (29). That is, *Endgame* is the first Beckettian drama to move from an external landscape to an internal one. It is the beginning of the hermetically sealed entropic world from which there is no escape, a world that will characterize Beckett's work henceforth.

Deirdre Bair argues that the dominant image in *Endgame*—Hamm in his wheelchair—comes out of Beckett's life (464–65). His aunt, Cissie Beckett, a talented painter who created a scandal when she married the penniless son of a Jewish antique dealer, died shortly before Beckett began work on this play. She had been crippled by rheumatoid arthritis that stiffened her body and forced her to spend the end of her life in a wheelchair. Beckett often took her for walks when he visited, pushing her along the coast while she watched ships in Dublin Bay through a telescope—like the one Clov uses. But Hamm is hardly the high-spirited Cissie. Rather, as Beckett has said, "he's a monster, not a human being" (Bair 468); a vociferous and ostentatious actor playing a postmodern Hamlet; a *hammer* who beats on Clov (*clou* is *nail* in French), Nagg (*Nagel* is *nail* is German), and Nell (a name which with the right British inflection becomes an approximation of *nail* in English, or *knell*, suggestive of the hammer and bell of church funerary services); the king surrounded by his pawns—and apparently Beckett was familiar with Marcel Duchamp's 1932 chess study called *Opposition and Sister Squares Are Reconciled*—in the last stages of a failed chess game, the endgame. It is true that neither Hamm nor Clov, Nagg nor Nell, embrace in Vladimir and Estragon's touching human gesture. But at least they are present for each other. At least each has the others with whom to pass the time. They may not be able to live with each other, but they certainly cannot live without each other.

In *Krapp's Last Tape* (1958), however, a play set sometime "in the future" (9), Beckett takes even that away in his continual movement toward the most minimal. Here the only other is the memory of oneself. Krapp-at-69—a grotesque near-sighted, hard-of-hearing, swollen-footed Beckettian clown with a white face, purple nose, and head of disordered gray hair—listens to a tape recorder, a machine Beckett had not seen before writing this piece, playing a tape of a strong and pompous Krapp-at-39. The young Krapp recalls the day his mother died and the day he renounced love. The impotent old Krapp, the antithesis of Hamm the Tragedian, feels so alone that he believes "the earth might be un-inhabited" (28). The table he sits at and the immediately adjacent area are blasted with strong white light that creates an image emphasizing his utter isolation and announcing what Hugh Kenner calls the Gestapo theme—"the spotlight bor-rowed from Nazi inquisitors and administrators of the American 'third degree' " (153). It is also the spotlight from a Puritan hell that calls for continual confession, a relentless examination of conscience. This play is a battle between the human (Krapp) and the inhuman (the tape recorder), between eros (desire on the punt—and for Beckett "this thing called love, there's none of it, it's only fucking" [Bair 481]) and thanatos (the mother's death). And the audience as well as

Krapp finds itself stuck in the mechanical repetition of "all that old misery" (26), again and again and again, since "once wasn't enough for you" (27).

It may be all old misery that he recalls, but at least Krapp—as his excremental name underscores—has a very physical self, a location for the pain he feels, something, as it were, to talk to. But when Beckett wrote his first radio play in 1956, he began dissolving even that. Suddenly the human evaporates and we are left with voices, radio waves, and static. As with the Unnamable, hurt and longing diffuse in the void. There is nothing left to see of drama except what goes on in the skullspace of our own minds. Geulincx's vision is complete. The mental world has been divorced from the physical one. In each radio play, as in *Endgame*, we are locked in a deranged consciousness, but here there is no possibility of an external universe. As Henry realizes in *Embers* (1959), a dramaticule whose title suggests the entropic drift Beckett's narrative system is caught in, "you will be quite alone with your voice, there will be no other voice in the world but yours" (116). Henry may or may not be walking by the ocean. He can conjure up sounds at will—horses galloping; his unloving child taking a music lesson; his wife and he first making love, like Krapp and his lover, by the sea. Perhaps, like Malone in his hospital bed, or the selfless Unnamable, Henry conjures up everything. Certainly he brings his suicidal father "back from the dead to be with [him], in this strange place" (95), and it is possible he calls up the voice of his wife, Ada, as well. In this way he is, like Hamm and Krapp, and to a lesser degree Vladimir and Estragon, another fictionalizer who believes that "every syllable is a second gained" (117). Yet, like the others, he feels himself in a gruesome purgatory, or worse, in a "hell," in the eternal agony of recollection and recoil, forced by some dark enigmatic impetus into "small chat to the babbling of Lethe about the good old days when we wished we were dead" (102).

This is, as Kenner has said (166), the paradigm for all the dramaticules Beckett will write from 1959 on. By the time we reach *Play* (1963), *Waiting for Godot* and *Endgame* have come to appear in retrospect as relatively conventional and even representational dramas. As the title suggests, *Play* has purified plot to its most generic and banal essence. We find a silly and vain man, a shrewish and cliché-filled Wronged Woman—perhaps, but not necessarily, the man's wife— and an archetypal Other Woman who appears to be on the verge of madness. All are doomed to recount their past lives, which are the stuff of drawing-room well-made plays.

The horrific enters into the stock plot through *how* they shall recount their past lives. These characters are like some hideous echo of Nagg and Nell in *Endgame* and Winnie in *Happy Days*, encased up to their necks in urns one yard high. The stage directions tell us that "it is necessary either that traps be used, enabling the actors to stand below stage level, or that they kneel throughout the play" (63), apparently because Beckett wants to create actual physical discomfort in his actors to accompany their general sense of disorientation. The characters' faces are "so lost to age and aspect as to seem almost part of the urns," their expressions "impassive," their voices "toneless . . . rapid . . . faint, largely unintelligible" (45). In other words, they are at the border between the human and the inhuman. None knows the other two are nearby. Each speaks a rambling monologue, each of which Beckett wrote separately, interspersing them only when each was completed, and each is compelled to confess his or her past sins. They speak only when solicited by the light, which Beckett has called "the inquirer" and which we are to think of "as no less a victim of his inquiry than [the other characters]" (Bair 567). Clearly the spotlight—the limit of the Gestapo theme, or what Beckett's director in Paris, George Devine, called a "dental drill" of light (Knowlson and Pilling 113)—is not particularly interested in its cross-examination, however, since it often switches from one character to another in midnarrative.

Worse, each character is compelled to confess his or her sins over and over again, precise and mechanical as Krapp's tape recorder. When the first "act" concludes, the stage directions instruct us to "Repeat play." When the second "act" concludes, we are given a "closing repeat" (61) that once more runs through the first few lines of the play. The indication is that the piece will rehearse itself *ad infinitum*, or almost so, since Beckett seems to have changed his mind from what he had decided in the published text. He wrote to George Devine saying that the repetition should not be exact. Rather, there should be "a slight weakening, both of question and of response, by means of less and perhaps slower light and correspondingly less volume and speed of voice." The result, he writes, should be an "impression of falling off . . . [a] suggestion of conceivable dark and silence in the end, or of an indefinite approximating toward it" (Bair 567). It is also the impression of greater and greater uncertainty. Some critics have argued that the second time through the audience members see a new play, since they can begin to put together the fragments they have heard the first time. But Beckett's revision seems to hint that though the audience members may see a new play, they certainly aren't seeing a more comprehensible one. Clearly the characters learn nothing through the infinite near-repetitions, and quite possibly neither does the audience, since as the light and voices grow weaker they also grow more indecipherable. What is louder confusion the first time through simply becomes fainter confusion the second.

Though the reader of *Play* can piece together some semblance of plot—though even in the text itself there are gaps—the viewer hears only some sort of an extension of Lucky's speech in *Godot*, and even this is quite a bit more than the spectator of *Breath* (1966) hears. Many at the time of its first performance thought Beckett had reached the pure articulation of the minimal here and that there was little he could do afterward. And many, as Knowlson and Pilling suggest (127), have since its first performance either treated it too reverentially or as a bad joke. Beckett had written it for Kenneth Tynan, who had asked him to do something for an erotic review to which Jules Feiffer, John Lennon, Edna O'Brien, and others were going to contribute. But one line of Beckett's skit turned out to read not "minimum light on stage littered with miscellaneous rubbish'' (91), as he had penned it, but "faint light on stage, littered with miscellaneous rubbish, including naked people'' (Bair 603). Beckett tried to have its performance stopped but could not. That performance took about 35 seconds. In print it takes 66 words:

Curtain

1. Minimum light on stage littered with miscellaneous rubbish. Hold about five seconds.

2. Faint brief cry and immediately inspiration and slow increase of light together reaching maximum together in about ten seconds. Silence and hold about five seconds.

3. Expiration and slow decrease of light together reaching minimum together (light as in 1) in about ten seconds and immediately cry as before. Silence and hold about five seconds.

Curtain

Here Beckett has turned a nondrama into an aesthetically terminal remnant. We are left without body, without self, without even voice. Fundamental sounds perhaps localize a being, perhaps typify a general emotional state, but there is no presence, no being really here. Perhaps we have another piece from beyond the grave or from a different dimension or from a postnuclear landscape or from a deranged individual's dreamscape. Perhaps, as Knowlson and Pilling indicate (127), we have an image that concretizes Pozzo's oft-quoted observation at the end of *Godot* that "they give us birth astride of a grave, the light gleams an instant, then it's night once more" (57). In any case, in *Breath* the essence of the human and of the dramatic has been immobilized, deformed, and disintegrated. Beckett has found the literary equivalent of John Cage's music, Barnett Newman's paintings, and autism.

The horrific in Beckett, of course, does not cease with *Breath*. Clearly it evinces itself, for instance, in the psychotic ramblings of the mouth in *Not I* (1972), or in the ghastly vision of an old man's white face centered on an all-black stage in *That Time* (1976), or in the agonized visage of the Protagonist as he stares at the audience at the conclusion of *Catastrophe* (1983). But one might argue in *Breath* such an impulse finds its most purely postmodern expression. Beckett's project falls not in the scope of eucatastrophic fantasy but of dyscatastrophic horror. It may be seen as a literature of negation that emphasizes the nightmarish at the expense of the visionary, the death of joy at the expense of the birth of hope. At its heart beats fear, uncertainty, sadomasochism, a sense of danger that threatens the reader-viewer's sense of normality both at the level of aesthetics and at the level of metaphysics. In this way, Beckett's project is part of a tradition in drama that reaches back to the beginnings of Western culture, but it is also a postmodern extension of this tradition, and it is an extension that radically challenges humanist assumptions about what it is to be a part of nature, what it is to be human, what it is to be sane, what it is to be safe.

Unlike eucatastrophic fantasy, then, which expresses that element of a culture that is fairly content with itself, dyscatastrophic horror—and particularly its postmodern form—expresses that element of a culture that believes itself in crisis. The horrific that takes the thematic and the structural to their limits registers a culture that believes itself in the midst of deconstruction, in the midst of a radically skeptical interrogation. The postmodern horror of Beckett, as well as that of writers as diverse as Genet in France, Weiss in Germany, Calvino in Italy, D. M. Thomas in Britain, Vargas Llosa in Latin America, Coetzee in South Africa, and Joyce Carol Oates in the United States, is a mode of discourse for a consciousness that believes ours is a culture *in extremis*, a culture in a between-times, what Umberto Eco calls "a new Middle Ages" (488). For the Italian semiotician and novelist, the parallels between the Middle Ages and the contemporary cosmos are striking. In both, he argues, "a great peace . . . break[s] down, a great international state power that had unified the world in language, customs, ideologies, religion, art and technology . . . collapses" (490). Eco cites, among other tendencies common to both periods, the Vietnamization of territories, ecological deterioration, neonomadism, a sense of insecurity, formalism in thought, art as bricolage, the development of universities-as-monasteries, and a society in permanent transition.

Obviously what is essential about these wildly imaginative claims is not their truth or falsehood. From one perspective, at any rate, comparing a given historical period with a brief moment in history separated from it by over 500 years seems at best pointless. But what is ultimately important about the claims is that one set of voices in our culture feels the need to make them. That is, their very *existence* is illuminating. Future sociohistorical critics may well abandon such claims and such terminology as the strange quirk of a given place and a given time in favor of others that better express their own biases. But what is overwhelmingly interesting is not how our age will be seen from a different temporal vantage point, since we unhappily shall not be there to partake of that optic. Rather, it is the sheer fact of the presence of an extreme version of the dyscatastrophic vision here, now. It is the sheer fact that for a subset of our society the horrific is the only reality of which our culture can make sense.

WORKS CITED

Aeschylus. *The Oresteia*. Trans. Robert Fagles. New York: Viking, 1975.
Alien. Dir. Ridley Scott. With Tom Skerritt and Sigourney Weaver. 1979.
Bair, Deirdre. *Samuel Beckett: A Biography*. New York: Harcourt, 1978.
Beckett, Samuel. "Breath." *First Love and Other Shorts*. New York: Grove, 1974.
———. "Catastrophe." *Ohio Impromptu, Catastrophe, and What Where*. New York: Grove, 1984.

————. "Embers." *Krapp's Last Tape and Other Dramatic Pieces*. New York: Grove, 1970.

————. *Endgame*. New York: Grove, 1958.

————. *Happy Days*. New York: Grove, 1961.

————. *Le Kid*. Unpublished and apparently lost.

————. "Krapp's Last Tape." *Krapp's Last Tape and Other Dramatic Pieces*. New York: Grove, 1970.

————. *More Pricks than Kicks*. New York: Grove, 1972.

————. "Not I." *Ends and Odds*. New York: Grove, 1976.

————. "Play." *Cascando and Other Short Dramatic Pieces*. New York: Grove, 1978.

————. *Proust*. New York: Grove, 1957.

————. "That Time." *Ends and Odds*. New York: Grove, 1976.

————. *Waiting for Godot*. New York: Grove, 1954.

————. *Worstward Ho*. New York: Grove, 1983.

————, and George Duthuit. *Three Dialogues*. 1949. Rpt. in *Proust and Three Dialogues*. London: John Calder, 1965. 97–126.

Cohn, Ruby, ed. *Samuel Beckett: A Collection of Criticism*. New York: MacGraw-Hill, 1975.

Corneille, Pierre. *Cid*. In *The Chief Plays of Corneille*. Trans. Lacy Lockert. Princeton: Princeton University Press, 1957.

Dante. *Purgatorio*. Trans. John D. Sinclair. New York: Oxford University Press, 1979.

Duchamp. Marcel. *Opposition and Sister Squares are Reconciled*. Brussels: L'Echiquier/ Edmond Lancel, 1932.

Eco, Umberto. "Towards a New Middle Ages." *On Signs*. Ed. Marshall Blonsky. Baltimore: The Johns Hopkins University Press, 1985.

Fletcher, John, and John Spurling. *Beckett: A Study of His Plays*. New York: Hill and Wang, 1972.

Ford, John. *'Tis Pity She's a Whore*. London: Benn, 1968.

Hobson, Harold. Review of *Endgame*. *The Sunday Times* (London) 15 July 1973:37.

Kenner, Hugh. *A Reader's Guide to Samuel Beckett*. New York: Farrar, 1973.

Kid, The. Dir. Charles Chaplin. With Charlie Chaplin, Jackie Coogan, and Edna Purviance. 1921.

Knowlson, James, and John Pilling. *Frescoes of the Skull: The Later Prose and Drama of Samuel Beckett*. New York: Grove, 1980.

Kyd, Thomas. *The Spanish Tragedy*. London: Oxford University Press, 1949.

Lovecraft, Howard Phillips. *Supernatural Horror in Literature*. New York: Dover Publications, 1973.

Lowry, Edward. "Genre and Enunciation: The Case of Horror." *Journal of Film and Video* 36.2 (Spring 1984): 13–20.

Psycho. Dir. Alfred Hitchcock. With Anthony Perkins and Janet Leigh. 1960.

Schlobin, Roger. "Fantasy versus Horror." *Survey of Modern Fantasy Literature*. Ed. Frank N. Magill. Englewood Cliffs, N.J.: Salem Press, 1983. 2259–66.

Shakespeare, William. *The Complete Works*. Baltimore: Penguin, 1969.

Texas Chainsaw Massacre, The. Dir. Tobe Hooper. With Marilyn Burns and Gunner Hansen. 1974.

Tolkien, J.R.R. "On Fairy Stories." *Essays Presented to Charles Williams*. Ed. C. S. Lewis. London: Oxford University Press, 1947. 38–39.

Webster, John. *The Duchess of Malfi*. Cambridge: Harvard University Press, 1964.

8

Multiplicities of Illusion in Tom Stoppard's Plays

Peter N. Chetta

One of the more interesting contemporary British playwrights who has had considerable success on both sides of the Atlantic is Tom Stoppard. The play that gave him international recognition was *Rosencrantz and Guildenstern Are Dead*, produced in 1967. The main characters, obviously, originated in Shakespeare's *Hamlet*. Stoppard creates for these characters an imaginary world interwoven with the world of Shakespeare's play yet having resonances of an absurdist modern play influenced by Samuel Beckett's seminal work *Waiting for Godot*. The innovation that Stoppard created of putting characters from a classic play by Shakespeare into a play that reflected a modern, late twentieth-century sensibility was very highly regarded at the time and is still in favor over twenty years later. Stoppard distinguished himself from Beckett and other absurdist playwrights by making this connection with Shakespeare. Audiences bring different perceptions to a work in which all the characters are original as opposed to a work that has familiar characters portrayed in a new light. The sense of disbelief is suspended to a different degree, certainly a more intense degree, when a new frame of reference has to operate for characters that previously existed in another work.

The idea of an author using literary characters that originated in a previous work goes back at least as far as the ancient Greeks. The epics of Homer are the repository for literally thousands of myths used over and over by subsequent poets. The classic Greek playwrights used the characters from mythology for their plays. But the mythology was part of the consciousness of the entire literate society. Aeschylus, Sophocles, and Euripides wrote plays dealing with the same characters and the same basic stories. But it was in their treatment of these materials that they displayed their art. It was in the difference in their philosophical as well as artistic outlooks that they were able to succeed in creating great works of art even though superficially they seemed to be covering similar ground. Stoppard differs from these in that he does not reinterpret old myths but rather presents previously created characters in an entirely new context.

This usage of Stoppard differs also from other earlier works in which there are several "worlds" juxtaposed by an author in an unusual way. For instance, in *Don Quixote* Cervantes presents characters in Part Two, such as the Duke and Duchess, who have read and are conversant with Part One, so that there is a double level of literary illusion operating throughout Part Two. Of course, Cervantes has the Don and Sancho also aware of what happened in Part One. One of the more amusing incidents in Part Two is when Don Quixote castigates the real-life author of a bogus Part Two denouncing it as obviously unauthentic. Another different and striking reuse of characters occurs in Vanbrugh's Restoration Comedy *The Relapse*. In this play, the main characters come from an earlier play, Colley Cibber's *Love's Last Shift*, one of the early sentimental comedies. In effect, *The Relapse* is a sequel written by an author other than the one who created the characters. In the twentieth century, Pirandello, in *Six Characters in Search of an Author*, presents characters supposedly from another unfinished play who interrupt an acting company to have the actors "complete" their story. Pirandello is playing with the concepts of theatrical illusion on several levels. Obviously, the acting company and the "six characters" all are played by actors and are all created by Pirandello. Stoppard's concept in *Rosencrantz and Guildenstern Are Dead* differs radically from Pirandello's since Stoppard's characters were created by Shakespeare and have a theatrical life that really preexists in a known text as opposed to Pirandello's characters who only exist in the one play.

In the 1950s, Tennessee Williams chose characters from several literary sources and invented new ones to interact in his vision of a limbo-like world in *Camino Real*. Some of the characters are historical, such as Byron and Casanova; and some are purely literary, such as Camille and Baron de Charlus, while Kilroy is Williams's embodiment of what was merely a name in World War II graffiti.

Stoppard, by contrast, takes two minor characters from *Hamlet* and gives them an existence in a play of their own, although restricting them to certain of the facts of Shakespeare's plot. Thus one could say these characters are neither totally original nor totally derivative. As Tim Brassell in his study of Stoppard writes, "What he has done is to take a fledgling nuance from Shakespeare's play and develop it with his own dramatic creations" (46).

Stoppard uses most of the scenes from *Hamlet* in which Rosencrantz and Guildenstern appear, but he does not faithfully conform to the Shakespeare play. Stoppard omits two Rosencrantz and Guildenstern scenes from *Hamlet* and omits lines from the scenes he does include. Brassell notes that our acceptance or rejection of what Stoppard has done depends on how we view the relationship between his play and Shakespeare's (46). Brassell cites John Weightman, for instance, who complains about the impropriety of Stoppard's handling of his heroes, since their not being properly connected up to *Hamlet* violates their origin in *Hamlet* (46). Robert Brustein feels that the nonconformity with *Hamlet* "violates 'the integrity of Shakespeare's original conception' " (Brassell 46). On the other hand, J. Dennis Huston contends that "when Stoppard arbitrarily manipulates and 'misreads' *Hamlet*, then, he consciously dramatizes both the modern playwright's bondage to and rebellion against Shakespeare's imposing presence" (47–48). Thus Rosencrantz and Guildenstern are turned into modern antiheroes.

William E. Gruber discusses the Stoppard play in terms of its literariness and its reverberations for a contemporary audience (23). There is no difficulty for Gruber in Stoppard's use of Shakespeare's material for his own purposes. For the critic of a modern playwright such as Stoppard, style, technique, utilization of material, and manipulation of reality are considered favorably by those who can align themselves with a modern sensibility. Those opposed say nay.

Stoppard begins his play with Rosencrantz and Guildenstern in a kind of existential or absurdist void waiting for some indication of their impending action since they were summoned to Elsinore by the King and Queen. This opening and subsequent scenes "backstage," so to speak, are directly influenced by the void in which Estragon and Vladimir find themselves in *Waiting for Godot*. The difference between the Stoppard play and the Beckett play is that Beckett's characters have no meaningful context whereas Stoppard's characters have *Hamlet* (Bassell 62). In the Stoppard play, then, two play worlds—not a play world and a real world—collide. But since Rosencrantz and Guildenstern are not aware of the fact that their world is a play world, in turn dependent upon yet another play world, they are constantly baffled and confused about the failure of all their assumptions about such matters as the numerical odds of heads and tails turning up in games of coin flipping or other operations of natural laws. Probability is not only absurdly determined by Stoppard but also determined by Shakespeare (Brassell 49).

Rosencrantz and Guildenstern try to prove that they have control over events, but they do not. They exist in a world that may seem absurd to them but is not absurd to the audience in the same sense. The situation in *Waiting for Godot* may be characterized as circular. Frequently in absurdist drama the end of the play returns to the beginning. But the situation in *Rosencrantz and Guildenstern Are Dead* is linear (Jenkins 40). The audience knows from the title of Stoppard's play, if not from a previous acquaintance with *Hamlet*, that there will be a definite concluding action for Rosencrantz and Guildenstern. As Brassell asserts, the audience's familiarity with *Hamlet* is obviously crucial to the irony of Rosencrantz and Guildenstern's situation; Stoppard's professed belief that it is not essential to an understanding of his play is nonsense (50). Anthony Jenkins finds that Stoppard's handling of the predicament that Rosencrantz and Guildenstern find themselves in about their identity fails to ring true. Vladimir and Estragon in *Waiting for Godot* have been robbed of a sense of identity by the crazy world in which they seem to exist. But even though the King and Queen may confuse Rosencrantz and Guildenstern, if they are to become human beings for the audience, they cannot really become confused about their identities themselves. They already have identities established for them in Shakespeare's play (41). Beckett has created a self-contained fantasy world in *Waiting for Godot*. But Stoppard has created a fantasy about two minor characters who already existed, literarily speaking, in a world created by Shakespeare.

Stoppard pursues this juxtaposition of the fantasy world of his play with the groundwork of Shakespeare's play by using two levels of language. The clash of Elizabethan language and colloquial language creates a deliberate incongruity to intensify the bewilderment of Rosencrantz and Guildenstern (Brassell 43). These seemingly incompatible elements should be seen as part of an ''ongoing dialetic'' that suggests the tensions of modern life (Gruber 26–27). The audience is shifted back and forth on a seesaw of language which helps to interfere even further with the suspension of disbelief.

Another method of creating disorientation is the manipulation of the scenes from Shakespeare. Obviously, Stoppard has intentionally chosen what he has included from *Hamlet* and what he has edited out. These choices result in a deliberate attempt to slant or direct the audience's perception of the characters of Rosencrantz and Guildenstern. By leaving out most of the exchange between Hamlet and Rosencrantz and Guildenstern in Act II, scene II, which would be taking place during the interval between Stoppard's first two acts, Stoppard eliminates the complicity of Rosencrantz and Guildenstern in the King's scheme to monitor Hamlet's behavior. Thus Stoppard can present the two of them as innocents (Brassell 43–44). The omission of Scene II and Scene III of Act III of *Hamlet* also diminishes Rosencrantz and Guildenstern's roles as minions and spies. In the omitted sections, in general, Hamlet is aware of the mission of Rosencrantz and Guildenstern, and his awareness culminates in his confronting Guildenstern in the ''playing'' on him as a recorder exchange in Act III, Scene II (Brassell 45). Stoppard is, in effect, preventing his two characters from being aware of Hamlet's displeasure with them so that they can be further bewildered by their roles in the larger drama of *Hamlet* and their predicament in their own play.

This fits in very nicely with the concept of Rosencrantz and Guildenstern as reflections of modern angst derived from T. S. Eliot's ''The Lovesong of J. Alfred Prufrock'' (Hayman 33). These two schoolfellows of Hamlet are merely ''attendant lords'' and ''essay tools,'' at times ''ridiculous'' and even fools. They do not have the capacity in their own natures to rival the princely hero of Shakespeare's play. This lack on their part makes the contrast with the royal trappings in the scenes from Shakespeare all the more poignant. The diminution of the protagonist from prince to attendant is completely in line with the celebration of tramps as protagonists in Beckett as well as Pinter (*The Caretaker*). Through Stoppard, we have Elizabethan nonentities as major dramatic figures in a modern play.

Another element of fantasy in the Stoppard play is his creation of a major role for the players, especially the chief player, of the ''Mousetrap'' play from

Hamlet. In *Hamlet*, Rosencrantz and Guildenstern mention to Hamlet that they have met the players on their way to Elsinore. Stoppard dramatizes this meeting and also has the players intrude on the "backstage" world of Rosencrantz and Guildenstern. But the players know that they are actors, so their presence creates another level of fantastic irony for Stoppard's heroes. In *As You Like It*, Shakespeare's melancholy Jaques states that all the world is a stage. This image is echoed in *Macbeth* and elsewhere. It would seem to be one of Shakespeare's pet metaphors, logically derived from his profession as actor and playwright. But there is a difference between a character in a play using the metaphor of the stage to describe the illusory in life, or the role-playing in the "stages" of life, and a playwright using actors, whose entire way of life is made up of creating illusions, as characters in a play. When actors are characters, different illusions operate.

In *Hamlet*, we do not know what happens to the players after they leave Elsinore. Stoppard provides further action for the players in order to emphasize one of his primary themes, that life itself is like theatrical illusion whether the individual is an actor, an attendant lord, a prince, or, no doubt, even a peasant. As Bigsby states, "[T]he theatrical metaphor is the dominant one in the play" (11). And it reverberates on several levels.

Stoppard's use of theatrical fantasy differs from Pirandello's use in several ways. Stoppard's characters preexisted in a play by Shakespeare in which a number of themes are explored, such as the nature of duty, the problem of resignation, the perception of one's role in life, and questions of the reality of life and death—in essence, a questioning of the "nature of things." Stoppard expands on these themes, adding to them a modern sensibility and a self-conscious exploration of theatrical illusion. His characterizations and the structure of the play force the audience to deal directly with his concerns since the characters directly confront the audience and make anachronistic jokes. The traditional boundaries of the stage are broken.

Pirandello, however, encloses theatrical reality within the framework of illusion. His six characters have no life outside their unfinished play. They are contrasted with his "actors" who presumably have a life away from the stage of the theater where they work. Pirandello uses this juxtaposition to explore theories of realistic drama and realistic stage techniques and concludes the play with a supreme trick of theatrical illusion. The audience gets caught up in the sordid story that the six characters at first tell and then enact. There is no breaking of the traditional frame of the stage even though we are confronted with an empty and bare stage at the beginning of the play. The director and the father (of the six-character story) argue about the nature of theater, reality, and illusion, but the audience brings no preconceptions to this play from another play or from a theatrical tradition as it does when it is confronted with Stoppard's play.

The audience for *Rosencrantz and Guildenstern Are Dead* brings *Hamlet* and the Theater of the Absurd with it. As Gruber puts it, "one senses the chilling presence of *Hamlet*, waiting menacingly in the wings" (34). Furthermore, the echoes of the absurdists, especially Beckett, proliferate in the scenes with the players as well as when the two protagonists are alone. In Act III, when Rosencrantz and Guildenstern are on the ship taking them and Hamlet to England, the players suddenly pop out of barrels. This may be a deliberate attempt on Stoppard's part to echo Beckett's use of garbage cans in *Endgame* or urns in *Play* (Rusinko 32). Or it may be a deliberate attempt to parody Beckett. On a more obvious level, the barrels echo the stowaway scene from the Marx Brothers film in which they take refuge in barrels. Since nonsensical comedy is supposed to be an influence on absurdist theater, the connection is fairly direct.

For all the frantic action in Stoppard's third act, the player had made his pronouncements in the second act about art and inevitability which project into the third act. Rosencrantz and Guildenstern never seem to be aware of their predicament. As the dramatic personifications of Stoppard's thesis, they are not permitted the eventual insight that Shakespeare gives Hamlet. They have been assigned specific roles in their world which can never be understood by them (Brassell 53). The player knows certain concepts about art that Rosencrantz and Guildenstern do not seem to be aware of, since they play parts that differ from the player in a foreordained script over which they have no control. The player, as an artist, seems to have control since he is always acting anyway. Stoppard has created different levels of fantasy in his play for the different characters. Rosencrantz and Guildenstern are trapped in what seems to be the emptiness of modern angst. Hamlet and Shakespeare's other main characters are trapped in the outline of Shakespeare's play. The players are only trapped in their profession; ironically they seem to be the most free in the last analysis.

Rosencrantz and Guildenstern will go to their deaths even though Stoppard has them find the changes in the letters of commission made by Hamlet after he discovers their mission to England to get him killed. On the one hand, they are incapable of changing their destiny to fulfill the course of action prescribed by the title of Stoppard's play, taken from the line in Shakespeare's text. On the other hand, the players are not going to their deaths. Actors "die" when they are unsuccessful or when they perform without an audience (Brassell 58). In the Stoppard play, the player reminds Rosencrantz and Guildenstern that they had walked away from the players when they were acting for the two in their encounter on the road to Elsinore. To actors, deaths in plays are not real, since nothing is real. Their life is acting; acting is the only reality. But Rosencrantz and Guildenstern are characters in a play, so they can die in that play. In fact, they *must* die in that play. So the death of Rosencrantz and Guildenstern has another ironic resonance.

Stoppard is playing fast and loose with many levels of literary and theatrical illusion. Eric Rabkin, in his study of the fantastic in literature, asserts that the fantastic is reality turned precisely 180 degrees around, but a reality nonetheless (28). Undoubtedly, there are several ways to create this reversal. One would be putting characters from someone else's play into a new play. Another would be frustrating the spectator's expectations by reversing these expectations completely. Stoppard's juxtaposition of the time levels of language, previously mentioned, seems to fit in with another thesis of Rabkin. Rabkin writes, "Most specifically, when linguistic perspectives continually shift within a given text, that is, when the ground rules of the narrative world are subjected to repeat reversal, we have Fantasy" (78). Stoppard uses characters as well as language in unexpected ways to create his own theatrical fantasy.

He enlarges on the paths taken by earlier absurdist dramatists such as Beckett. Beckett creates a closed, dead-ended world which, in his profound gloominess, is supposed to represent human nature. Stoppard creates a world in which colorful scenes from Shakespeare's Danish court and playful players clash with the gloom of two minor characters who were in Shakespeare's play on the fringe of seemingly great action. If modern audiences can still find *Hamlet* a meaningful dramatic experience, then the concerns of Shakespeare and, by association, Stoppard are still very relevant.

Stoppard used the technique of mixing levels of fantasy again in *Travesties*, written several years after *Rosencrantz and Guildenstern Are Dead*. In this later play there are even more levels of fantasy in operation than in the earlier play. This time, instead of fictional characters, there are historical characters mixed in with characters derived from Oscar Wilde's *The Importance of Being Earnest*. It is Stoppard's conceit that certain real-life characters who happened to be in Zurich at the same time, in 1918, were all involved with each other, even though there is no basis in real fact that any of them were, except for two. Stoppard presents us with a play in which James Joyce, Tristan Tzara, and Nicolai Lenin are involved with a minor British consular official named Henry Carr and an amateur production of *The Importance of Being Earnest*. Joyce and Carr were really involved with that production. But the others were hardly likely to be even vaguely in contact with each other in any way. Lenin was on the verge of returning to Russia in the notable closed train. Tzara was a figure in the Dadaist movement in art. James Joyce was enduring part of his lifelong exile from his native Dublin. Once again, expectations on the part of an audience are reversed and played with in brilliant fashion.

In an interview conducted by Ronald Hayman, Stoppard made some comments that might enlighten us on his general mode of operation. He contends that in his plays there is no static viewpoint on the events: "There is no observer. There is no safe point around which everything takes its proper place, so that you see things flat and see how they relate to each other" (Hayman 141). Stoppard refers to an article by critic Clive James in which the latter made an analogy: "Although the Einsteinian versus Copernican image sounds pretentious, I can't think of a better one to explain what he [James] meant—that there's no point of rest" (Hayman 141). Stoppard does not need or want to base his plays in any particular realm of reality. He creates his own world. When Hayman, in the interview, questioned him on the "bumping up against each other" of the styles in *Travesties*, Stoppard replied as follows: "Yes, I just wanted to dislocate the audience's assumptions every now and again about what kind of style the play was going to be in. Dislocation of an audience's assumptions is an important part of what I like to write. It operates in different ways" (140). This procedure fits in with Rabkin's theories on fantasy referred to above. Just as there were clashes of Elizabethan and colloquial languages in *Rosencrantz and Guildenstern Are Dead*, so there are parodies of the styles of Joyce, Tzara, and Lenin in *Travesties* (Rusinko 46).

Despite his acknowledgment of the parodies, Hayman does not feel that the fantasy is carried far enough: "Although Tzara and Joyce are both accommodated more comfortably than Lenin into the scheme of the play, Stoppard does not pick up all the cues that Dada and Joyce offer him for trying out new kinds of theatrical writing" (126). Hayman does feel that the treatment of Lenin comes closer to historical accuracy, but he also feels that the lecture at the beginning of the second act is a failure because it merely functions as background on Marxism and Lenin and does not advance the action (124–25). Rusinko also finds fault with the lecture as follows: "It is straightforward and serious, in keeping with the prosaic style of Lenin, but out of keeping with the rest of the play" (53). But Rusinko has nothing but praise for the play in general:

The three styles of discourse—dadaist, Joycean, and the somberly Leninist—with their sharply contrasting natures are, at the very outset of the play, the beginning of what develops into the most intoxicating reinvention of language on the modern English stage. Indeed, the theft of Wilde's plot, the fictionalizing of the meeting of the three revolutionaries, and the expected Stoppardian debate of ideas seem but a structural excuse for the luxurious indulgence in language for its own sake, an indulgence that only increases in speed, color, and intensity as the action progresses. (48)

Stoppard's use of the clashes of linguistic styles, then, provides much of the fantasy.

But there is fantasy also in the overall structure of the play. Stoppard brings to life "a Zurich landscape that exists only inside Carr's head, where fact, fiction, and jumbled reminiscence whirl around in glorious abandon" (Brassell 138). Jenkins characterizes Carr's memory as prejudiced, rusting, and a contorted filter (116). Rusinko believes that the "use of Carr's unreliable memory as a filtering consciousness for the world shaking events of the time" provides for the shuttling back and forth from present to past (489). Stoppard is then freed from conforming to any historical accuracy as he freed himself from adhering to Shakespeare's characterizations of Rosencrantz and Guildenstern when it did not suit his purpose. Stoppard is creating his own world of fantasy using other worlds as his springboards.

Stoppard uses echoes and parodies of lines from Wilde's *The Importance of Being Earnest* as another means of bouncing the audience from one level of fantasy to another. He does not use chunks of the play as he did with *Hamlet* in *Rosencrantz and Guildenstern Are Dead*. Instead, as Brassell puts it, "Here [in *Travesties*], however, the whole point of the play-within-a-play concept is the absence of any real mutual dependence of the one on the other'' (140). Gwendolyn and Cecily are the young, romantic ladies in the Wilde play. In *Travesties*, Gwen is Joyce' secretary who falls in love with Tzara. Cecily is a librarian who falls in love with Carr. Reflecting the twists of the Wildean farce in the confusion of mistaken identities, Tzara and Carr "find themselves reenacting situations analogous to those of Jack/Ernest Worthing and Algernon in Wilde's play'' (Rusinko 47). There is also a mix-up of manuscripts of Joyce and Lenin similar to the mix-up of the handbag and the baby in the Wilde play.

Circles and tangents of literature proliferate in the fantasy world of Stoppard's play when he uses the material of other playwrights. And there are other circles and tangents in *Travesties*. Stoppard creates a proliferation of ironies. The real Carr and Joyce had a dispute resulting in litigation over Carr's claim to be reimbursed for a costume that, it was later judicially determined, was an ordinary suit which could be worn otherwise. This suit escalated into counterclaims and a suit for libel, all of which eventually fizzled out. Joyce got his revenge on Carr by naming a drunken, loutish soldier Carr in the "Circe" section of *Ulysses*. Stoppard, in effect, has Carr get his revenge on Joyce in *Travesties* by having Joyce wind in and out of the action in an unfavorable light, somewhat ineffectual, and reduced to jokiness (Brassell 142–49). Stoppard, the agile manipulator of fantasy, is working here at his best.

Further aspects of fantasy can be seen in Stoppard's playing with the probability of subsequent events which have historically already taken place but are seen from hindsight to have been preventable. Rosencrantz and Guildenstern could have prevented their deaths since they knew the contents of the commission but foolishly deliver it anyway. Carr could possibly have somehow prevented Lenin from making the train trip that resulted in a violent change in the course of world history. We can be powerfully intrigued by all the "if only's" and "what if's" that Stoppard so tantalizingly dangles before us. We become dazzled by the possibilities, elevating us further into the realm of fantasy.

Through his use of all the literary devices discussed above and his creation of a multiplicity of levels of fantasy and illusion, Tom Stoppard demonstrates that he should be ranked as one of the best exponents of fantasy in modern drama.

WORKS CITED

Bigsby, C.W.E. *Tom Stoppard*. Harlow, England: Longman, 1976.

Brassell, Tim. *Tom Stoppard: An Assessment*. New York: St. Martin's, 1985.

Gruber, William E. " 'Wheels within Wheels, Etcetera': Artistic Design in *Rosencrantz and Guildenstern Are Dead*." *Tom Stoppard: A Casebook*. Ed. John Hartz. New York: Garland, 1988, 21–46.

Hayman, Ronald. *Tom Stoppard*. London: Heinemann, 1977.

Huston, J. Dennis. "Misreading *Hamlet*: Problems of Perspective in *Rosencrantz and Guildenstern Are Dead*." In *Tom Stoppard: A Casebook*. Ed. John Hartz. New York: Garland, 1988. 47–66.

Jenkins, Anthony. *The Theatre of Tom Stoppard*. Cambridge: Cambridge University Press, 1987.
Rabkin, Eric S. *The Fantastic in Literature*. Princeton: Princeton University Press, 1976.
Rusinko, Susan. *Tom Stoppard*. Boston: Twayne, 1986.
Stoppard, Tom. *Rosencrantz and Guildenstern Are Dead*. New York: Grove, 1967.
———. *Travesties*. New York: Grove, 1975.

9

Leivick's *The Golem* and the Golem Legend
Carl Schaffer

I know not if mine is the guilt;
  Must my hands with blood be stained?
Must my mind on murder be bent?
  For this, God, did'st thou give strength to my limbs?

(Chayim Bloch, written en route to the front)

"Invention," Mary Shelley once said, "does not consist of creating out of void, but out of chaos" (8). So it was, too, with the creation of Halper Leivick's extraordinary verse play *The Golem*, a work which, drawn from the same stuff of legend as *Frankenstein*, has been called "the highest achievement in Yiddish poetry" (Samuel Niger in Madison 357). According to Leivick's own account, the drama's real origins can be traced to a series of chaotic events that occurred on a winter day when he was seven years old. First, while passing a church on his way to *cheder* (religion class), the young Leivick was suddenly confronted by a large Polish man who knocked off his hat, sent him with a blow to the ground, and shouted, "Dirty Jew! [*Zhid!*] When you pass our church you have to take your hat off!" Leivick was overwhelmed by this unexpected outburst of hatred. Afterward, when he arrived at last at *cheder*, the lesson for the day was on the sacrifice of Isaac, a tale that shocked him beyond belief. "But what would have happened," he asked the rabbi in tears, "had the angel *come one moment too late*?" The rabbi's assurance that angels never came late brought him no solace. Still later, when the lesson was over, Leivick passed the great courtyard of Count Yassevitch, who was reputed to keep his demented son behind bars, and decided, on an impulse, to wait before a grated window to see if he could catch a glimpse of "this man of pain and suffering," as he later described him. To his surprise, the wish came true. Through the window he saw appear a "giant, the black hair of his head and face—dishevelled, wild,'' a sight that filled him with such fright and compassion that, in an effort, as he later said, ''to do something to make him joyous,'' the boy stuck out his tongue to the frozen bar and suddenly found himself stuck fast to it. For the fourth time that day Leivick was flooded with terror. He pulled himself free, felt his mouth fill with blood which spilled onto his clothes, and ran home, where he fell into a fever. But that day would remain with him for the rest of his life. ''Four moments, four sharp experiences,'' he would say later, ''in one day in the life of a seven-year-old. They would be too much even for an adult. How much more so for a child. . . . These four events of a single day left a permanent imprint upon my entire life and became the undertone of all my later poems and plays, the undertone of my existence as a Jew and of my fate as a Jew'' (218–20). This, we must remember, from a man who had survived hard labor in the Russian prisons and exile in Siberia. Nevertheless, the pain and pathos experienced that day, coming, as the boy saw it, from man, from father, from God, from one's own inherent mortal limitations, defined for him forever the lot of the Jew and of the human condition.

That, of course, is the role of the golem in his drama. By now, most of us are familiar with the mythical figure of the golem—a man-made creature created, through cabalistic magic, in a shadowy duplication of the original act of divine creation by which man himself was formed. The most famous golem, that on which the golem of Leivick's play is modeled, was that of the famous Rabbi Judah Loew of Prague, called also the Maharal. He was a man of great learning in both religious and secular spheres, especially mathematics and astronomy, an intimate acquaintance of such noted scientists as Johannes Kepler and Tycho Brahe, the latter of whom is said to have arranged his audience with the emperor; indeed Judah Loew does not seem to have been interested in magic at all. Nevertheless, according to popular belief, when the Jews of Prague were about to endure still another pogrom because of the blood-libel brought against them by the malicious priest Thaddeus, the Maharal created a golem to protect them from their enemies.

Blood-libel, for those who are unfamiliar with the term, is the accusation that Jews periodically slaughter a Christian child for ritual purposes, usually at the time of Passover, when, it is said, the blood is used for the Seder feast. Absurd as the charge sounds, retaliatory pogroms due to charges of ritual murder have been responsible for Jewish deaths since 1144, when in Norwich, England blood-libel made its first known appearance, until the last documented occurrence in Poland in 1946. The most famous case is that of Hugh of Lincoln, who was found dead in a well in 1255. In that instance 994 Jews were implicated and charged with ritual murder, according to the account of Matthew Paris. Hugh himself was canonized, and a shrine at the well is visited to this day (Hill 217–38).

Against the historical backdrop of this real peril of the blood-libel, stories of Rabbi Loew's role in thwarting the accusers abound; they begin, in fact, from the day of his birth. As one story tells it, when, on the eve of Passover, his mother felt her first birth pangs and cried out, members of the household ran out into the night in search of a midwife and came across a man carrying a large, suspicious-looking bundle. It turned out to be the corpse of a child, and the man confessed he had been hired by anti-Semites to plant it in the cellar of Rabbi Bezalel, who would consequently face the blood-accusation. Rabbi Bezalel then knew the role the newborn infant would play in rescuing Jews from the blood-libel and named him accordingly, after Genesis 49:9: "Judah is a lion's whelp; from the prey, my son, thou art gone up." Perhaps Leivick was drawing on this story when he named his Maharal Aryeh (that is, Lion) Levi, rather than Judah Loew, to underscore the nobility and, indeed, ferocity of the Prague scholar who created the ultimate warrior.

That Judah Loew was believed to have conjured into being a golem is a tribute to the regard in which he was held. For in Jewish lore it is only the greatest of mystics who are able to perform this feat—perhaps because it takes even the most learned of scholars three years to understand the requisite *Sepher Yetsirah*, *The Book of Formation*. For example, Abraham and his teacher, Shem, the son of Noah, are said to have studied it for this length of time and then were able to create a world. It is true, of course, that there are instances in Jewish lore where life is created by unworthies: the magicians of Egypt whom Moses faced brought their staffs to life as snakes; Paracelsus is said to have created a man out of blood and urine and semen. In other cases, the feat is done by means of a kind of cabalist plagiarism, when the *shem ha-mephoresh*, God's Ineffable Name, is discovered and used improperly. In the Talmud *Sota*, for example, we read that Jeroboam's bull idol was made to speak when one of the names of God was carved into the muzzle (*Sota* 47a; Scholem 182). And a similar story is told about an idol of Nebuchadnezzar brought to life when the Jewish high priest's diadem, inscribed with the tetragrammaton, is placed on its head (Scholem 182).

Nevertheless, despite these unusual cases, it still holds true that, in Aggadic legends, only a few rare souls are capable of creating life. It is said that Rabbi Abraham Ibn Ezra created a man and said, "Turn back!" and the creature became what it had been before—although what that had been is not reported (bin Gorion 752). We are told that Rava created a man and sent him to Rabbi Zera. When the man did not reply when spoken to, Rabbi Zera recognized him as a golem and said, "You must have been made by the companions [members of the Talmudic academy]. Return to your dust." Another story tells us that "Rav Hanina and Rav Oshaya busied themselves on the eve of every Sabbath with the Book of Creation." After three years of study, "they made a calf one-third the natural size and ate it" (Scholem 166; *Sanhedrin* 65b). Ben Sira, with his father, Jeremiah, created a man on whose forehead was written *emeth*, or *truth*. To destroy the golem they reversed the combinations of letters by which he was created and erased the first letter, aleph, from *emeth* so that it read *meth*, or *he is dead* (Scholem 179). Other versions, interestingly enough, have the inscription read *Adonai Elohim emeth, the Lord God is truth*. When the aleph is erased, it reads *the Lord God is dead*—a fact that reveals, as Gershom Scholem has aptly pointed out, a strong element of blasphemy in golem making. In golem making, man, the creation, sets about to usurp the role of creator (Scholem 181). And finally, we read of Ibn Gabirol, in a story that perhaps inspired the creators of the film *Weird Science*. In the story, Gabirol creates a woman to serve him—unlike in the film—for chaste purposes. We are told, "When he was denounced to the authorities, he showed them that she was not a full or complete creature. And he restored her to the [hinges] and rounds of wood of which she had been constructed" (bin Gorion 752; Scholem 199).

Most interesting about the last tale is the material from which the golem is said to have been made, for in almost every version of the golem stories the creature is made not of wood but from virgin earth, as in fact it is in Leivick's play; for, as we know, such was the stuff of Adam. Indeed the only place in the Bible where the word *golem* is used is in the psalm traditionally understood to be in Adam's voice—Psalm 139–16:

> galmi ra'u ayneha
> vi'al sifriha kulam yikatayvu
> yamin yutzaru
> vilo ehad bahem.

> (Thine eyes did see my substance, yet being unperfect;
> and in thy book all my members were written,
> which in continuance were fashioned,
> when as yet there was none of them.)

Inherent in the verse is the idea that the creation of man, like the creation of the universe, was brought about through the power of language, specifically the Hebrew language. It is for this reason that golem making requires the use of the *Sepher Yetsirah*, *The Book of Formation*, an esoteric work that explains this process. (Some attribute the authorship of this work to Akiba ben Joseph; others, such as Judah ben Barzilai, go so far as to say that God first created *The Book of Formation*, then looked into it, and created the world.) That man himself began as a golem is posited specifically by Aha bar Hanina, among others, who states that the day Adam was created had twelve hours: "In the first hour his [Adams's] dust was gathered; in the second it was kneaded into a shapeless mass [a golem]; in the third, his limbs were shaped; in the fourth, a soul was infused into him; in the fifth he stood on his feet" (*Sanhedrin* 38b; Scholem 161; Ausubel 603). Another interpretation of the psalm by Rabbi Berakhya claims that man was created first, but, as God did not want it to be thought that man had had a hand in creating the world, he set him aside in a golem state and only on the sixth day infused him with soul. Eleazar of Azariah claims that in his golem state Adam stretched from one end of the world to the other, and Judah Bar Simeon expands on the interpretation, explaining that, as he watched the universe come into being, Adam saw, in a week-long glory of vision, all the generations of men that were to come.

The process of golem making is described in various sources. Eleazer of Worms outlines the golem-making steps in his commentary on *The Book of Formation*. He omits, however, the exact details on the proper combinations of the Hebrew alphabet. Two or three adepts are required, a restriction based on the story of the golem of Ben Sira, the seer who was told by a heavenly voice that a companion was needed for golem making to be successful, and he thus sought out his father, Jeremiah. Pseudo-Saadya's directions add an additional element: along with detailed instructions on the proper combinations of the alphabet, the golem makers, as they chant, circle around the kneaded earth they have buried in the ground. To destroy the creature, they reverse the combinations of letters and circle in the opposite direction. (This is the method used by Rabbi Loew and his disciples in the novel *The Sword and the Golem*.) There is a danger involved in this process: Rabbi Ishmael ben Elisha and his students, for example, circled in the wrong direction and found themselves sunk into the earth up to their waists, until the rabbi realized his mistake and turned around. Still another set of golem-making instructions is given by Abraham Abulafia, who maintains that the earth—exactly weighed (although the amount is not given)—must be mixed by blowing it into a bowlful of pure water, a process reminiscent of God's divine inspiration of spirit into Adam.

Much of this stuff of Jewish lore is used by Leivick in his verse drama. The play opens with a golem-making ritual that seems to be in accordance with the version given by the sage of Judah Loew's birthplace, Eleazer of Worms: beside a river the Maharal is leaning over a figure of kneaded clay and sends for his disciples Isaac and Jacob. That the Maharal should by extension be associated with Abraham is entirely appropriate, for it is Abraham, father of all Jews, who is said to have known the mystery of creation and who could create souls; indeed old manuscripts of *The Book of Formation* bear the additional title of *Othioth d'Avraham Avinu, Alphabet of Our Father Abraham* (Scholem 170–71). This understanding no doubt stems from the final chapter of the *Sepher Yetsirah*, in which we read:

> When Abraham, our father, may he rest in peace, came: he
>   looked, and
>   saw, and
>   understood, and
>   explored, and
>   engraved, and
>   hewed out, and
>   succeeded at Creation as it is said, "And the bodies they had made in
>   Haran" [Genesis 12:5].
>
> The Lord of All—may His Name be praised forever—was
>   revealed

to him, and

He set him in His bosom, and

He kissed him on his head, and

He called him Abraham, my beloved [Isaiah 41:8], and

He cut a covenant with him and his seed forever, as it is said "And he
    believed in YHVH, and He considered it to him for righteousness"
    [Genesis [15:6], and

He cut a covenant with him between the ten fingers of his hands, and that it
    is the covenant of the tongue, and between the ten toes of his feet, and that
    is the covenant of the circumcision, and

He tied the twenty-two letters of the Torah in his tongue, and

He revealed to him His secret:

    He drew them through Water,

    He burned them in Fire,

    He shook them through the Air,

    He kindled them in the Seven Stars

    He led them through the twelve constellations. (Blumenthal 1: 43–44)

The Maharal, then, the creator of life, is Abraham, and the implied presence of
all three patriarchs seems to suggest a state of completion—so, too, with the
naming of the three elements. The *Sepher Yetsirah* tells us, "There are three
mothers that are three fathers, Fire, Air, and Water" (ben Joseph 27). Each
patriarch is associated with his own element; thus the golem, made of earth,
brings together all four elements of being. Furthermore, we are told in cabalistic
tracts that the human soul itself is a tripartite entity, or, to be more precise, three
separate but unified entities, each of which is also identified with a particular
element. In *The Zohar*, the largest and most important cabalistic work, attributed
to the great Rabbi Shimon ben Yochai,[1] we read:

Now the soul is a compound of three grades, and hence it has three names, to wit, *nefesh*
(vital principle), *ruah* (spirit) [the aspect responsible for moral behavior], and *neshamah*
(soul proper). *Nefesh* is the lowest of the three, *ruah* is a grade higher, whilst *neshamah*
is the highest of all and dominates the others. These three grades are harmoniously
combined in those men who have the good fortune to render service to their Master. For
at first man possesses *nefesh*, which is a holy preparative for a higher stage. After he
has achieved purity in the grade of *nefesh* he becomes fit to be crowned by the holy grade
that rests upon it, namely *ruah*. When he has thus attained to the indwelling of *nefesh*
and *ruah*, and qualified himself for the worship of his Master in the requisite manner,
the *neshamah*, the holy superior grade that dominates all the others, takes up its abode
with him and crowns him, so that he becomes complete and perfected on all sides. (2:
280)

Further on, we are told:

Observe that *nefesh*, *ruah*, and *neshamah* are an ascending series of grades. The lowest
of them, *nefesh*, has its source in the perennial celestial stream, but it cannot exist

permanently save with the help of *ruah*, which abides between fire and water. *Ruah*, in its turn, is sustained by *neshamah*, that higher grade above it, which is the source of both *nefesh* and *ruah*. When *ruah* receives its sustenance from *neshamah*, then *nefesh* receives it in turn through *ruah*, so that the three form a unity. (*The Zohar* 2: 281)

Especially interesting in this passage is the assertion that the degree of one's soul hinges upon the degree of service to one's master—that is, God. Man, like the golem, is created to serve. But whether the golem truly has a soul has been much debated. Me'ir ibn Gabbai maintains that the golem has *nefesh* but no more. But Moses Cordovero asserts that the golem—although he does not use that term—has none of the three degrees of soul mentioned in *The Zohar* but has a kind of vital spirit, called *hiyyuth*, higher than the animal soul. This is why a golem cannot constitute a quorum and why, according to Rabbi Zera, destroying a golem does not constitute murder (Scholem 194–95).

Whatever the nature of the vital force animating the golem, man's creation, unlike God's, must be imperfect because the creator is imperfect. For example, in the incident related earlier, where Rabbi Zera recognized Rava's golem for what it was when it did not answer, we are told, "But if not for his sins, he would have answered." The golem lacks speech, then, because of its creator's flaws; indeed, a recurring feature of the golem legends is that the creature always contains some inherent defect—most often, the power of speech. Bahya ben Asher says of Rava's golem that it was mute because it had no rational soul, which is the source of speech. Another opinion states that it is possible to give a golem the power to speak but not to procreate or reason, "for this is beyond the power of any created being and rests with God alone" (Scholem 193–94).[2]

Leivick's golem can speak; and since it becomes familiar with, and is rebuffed by, the Maharal's granddaughter Devorale, we know it has sexual urges as well. Its defect is of a different kind; it comes from a flaw within its creator, and this is the impetus for much of the action of the drama. For the Maharal is making his golem not for the divine knowledge and ecstasy mystical creation brings but to bring down the enemies of his people. Even before the golem is brought to life, its vital force appears to the rabbi and begs him to forego the final step. "The whole night through you kneaded me," the dark figure tells him. "With coldness and cruelty you shaped me" (226). And even the Maharal himself recognizes that his golem has not been created in the prerequisite state of spiritual purity:

A darkness has invaded the desire
I strove so hard to render holy, pure,
With words of fear I have myself
Produced a flaw within the heart to be. (125)

Compounding the problem, another dark figure shows itself, that of the Maharal's nemesis, the priest Thaddeus, who causes—or perhaps merely emblemizes—the immeasurable hatred of the rabbi for those who would harm his people. Seeing the venom in the Maharal's eyes, the figure cries out that he has

> . . . never chanced to see two Jewish eyes
> That looked upon me with the true fury,
> With murderous rage and hate, as yours do now
> They seem the eyes of some Golem run wild. (127)

This hatred, which fills the Maharal during the creating process, mars the creation forever, resulting not in raising the mystical communicant to a more apotheosized level but in lowering him toward the level of his creation. Indeed, as Scholem has observed, "The danger is not that the golem, become autonomous, will develop overwhelming powers; it lies in the tension which the creative process arouses in the creator himself. Mistakes in carrying out the directions do not impair the golem; they destroy its creator" (191). Such is the case, for example, with the Jewish golem described by Jakob Grimm, which grew so tall that its creator found to his horror that he could no longer reach the creature's forehead to erase the *aleph*. He tricked it by having it pull off his shoes, erasing the letter when the huge golem leaned over; but the clay monster fell over and crushed him. In Leivick's play, this golem, too, will grow: beginning life as almost a robotic creature, dumbly obeying the orders of the Maharal in the manner related by the earlier legends of the Loew golem, he becomes more and more human as the play progresses—a concept that is also used in the film *D.A.R.Y.L.* and, more recently, *Terminator 2*.

The Maharal is not blind to Joseph's potential for growth. Even in the second scene, called "Walls," he tells him:

> The mighty powers now begin to surge within you.
> They cleanse themselves a path into your soul.
> The dark blackness of your other being
> Has not released your head and heart
> And from within you speak its unclean curses. (135–36)

Leivick's golem, then, unlike the usual sort, does have a soul. One is tempted to see the as yet unreleased "head and heart" as the second and third stages, the *ruah* and *neshamah*, of that soul, an interpretation especially inviting when we recall Chaim Bloch's statement that "Some regarded the golem as a 'ghost' of Rabbi Loew" (Bloch 76; Scholem 189). By mirroring the Maharal's unsurfaced and unrealized anger and hatred, the golem works as his doppelganger and brings before him, as it grows, the terrible truth of this flaw within his own soul. In the play, this hatred is symbolically represented by the color red, which appears and reappears in a series of gradually intensifying images. We see it in the first scene in the red of violence seen by the disciple Isaac in a chaotic dream;

in the second scene, in the fiery walls the golem sees and cowers from; in the third scene, in the vision of fire and blood in the Maharal's dreams; in the fourth scene, in the invisible fire intuitively seen by the beggar when the golem enters; in the fifth scene, in the images of red conjured by Thaddeus with his accusation of the blood ritual and the impending pogrom; and, in the sixth scene, in the wounds of the Young Beggar, who is the messiah, and his vision of the "crimson night." In the hallucinatory seventh scene, a collage of sound and sense, we see the hatred in the "reddest wine . . . brightest far than blood" of Elijah's cup, in the blood of love which Thaddeus claims for Christ, in the vials of blood taken from a child Thaddeus has slaughtered to lay blame on the Jews, in the bloody cruciform gashes the golem dreams are on the Maharal's face, and, as the scene closes, in the Maharal's last words to him: "The word is—blood." That, of course, prefigures the final scene, where the red of martyrdom appears in the Jewish blood that the golem spills in the great synagogue. Only then does the Maharal see the result of his own hatred as well as the terrible truth about the redeemer he has created.

That Leivick's golem should emerge as a messianic figure should not be surprising, for the redeemer/messiah is central not only here but to much of Leivick's work. His play preceding *The Golem* was *The Messiah in Chains*; a later drama (1932) was entitled *The Salvation Comedy—The Golem Dreams*. It is not by chance that the golem in this play is called Joseph, for, in Jewish tradition, there are two messiahs: the messiah of the House of David, the deliverer who will restore peace and order to the world and return the Jewish people to their promised land; and the messiah of the House of Joseph, who will precede the other in the time of Armageddon, battling the hordes of Gog and Magog until he falls before the gates of Jerusalem. There, it is said, he will remain for 40 days until the messiah of the House of David comes and resurrects him. Death and resurrection are, of course, integral to the legend of the golem, but we must remember, too, that it is only in the later golem stories that the creature is used as a guardian/deliverer. The cabalist originally created the golem for the mystical experience alone, the momentary knowledge of creation culminating in a kind of spiritual ecstasy. This is why the golem is returned immediately afterward to its original dust. To use the golem for material purposes is to abuse this knowledge. In the example cited before, when Rav Hanina and Rav Oshaya, after three years of study, created a calf and ate it, they immediately forgot all they had learned, and it took three years more of study before they could duplicate the feat.

In the corpus of the Rabbi Loew legends, the golem is used in a period of great crisis when it is deemed that it is nevertheless not yet time for the true messiah to come. This is exactly why the Maharal creates Joseph in the play. The impending catastrophe is real, so real, in fact, that the messiah and the prophet Elijah actually make their appearance in the play in the guise of the Young and Old Beggar. This is in line with the Jewish tradition of the *lamed-*

vovniks, the 36 righteous men who walk the earth, unknown to any but the most pious, who redeem mankind by virtue of their good deeds. One of these, it is said, is the messiah, who may not, indeed, know his identity himself.

The great Maharal, of course, *does* recognize them, but, surprisingly, he becomes angry that they have come ''unbidden,'' as he says, and orders them off. Later, in the scene called ''Unbidden,'' he explains why, telling the Old Beggar,

> Why did you have to bring him [the messiah] here?
> To let him see the face of death and danger?
> What can he do for us? What should he do?
> The world has not exhausted yet
> Its store of cruelty, on us.
> Has *each* of us in every land felt
> The butcher's knife against his throat?
> Has he yet heard the final groan?
> Or seen the last of lifted swords?
> How could he say he saw or heard
> If my throat stands unslaughtered here,
> If my body is unburned?
>   . . . He must be *the last* . . .
> And woe to him if he should try
> To intercede for us against our will. (185)

In other words, the messiah's time will come only when the last Jew on earth faces extermination. The Prague crisis, extreme as it may be, does not approach Armageddon. And, indeed, the golem Joseph does seem capable of averting it. When Thaddeus and his disciple hide two vials of blood from a child they have slaughtered, the golem unearths them and drives off the two monks. Here Leivick plays with another Rabbi Loew legend: where before it is the rabbi who can render the golem invisible by means of an amulet, here the creature is able at will to become invisible, which it does when it is bidden to do violence. It is almost as if it is a side of itself that it wishes not to see; for, as we have said, it belongs not to it, but to its creator. Forced to witness the pathos of the human condition, and to experience it, he finds the mission he has been created to fulfill more and more horrifying. This realization comes slowly and begins at an early stage of the play when the Maharal, wisely seeing that Joseph is capable of running amuk, orders him to Tower Five, where he sees mendicants, cripples, outcasts, and other sixteenth-century bag people who have found shelter there. The sight is heartrending, and Joseph reacts to it in a manner similar to the way the narrator of still another doppelganger tale, ''Bartleby,'' reacts to the news of the dead scrivener's past experiences in the Dead Letter Office[3]: he is overwhelmed by an epiphany of compassion. As Joseph confesses:

> . . . I thought I would not care,
> That I would leave these ruins and their call

And let the moaning die in the tower's void.
I thought this. But, you see, within my heart
A love awoke, a longing, and a shiver shook my frame. (199)

Certainly we may see here the awakening of the *neshamah*, the highest state of the human soul. It is at this point that we see Joseph truly rising to the level of a *lamed-vovnik*, a righteous one—indeed, to the level of a messiah. At the same time, as a golem, he has been created for a role now contrary to his nature. This is his martyrdom. Leivick, understanding this irony, brings Joseph together in an intensely lyrical, climactic scene with the Jewish messiah (the Young Beggar), dragging his chains, and Christ, called simply The Man with the Cross. Cross, chain, and the golem's axe thus form a poignant trinity of symbols emphasizing the particular martyrdoms of each messiah. Each savior, as he enters the subterranean caverns under Tower Five where Joseph has thwarted Thaddeus, entreats the golem for something to drink, and to each Joseph offers one of the two vials of blood he has unearthed. Both the Jewish and Christian messiahs taste a vial and are horrified, and Joseph enjoins them to put them back: to taste blood is a martyrdom to be endured only by the golem-messiah.

But if Joseph has risen to such a height, what of the Maharal? The answer, ironically enough, is given through his archenemy Thaddeus. Earlier in the play, we remember, the figure of Thaddeus remarked that the eyes of the Maharal, burning with anger, seemed like those of "some Golem run wild"; later, in Tower Five, Thaddeus, indicating a hunchback, tells the Jews cloistered there that they "wear their anger as he wears his hump." So, too, with the Maharal: Anger and hatred have deformed his soul and brought him down to the level of a golem. That Leivick is suggesting a reversal of roles between creator and created can hardly be denied. In the visionary seventh scene, Joseph is visited by the figure of the Maharal, just as Joseph's figure appeared before Judah Loew in the opening scene; by the final scene, it is Joseph who, to the astonishment of the shammes, sends for the rabbi.

It is fitting, then, that Joseph's encounter with the other two messiahs, along with the Maharal's shape, should culminate with the actual appearance of the Maharal, who commands Joseph to complete his mission of violence. This Joseph will do, although in a manner that will leave the Maharal horror-stricken. For Joseph has come to a self-knowledge that places him beyond his creator's grasp. "I know all now," he tells the Maharal. "Your hand / Lies over me but you are not with me."

These final words foreshadow the tragedy to come. For it is Joseph's hand that raises itself over the Maharal, who is now forced to confront the fury of his own hatred. Joseph's hand, however, is unable to descend on its creator; instead, the golem bursts into the synagogue and wreaks havoc, murdering two of the congregation with his axe, and the blood the Maharal sought to save is shed. "Are you aware whose blood it was you have spilled?" the Maharal shouts. "Jewish blood," the golem answers. It is not a distinction that would have been made by Leivick, who as a boy had felt his heart lunge at the plight of Count Yassevitch's son and who became the gentle socialist and egalitarian sentenced to prison and exile in Czarist Russia for decrying that regime's oppression of its people.

The Golem, then, is a play about the height and depth of man's soul and the possibility for both glory and destruction in those creations drawn from the chaos and void of his being. It is a truth as valid today as it was in sixteenth-century Prague or in first-century Jerusalem and Tiberias where the great Jewish mystics walked. It seems fitting to close this essay with the words of the foremost scholar of Jewish mysticism in our time, Gershom Scholem, at whose tongue–in–cheek suggestion a sophisticated computer facility designed for military use was named *Golem Aleph* (*Golem Number One*). At the dedication ceremony of *Golem Aleph* in Rehovot, Scholem said,

All my days I have been complaining that the Weizmann Institute has not mobilized the funds to build up the Institute for Experimental Demonology and Magic which I have for so long proposed to establish there. They preferred what they call Applied Mathematics and its sinister possibilities to my more direct magical approach. Little did they know, when they preferred Chaim Pekeris [the computer's inventor] to me, what they were letting themselves in for. So I resign myself and say to the Golem and its creator: develop peacefully and don't destroy the world. *Shalom.*

NOTES

1. Gershom Scholem's exhaustive research leaves little doubt that the true author of *The Zohar* was Moses de Leon, a thirteenth-century Spanish cabalist. See his Fifth Lecture in *Major Trends in Jewish Mysticism* (New York: Schocken, 1961).

2. According to Rabbi Meier ibn Gabbai, it is *ruah* that endows one with the property of speech, while *neshamah* provides the property of intellection. *Hiyyuth* is in actuality a fusion of *nefesh* and *ruah*; thus it is possible for a golem to speak. See Moshe Idel's *Golem: Jewish Magical and Mystical Traditions on the Artificial Anthropoid* (Albany: State University of New York Press, 1989).

3. For a fuller explanation of the doppelganger motif in Melville's story, see my article, "Unadmitted Impediments, Unmarriageable Minds: Melville's 'Bartleby' and 'I and My Chimney,' " in *Studies in Short Fiction* 24.2 (1987): 93–101.

WORKS CITED

Ausubel, Nathan, ed. *A Treasury of Jewish Folklore*. New York: Crown, 1948.
ben Joseph, Akiba. *The Book of Formation: Sepher Yetzirah*. Trans. Knut Stenring. New York: Ktav, 1970.
bin Gorion, Micha Joseph, comp. *Mimekor Yisrael: Classical Jewish Folktales*. Ed. Emanuel bin Gorion. Trans. I. M. Lask. Bloomington: Indiana University Press, 1976.
Bloch, Chayim. *The Golem: Mystical Tales from the Ghetto at Prague*. Trans. Harry Schneiderman. Blauvelt, N.Y.: Rudolf Steiner, 1975.

Blumenthal, David. R. *The Merkabah Tradition and the Zoharic Tradition.* New York: KTAV, 1978. Vol. 1 of *Understanding Jewish Mysticism.* 2 vols.

Glut, Donald F. *The Frankenstein Legend: A Tribute to Mary Shelley and Boris Karloff.* Metuchen, N.J.: Scarecrow, 1973.

Hill, Sir Francis. *Medieval Lincoln.* Cambridge: Cambridge University Press, 1965.

Idel, Moshe. *Golem: Jewish Magical and Mystical Traditions on the Artificial Anthropoid.* Albany: State University of New York Press, 1989.

Leivick, Halper *The Golem.* In *Three Great Jewish Plays.* New York: Applause, 1986.

Madison, Charles A. *Yiddish Literature: Its Scope and Major Writers.* New York: Ungar, 1968.

Patai, Raphael. *The Messiah Texts.* Detroit: Wayne State University Press, 1979.

Scholem, Gershom. *On the Kabbalah and Its Symbolism.* Trans. Ralph Manheim. New York: Schocken, 1969.

Shelley, Mary. *Frankenstein: or, the Modern Prometheus.* Ed. M. K. Joseph. London: Oxford University Press, 1969.

Sanhedrin. Trans. Jacob Schachter and H. Freedman. In *The Babylonian Talmud: Seder Nezikin.* Vol. 3. Ed. I. Epstein. London: Soncino, 1935.

The Zohar. Trans. Harry Sperling and Maurice Simon. 5 vols. London: Soncino, 1934.

10

Dream on Monkey Mountain: Fantasy as Self-Perception

Robert J. Willis

Derek Walcott, a Third World poet and dramatist, born in the Castries, St. Lucia, began writing poetic dramas in 1948 with his first play, *Henri Christophe*, a play about the Haitian Revolution. Walcott has written 15 plays, which have been produced and published, and 10 volumes of poetry, seven of which must be called major collections (Jones 270). His own life as a "divided child"—he is the son of parents of mixed European and African descent—embodies one of the prime tensions of the West Indian experience.

Walcott's arch hero, Makak, in *Dream on Monkey Mountain* is taken from the author's early years in St. Lucia where Walcott recalls a childhood memory of an old, undisciplined woodcutter, who reflects regional history. Two of the major themes of the play are racial inferiority (Makak's French Patois name implies an apelike figure) and the thwarted potential of an independent spirit, "living on his own ground, off its elemental resources" (Ismond 70). Walcott's drama illuminates the tragic struggle of Makak, his hopes, his fears, and his temporary freedom, which is itself a dream. Makak is a microcosm of all poor West Indians who suffer; he is offered a seeming identity only to return to his mountain hermitlike life, with dreams defeated again. The play, however, leaves the audience with a hopeful vision: Makak must and will descend again from his mountain isolation to face reality, regardless of the cost.

Walcott, in his introduction to *Dream on Monkey Mountain*, credits the theater as an outlet to show the legacy of racial oppression and subjugation of the West Indian natives "[B]eing poor, we already had the theatre of our lives which we share with the agony of actors of all time" (*Dream* 5, 6).

Dream on Monkey Mountain is a mythic drama, a ritualized play of the West Indies, combining fantasy, obeah, music, dance, and poetry to expose the deeper, unconscious sources of identity and the nature of freedom. The cast includes seven black men, one white woman dancer-singer, a male chorus, drummers, and music. The play was first presented by the Trinidad Theatre Workshop in Toronto in 1967. Other productions were presented in the Eugene O'Neill Memorial Theatre in Connecticut; the Mark Taper Forum in Los Angeles; and in New York, where the play won the Obie Award for the best foreign play in 1970–71 (Hamner 84). In the 1971 production at St. Mark's Theatre, the White Goddess appeared singing in a huge cutout of the moon. When Makak's hallucination is over, the moon sinks into the sea. Edith Oliver, in her review of the play, tells how the setting, choreography, costumes, and lighting enhance the mood of the play (84). In this play, characters exchange roles, assume aspects of the protagonist's dominant personality traits, and serve as symbols; one who is twice killed returns alive again in the epilogue.

The play, ripe with satire, is structured around a series of interrelated themes within dream sequences echoing Cervantes' *Don Quixote*. In these dream episodes, the protagonist, Makak, discovers his true self, neither God nor beast, only a man, an old black man who eventually learns his name and identity.

Walcott generously credits Brecht; Oriental artists; and Robert Graves's *The White Goddess*, who appears in Makak's dream as the white apparition representing inauthentic and limited African identity, for his inspiration. The play is also rich in puns, metaphors, and verbal play of fast-paced Calypsonian rhetoric. Unlike Brecht's productions, Walcott's plays demand a different kind of disciplined actor, dancer, and singer more like those who perform in Kabuki theater. All of these elements, including dream sequences and the introduction of the White Goddess, merge in *Dream on Monkey Mountain*.

Walcott's protagonist, Makak (monkey), who is an extension of Walcott's hero in his drama *Henri Christophe*, is a coal-burner who represents not only the blacks' righteous rebellion against the white master but also the heretical step of rejecting the equally oppressive role imposed by black racists. In a note on the production, Walcott, somewhat reminiscent of Strindberg, allows the producer freedom to amplify: "The play is a dream, one that exists as much in the given minds of its principal characters as in that of its writer" (*Dream* 208). Walcott also suggests Sartre's prologue to *The Wretched of the Earth* as another source of his theme: "Thus in certain psychoses the hallucinated person, tired of always being insulted by a demon, one fine day starts hearing the voice of an angel who pays him compliments" (211).

In the Prologue, Makak has been jailed for being drunk and disorderly. He shares his cell with two fellow prisoners, Tigre and Souris, who merge with his hallucination and share his quixotic experiences, as does Makak's jailer, Lestrade. The names of the characters suggest fable: Lestrade, neither black nor white, is a straddler. *Makak* means *monkey*, taken from the name of the mountain where he lives. His two companions are the tiger and the mouse. Corporal Lestrade, like Charles Fuller's Sergeant Waters in *A Soldier's Play*, ridicules backward blacks. He attempts to prove that Makak is an old ape who must be told how to act and what to do: "Animals, beasts, savages, cannibals, niggers, stop turning this place into a stinking zoo" (216).

When Lestrade interrogates Makak about his race, Makak replies, "Tired," a one-word declaration of long-standing prejudice. Then Makak relates his dreams, claiming "All I have is my dreams and they don't trouble your soul" (225). The prisoner goes on to tell about his vision of the White Goddess on Monkey Mountain who calls out his "real" name and not the one he uses (228–35).

In Scene One, Makak is on Monkey Mountain with his friend, Moustique, whom he tells about his dream and the lady, the root of his problem, in his vision. Makak declares that the lady, after talking all night, commands him to regain his African birthright (236). He has been living all of his life, without a wife or children, on Monkey Mountain, working at his charcoal pit. Moustique does not believe his story but, like Sancho Panza, decides to accompany his "king" on his misadventures. The two men mirror the play's black consciousness in that both lack any positive identity, underscored by Moustique: "You black, ugly, poor, so worse than nothing. You like me, small, ugly with a foot like an 'S' " (237). Obviously, Makak had one identity throughout his life—subhuman. His hallucinations slowly give him dignity and eventually his God-given identity of a man. The two travelers set out to prove Makak's birthright in a series of misadventures. The episodes are laced with satire and humor: "Saddle my horse, if you love me, Moustique, and cut a sharp bamboo for me. . . . Makak will walk like he used to in Africa, when his name was Lion!" (240). Reluctantly, Moustique agrees to follow his master, but adds, "Is the stupidest thing I ever see" (242). To the music of flute and drum, they sally forth down the mountain to glory.

On their first encounter, Makak is instrumental in restoring a dying man to life. Corporal Lestrade, informed about the local "savior" appears in wig and gown, deriding the crowd's delusions: "It's the cripples who believe in miracles. It's the slaves who believe in freedom" (261–62). Moustique is quick to seize the opportunity for gain, like many other trickster heroes of West Indian folklore who convert faith and trust into a profitable enterprise. Caught impersonating his master, Moustique is beaten to death by a crowd of villagers who discover his attempt to be the miracle-working Makak.

In what appears to be reality, Makak is back in his cell with Souris and Tigre, enduring Lestrade's pointedly contradictory defense of white justice. In an attempt to sublimate his own problem of racial identity, Lestrade—once again echoing Fuller's Sergeant Waters—screams: "This ain't Africa. This is not another easy-going nigger you talking to, but an officer!" (280). Angered, Tigre plans an escape for himself, Souris, and Makak who pretends madness to bring Lestrade to his cell where he stabs him. After they leave the jail, the corporal rises and explains to the audience that the act is only what they dream of—their dream of revenge. As Lestrade begins his hunt for the fugitives, he warns: "Attempting to escape from the prison of their lives. That's the most dangerous crime. It brings about revolution'' (286–87). Going through the forest on their way to Monkey Mountain (Africa), the fugitives become hungry. Makak dries ganja to smoke and tells Souris and Tigre that they will not need food when they smoke the plant. As the chorus chants, ''I am going home to Africa,'' Makak announces ''The mind can bring the dead to life. It can make a man a king. It can make him a beast'' (291).

Lestrade, searching for the escaped prisoners, meets Basil, another apparition, a coffin maker and spirit of death, who admonishes the corporal and demands he repent his sins. Lestrade does not know if he is in the real world or in a dream himself. Coming upon Makak and the others, who see Lestrade apparently talking to himself, the officer, thinking of his sins, ''goes native'' and becomes the most fanatic convert to Makak's back-to-Africa movement. At this point, Makak himself is caught up in the frenzy for power and revenge. Makak promises to make Tigre a general when they arrive in Africa. Meanwhile, Makak is crowned king by his three followers. Souris is also converted totally to Makak's dream. Throughout the play all of the major characters, at one time or another, question their racial identity, their place in life. Makak wavers between reality and illusion. Another dream-death takes place when Lestrade drives a spear through Tigre, who, like Moustique, seeks only monetary gain from his newfound position of power.

In a quick change of scene, they are transported to Africa, and Makak sets up court and judgment is passed on the history of racial oppression. Lestrade insists on death for all the accused, including Makak's White Goddess. In one of the wittiest and most entertaining scenes in the play, Basil, who reappears in Africa, reads a list of the offenders, including Aristotle, Shakespeare, The Phantom, Mandrake the Magician, and Al Jolson.

The revolutionists then consider the enemies' fate. Basil asks if the Pope is to be spared. A unanimous negation is the tribe's response. The same reaction is rendered at the names of the President of the United States, the Republic of South Africa, and the Ku Klux Klan. Also in this dream sequence, congratulatory letters arrive from several golf and country clubs. A gilt-edged doctorate from Mississippi University arrives, along with the Nobel Peace Prize, an autograph of Pushkin, the Stalin Peace Prize, an offer from the United Nations, a sliver of bone from the thigh of Lumumba, and an offer from Hollywood. The scene then shifts from satire to ''tragedy.'' With the beheading of the White Goddess, Makak gains his total freedom—by killing his ''problem'': ''She is the white light that paralysed your mind, that led you into this confusion. It is you who created her, so kill her! Kill her!'' (*Dream* 319). Moustique is also executed (his second death) for having betrayed the original dream. In this court, there is no room for personal relationships; there is only racial retribution.

The Epilogue makes it clear that the play's action has been real only in Makak's mind. He has cut through illusion to discover his essential self. Makak, the ''Being'' without an identity, without manhood, now has rejoined the world, taking on his ancestral name. His name is his identity; Makak, as the world has considered him, is a new man, equal to all other men and women. When he wakes in his jail cell, he recollects that his legal name is Felix Hoban. Moustique comes to take him from the jail and discovers Makak to be a new man. Together they set out for Monkey Mountain. Makak's last words are a prayer for the future: "Makak lives where he has always lived, in the dreams of his people! Other men will come, other prophets will come, and they will be stoned, and mocked, and betrayed. But now this old hermit is going home, back to the beginning of this world" (*Dream* 326).

Walcott dismisses revenge as uncreative. Makak, after experiencing his dream, realizes he is a man, a man living off his own land and its native resources. He has found his own roots, which are just as sacred to him as the white man's roots are to the white man. It is his self-imposed image that Makak has learned to dismiss, not by seeking revenge on the oppressors such as Lestrade but by seeking in himself a positive image. His racial identity has been made up of a complex historical legacy, but this should not deter him from creating a new vision of renewal with dignity and purpose. This theme is reiterated throughout Walcott's work.

Makak has thus gone through the whole cycle from woodcutter to king to woodcutter again, but his experiences will keep alive the dreams of the people of the Caribbean, a dream of freedom that must be maintained in the colonized world. The play reawakens the anger at the legacy of bondage in the minds of the oppressed, but it also, in glorifying and idealizing Africa, displays the power of the theater in everyday life. The awakening of the colonized consciousness is seen in the acting out of the hallucinations of this old charcoal maker who refuses to accept the forced identity of a subhuman.

As the play ends and the house lights go on, the audience may doubt the fantasy of the play, for outside of the world of the theater, humans are still irrational. They still consult the astrologer; they still cross their fingers and knock on wood; and they are still, in a sense, religious. Then, as the house lights again dim, the actors renew their cult of nakedness. Life begins again every night when the house lights go out. Rehearsals are also life. They have accepted the twilight. Walcott teaches us that in the theater all the races are one race. He believes that there is no such thing as black or white literature. He notes that the reception of this play in New York (the critics viewed the play as part of the "Get Whitey Syndrome") would not be acceptable to a West Indian audience. What Makak recognizes after he awakes from his nightmare-dream is the lesson he learned from the horror of the blacks' actions in Africa—tribes slaughtering each other—that human cruelty is raceless. Makak has come to realize that the first step in getting rid of his fear of everything white is his need for freedom and identity. The world can and must dispossess prejudice at all levels. Makak has given us a new meaning of life.

WORKS CITED

Bell, Hesketh J. *Obeah: Witchcraft in the West Indies*. New Haven: Negro Universities Press, 1970.

Brown, Lloyd. "Dreamers and Slaves." *Caribbean Quarterly* 17.3–4 (1971): 39.

Colson, Theodor. "Derek Walcott's Plays." *World Literature Written in English* 12 (1973): 90–91.

Graves, Robert. *The White Goddess*. London: Faber, 1961.

Hamner, Robert. *Derek Walcott*: Boston: Twayne, 1981.

Ismond, Pat. "Self Portrait of an Island." *Journal of West Indian Literature* (1986): 59–73.

Jones, Dennis. "Derek Walcott." *Dictionary of Literary Biography, Yearbook* 16 (1981): 1270–77.

King, Bruce, ed. *West Indian Literature*. London: Macmillan, 1979.

Oliver, Edith. Review. *The New Yorker* 27 March 1971: 83–85.

Ramchand, Kenneth. *West Indian Literature*. Nairobi: Nelson Caribbean, 1980.

Rodman, Selden. "Derek Walcott." *Tongues of Fallen Angels*. New York: New Directions, 1974. 233–59.

Simons, G. L. *The Witchcraft World*. New York: Harper and Row, 1974.

Walcott, Derek. "The Caribbean." *Journal of Interamerican Studies and World Affairs* 16 (1974): 12.

———. *Dream on Monkey Mountain and Other Plays*. New York: Farrar, 1970.

———. "Man of the Theatre." Interview. *The New Yorker* June 1971: 30.

11

Spalding Gray's *Swimming to Cambodia*: A Performance Gesture

Jessica Prinz

> Laughter today—and this helps to explain why it often has a hollow sound and why so much contemporary humor takes the form of parody and self-parody—comes from people who are all too well aware of the bad news but have nevertheless made a determined effort to keep smiling.
>
> Christopher Lasch

Spalding Gray walks onstage at the Performing Garage in Soho. He sits down at a simple wooden table, takes a small sip of water, and begins to talk. He talks about his role in the making of *The Killing Fields*; he talks about Thailand, Cambodia, New York, and mostly he talks about Spalding Gray. Richard Schechner defines Gray as a pioneer in the new experimental theater of the 1980s, with its tendency toward the personal, the private, the monological, and the narcissistic. "By the 1980's," Schechner says, "the definitive mark of experimental theatre was one person alone in a small space" (34, 36). Neither classic theater, film, or literature, *Swimming to Cambodia* is nevertheless available to us in all of these forms—as drama, film, and text. Certainly we can read the book *Swimming to Cambodia*, but we would miss the essence of Gray's performance: his presence, his intonations, his facial expressions, vocal inflections, dialects, and gestures. These are indispensible elements of the new performance mode that Gray is helping to generate.

In *Swimming to Cambodia* Gray explores what it means to confront the fantastic but nevertheless true and tragic history of Cambodia. Within the performance, the simple set and staging, the minimal props, and quotidian talk are all, I will argue, a reaction to or defense mechanism against the fantastic and seemingly impossible facts of history. Tzvetan Todorov's definition of the fantastic is the most pertinent here: the fantastic causes the spectator to hesitate between supernatural and natural explanations of an event. "The fantastic," he says, "confronts us with a dilemma: to believe or not to believe" (83).[1] If in the "uncanny," supernatural events are explained as natural, in the "marvelous," supernatural events are accepted as such. But the fantastic hesitates between these two poles. While *Swimming to Cambodia* does not treat the supernatural, per se, it does describe and produce an epistemological hesitation of this kind. Gray is uncertain about where to locate "reality." The real history of Cambodia is impossible to understand and "much too far to swim to." The discussion of these issues will begin with an analysis of that quintessentially dramatic element: gesture.

As a concept addressed by psychologists, anthropologists, semioticians, and theoreticians of the theater, gesture is an interdisciplinary concept especially suited for an analysis of Gray's intermedial art. Interestingly enough, theorists in all of these disciplines strive in varied ways to separate gesture from language. Motivated by objectives defined by their own fields, they nevertheless almost univocally and universally dissociate the verbal from the gestural.

Antonin Artaud, Bertolt Brecht, and Jerzy Grotowsky, despite their differences, all celebrate a drama that is primarily gestural and only secondarily linguistic. Artaud, for instance, is opposed to the dominance, indeed tyranny, of speech in the theater (80–81) and argues that theater is poetry in space, not in language (30). Brecht's A-Effect, or alienation effect, calls for a heightened self-consciousness to gesture, as in Chinese acting, where the actor is seen to observe his own gestures (139), or through purposeful contradiction between gestures and speech (Pavis 83). Thus in his study of Brecht, Benjamin repeats: "Epic theatre is gestural. . . . The gesture is its raw material" (3). For Grotowski, too, theatrical gesture is not subordinate to a language that it illustrates. Gesturality is supposed to free itself from discourse and form an autonomous semiotics for itself (Pavis 87). According to Grotowski, it is only the "hypersensitive professor" who expects the theater to be a realization of a text (31).

Ray L. Birdwhistell is an anthropologist who has founded the science of gesture, *kinesics*. Although his work continuously draws analogies between gestures and language, Birdwhistell emphasizes repeatedly that gesture is an extralexical activity ("Kinesics" 536). In a 1968 essay on gesture, Julia Kristeva even more emphatically argues for a nonlinguistic model of gesture. For her it is important to see gesture as nonrepresentational; it is, she says, indicative but not signifying. This nonlinguistic and nonrepresentational concept of gesture allows her to create a semiotics that does not privilege language (Pavis 84).

Finally, if we turn to the analysis of gesture by psychiatrists and psychologists, the conclusions are surprisingly similar. John P. Spiegel and Pavel Machotka begin their book *Messages of the Body* with this assertion: "To say that the communication system of the body is not like a linguistic system is not to deny that it is a set of coded messages; but its code and the program of encoding and decoding its messages probably bears a closer resemblance to music, drama, and the plastic arts than to words and language'' (5).

What these various theories do is help to foreground the surprisingly linguistic quality of Gray's acting in *Swimming to Cambodia*. In this performance piece, Gray's gestures mirror and reinforce the spoken text. Using the ordinary language of everyday talk, including its slang and sometimes profanity, Gray's facial expressions and gestures almost always translate the verbal into a visual and gestural code.[2] This code switching merely produces a semantic redundancy (Exhibits 11.1 and 11.2).

There is a consistent reciprocity of gesture and text in Gray's work. Why, we might ask, does such a contemporary, even avant-garde artist, use gesture in such a traditional way? Why is gesture here an accessory to speech?

In her essay "Redundancy and the 'Readable' Text," Susan Rubin Suleiman reminds us that, despite the negative connotation redundancy has in ordinary speech, linguists and information theorists view redundancy as a positive term, for without some redundancy communication is impossible. Clearly, Gray is determined to communicate with his audience, and as many theorists have noted, the postmodern audience is a wide one. Unlike the modern avant-garde, which was determined to antagonize, provoke, and even cancel its relation to the audience, along with other contemporary performance artists, Gray is determined to engage and communicate with it. Scholars as different as Harold Rosenberg, Fredric Jameson, Andreas Huyssen, and Umberto Eco have all noted this shift in postmodernism—the merging of high art and popular culture, fine art and mass media techniques, a shift in the relation to the audience so that the purpose is, as Eco says, to "reach . . . a vast audience" (72).

The intermedial redundancy of *Swimming to Cambodia* ensures coherence and disambiguation, effecting greater communication between the performer and his audience. Yet the performance itself outlines numerous parables of failed communication. What does it mean to live in Manhattan, where people do not have a common language? The implications, for Gray, are finally political.

But I say . . . how . . . how does a country like America, or rather how does America because certainly there is no country like it, begin to find the language to negotiate or talk with a country like Russia . . . if I can't even *begin* to get it with my people on the corner of Broadway and John Street? (*Swimming*, film version)

Acutely aware of the problematics of communication, Gray devises a performance mode that will establish communication with his own audience as effectively as possible.

The gestures within *Swimming to Cambodia*, like all gestures in the theater, help to extend Gray himself as an actor. In an excellent analysis of gesture, Patrice Pavis writes:

The essential function of gesture is its capacity to designate the situation of the utterance, its being deictic, [or] a sign which refers to the presence of the stage and the actor. . . .

Exhibit 11.1. Gray talks to Buffy, his upstairs neighbor back in white, homogenous Boston. They've got the common language, and so Buffy turns down his hi-fi. Image from the videotape, *Swimming to Cambodia*, used courtesy of Spalding Gray.

Exhibit 11.2. Gray impersonates his girlfriend, Rene, who is hurling obscenities on the phone at their upstairs neighbor in Soho. The music on the quadrophonic torture box goes louder. They do not have the common language. Image from the videotape, *Swimming to Cambodia*, used courtesy of Spalding Gray.

Gesture is not dissociable from the actor who produces it . . . the actor is always anchored on the stage of innumerable corporal deictics, beginning with attitude, glance and mere physical presence. (83–84; see also Elam 73)

Hence a primary function of gesture in *Swimming to Cambodia* is deictic, pointing to Gray's central presence in the action. In keeping with the narcissism built into the monological and autoperformative mode, many of Gray's gestures are self-directed. The focus of the performance is Gray himself as performer, character, and actor. Not only is he at the center of the narrative but symmetrical gestures often locate him at the center of a visual field (Exhibit 11.3).

Paradoxically, despite all this signalling of the self, Gray is presented in a way that also calls presence into question. Both Richard Schechner and Philip Auslander have noted that Gray enacts various Gray personae, creating a scene for his multiple selves. James Leverett writes, "It has gradually become Gray's chosen lot simultaneously to live his life and to play the role of Spalding Gray living his life, *and* to observe said Gray living his life in order to report on it in the next monologue" (xii). This self-diffraction is most pointedly expressed when Gray describes his excitement at the beach at Phuket, where he goes swimming with his friend Ivan: "I'd run down the beach and look back to try to see us there in the surf and each time I'd miss myself and then run back to try to be in it all again. Then down the beach and back and down the beach and back. . . . " (*Swimming*, Film version)

Gray's performance is self-reflexive at a variety of levels and in many ways concerns its own involution. The narrative offers a metaphor for its own self-reflexiveness, as Gray describes a teak table he saw at the Vietnamese embassy:

This table was exquisite. . . . On the surface there was a hand-carved, three-dimensional relief of elephants tearing down teak trees with their trunks in order to make the table—so you see, it was a reflective table—it told a story about itself. In fact, it was doubly reflective, even reflexive, because it had a piece of glass over it and every so often I would catch a reflection of myself in the glass. (*Swimming* 65)

Like the teak table, Gray's narrative is about itself, and it is also about his trying to catch glimpses of himself within it.

Swimming to Cambodia is a film about a film, a performance about performing, and a dramatic event that analyzes and describes acting. The Stanislavski "method" is satirized throughout the monologue, especially in Gray's description of Ira Wheeler trying to do an emotional memory and being on the verge of tears and in a deep funk all day, while the car in which they sit systematically falls to pieces. When Gray starts talking to the driver, Wheeler gets outraged and yells, "Will you stop talking. . . . I'm trying to have an emotional memory." Gray responds, "This man is about to get killed by an elephant. Try *that* one." "You would be amazed at what some people went through to get into character for this film," says Gray. The spoofs on Stanislavski accomplish at least two things in the narrative.

Exhibit 11.3. Gray's symmetrical gestures position him at the center of the visual field. Image from the videotape, *Swimming to Cambodia*, used courtesy of Spalding Gray.

First, they emphasize how nonnaturalistic Gray's own acting style is. We never for a moment forget that his gestures in *Swimming to Cambodia* are the artificial products of a staged body. While his gestures are surprisingly *linguistic*, they are not therefore naturalistic or realistic (in the Stanislavsky mode). Rather the impetus of Gray's acting style is to undercut and resist realism in the way that many theorists of the theater advocate (Artaud, Brecht, Meyerhold, Witkeiwicz). In the performance piece *The Terrors of Pleasure*, Gray talks about the desire to find a piece of property with streams and rivers and describes how he became obsessed with water; then he pauses and takes a sip of water from a glass. The heightened literalism does not serve realism but undercuts it.

Second, and more important, the Stanislavsky method does not work in a situation, like that described by Gray, in which the boundaries between the illusory and the real have disintegrated:

You don't have to Method-act. When those helicopter blades are whirring overhead, you shout to be heard. You don't have to Method-act when you look down and see a Thai peasant covered with chicken giblets and fake blood in 110-degree weather for fifteen hours a day for five dollars a day. (If they're real amputees they get seven-fifty.) It's just like the real event! (*Swimming* 55–56)

Where does acting leave off and reality begin? For Gray, life is an arena in which everyone acts for others. The Thai prostitutes deserve Academy Awards for their performances—they are so *apparently* happy. When Athol Fugard advises Gray to go home (saying there's no difference between Thailand and Krumville), Gray wonders with whom Fugard has been studying acting. "I wanted to say goodbye like a man," says Gray, "and if I couldn't be one, I was going to *act* like one. . . . And I went around to each person and acted as though I'd made up my mind" (*Swimming* 101). People don't have to act naturalistically, Gray seems to be implying, because they always are acting naturally already.

But the confusion of illusion and reality is even more pervasive and profound than this in *Swimming to Cambodia*, and it is this confusion that produces the "fantastic" within it. Here the distinction between the real and the simulated has dangerously dissolved. Gray gets into a helicopter and says, "I felt like I was in a movie, like I was in *Apocalypse Now*, and then I realized that I *was* in a movie!" (*Swimming* 55). The beautiful beach at Phuket is like "one big piece of calendar art" and Gray goes swimming on "a perfect Kodachrome day." Walking into a bar with Pat Pong is like stepping into a scene in *The Deer Hunter* (*Swimming* 40). The producers of the *Killing Fields* build a real swimming pool and tennis court at a hotel in Wahen in order to better simulate the Hotel Phnom Phen. Spalding Gray points to a map of Cambodia, duplicating an image from *The Killing Fields*; it appears when Sidney Shanberg watches a video that shows Richard Nixon on television pointing to a map of Cambodia. "Are those burning villages or burning tires set out by the special effects crew?"

asks Leverett; "Is this history or just another take?" (*Swimming*, film version).
Certainly we are in the realm of Jean Baudrillard's "Precession of Simulacra,"
where the mass media neutralize reality and the hyper-real and simulation sup-
plant it.

Postmodern works like *Swimming to Cambodia* enact and describe the simulation process that Baudrillard describes. Throughout *Swimming to Cambodia*
Gray struggles with the relation between reality and its replica, more specifically
between the real history of Cambodia and its simulation in *The Killing Fields*.
One might say that his monologue is an effort to kill the field of simulation
produced by *The Killing Fields* in order to apprehend the "reality" behind it.
In this sense it is an effort to "real"ize the fantastic, to make it real, to achieve
a sense of reality. But that reality threatens to slip from Gray's grasp—and
ours—intertwined as it is with the media and mediated images.

In his fascinating account of contemporary culture entitled *The Minimal Self*,
Christopher Lasch maintains that the confusion of illusion and reality in contemporary media culture contributes to the narcissism of the 1980s (19). Epit-
omizing this wide cultural phenomenon, *Swimming to Cambodia* is narcissistic
in both its form and content. Gray tells us that John Swain was the most narcissistic of the reporters, because he had come to watch himself being played
in *The Killing Fields*. Then how much more narcissistic is Gray himself who
creates a two-hour monologue concerning his own bit part in the film? The first
scene in *Swimming to Cambodia* describes a hotel that Gray calls "the pleasure
prison," where the crew is indulging in what the Thais call *sanug*, or pleasure.
Gray's search for a perfect moment is a narcissistic urge to merge with the
environment. At one point he says it is "like falling in love . . . with yourself"
(*Swimming* 5). One form of self-indulgence is replaced by another, but pervading
all is irony and self-parody: "What am I doing lying on the beach like an old
hippie at forty-two years old, trying to have Perfect Moments in Thailand? What
am I doing searching for Cosmic Consciousness? . . . Go directly to Hollywood
and get an agent! Go! Get an agent!" (*Swimming* 91–92). Exhausted from this
"epiphany," Gray falls asleep only to be awakened by the words "Boat people!
Boat people" which someone is shouting on the shore. Thus the search for self-
fulfillment and self-gratification is both presented and ironized as Gray questions
what it means to pursue pleasure in the context of suffering.

Lasch's book is especially helpful, for it allows us to see contemporary narcissism not as an idle, meaningless self-absorption but as an understandable and
justifiable survival or coping mechanism in the face of historical barbarism.[3]
The narcissistic age is beset by fears that develop not only from its historical
awareness but also from the realization that the holocausts of the past may
prefigure even more radical atrocities, including the annihilation of humanity
itself (Lasch 103).

Thus Gray's character, Jack Daniels, who is chained in a waterproof chamber,
high on coffee and blue-flake cocaine anxiously awaiting the moment when
he can finally fire his nuclear missile at the Russians, allows Gray to voice his

own anxiety about nuclear war. Gray is directing his satire not at the U.S. Navy, or patriotism, or the military, but at a casual, irresponsible desire to use atomic weapons. "I can tell you I thought I was looking my death in the face," he says. The threat of nuclear war, the memory of holocausts in Germany and Cambodia, the fear of ecological disasters create a climate of crises in which narcissism itself, according to Lasch, becomes a form of survivalism. Gray's perfect moment is not a romantic transcendence but a brief instant freed from "phobias," anxieties, and fears; when it is over, he is back in "fearful time" again.

Swimming to Cambodia negotiates the relation of the political and the personal, the historical and the biographical. The double-layered backdrop of the performance captures this tension between personal, even narcissistic, experience (in the blue sky) and historical/political awareness (in the maps).

The central activity of *Swimming to Cambodia* is memory—both personal and collective. Our way of coming to know and understand history is entirely problematic ("We don't know what went on," he says). "I titled this work *Swimming to Cambodia*," he explains, "when I realized that to try to imagine what went on in that country during the gruesome period from 1966 to the present would be a task equal to swimming there from New York" (*Swimming* xvi). The truth is beyond our imagination. Hence history is portrayed in a curiously mediated way. Facts are presented as reported discourse, information is gleaned from eyewitness reports, and even American history is conveyed by an outsider. *Swimming to Cambodia* does not deny the existence of the past; it does question whether we can ever know that past in any other than a mediated way—like the forms of mediation (books, videos, films) through which Gray's own performance may very well come to us.

How does one comprehend the history of the twentieth century, with its holocausts in Germany and Cambodia? As Lasch observes, the only art appropriate to such atrocity is a minimal art, an art stripped bare and reduced to its simplest counters. A desk. A map. A glass of water. A single man talking:

And they were laughing. There was a lot of laughter, a *lot* of laughter. And eyewitnesses said that if you pleaded for your life, they laughed harder. If it was a woman pleading for her life, they would laugh even harder. And they would take the half-dead bodies and throw them into American bomb craters, which acted as perfect graves. It was a kind of visitation of hell on earth. Who needs metaphors for hell, or poetry about hell? This actually happened. Here on this earth. Pregnant mothers disemboweled, eyes gouged out, kids (children) torn apart like fresh bread in front of their mothers. And this went on for years until two million people were either systematically killed or starved to death by the same people. And nobody can really figure out how such a thing could have happened. (*Swimming*, film version)

Viewed in this way, history is difficult if not impossible for the psyche to assimilate. It seems both real and fantastic, so Gray must repeat, "This actually happened. Here on this earth." According to Kristeva's analysis, the abject—

the horrible—borders the fantastic, fuses the imaginary and the real: ''The corpse, seen without God and outside of science, is the utmost of abjection. It is death infecting life. Abject. It is something rejected from which one does not part. . . . Imaginary uncanniness and real threat, it beckons to us and ends up engulfing us'' (4). The abject is experienced both inside and outside the self: ''Excrement and its equivalents (decay, infection, disease, corpse, etc.) stand for the danger to identity that comes from without: the ego threatened by the non-ego, society threatened by its outside, life by death'' (71). Rather than repressing the abject and the horrible, Gray exposes them—both within himself and outside. *Swimming to Cambodia* begins with a story about a bad drug trip:

Up it came, and each time the vomit hit the ground I covered it over with sand, and the sand I covered it with turned into a black gauze death mask that flew up and covered my face . . . until I looked down to see that I had built an entire corpse in the sand and it was my corpse. (*Swimming*, film version)

The abject thus operates at a variety of levels within the monologue: physical (nausea), personal (death), and political (autohomeogenocide). Gray's laughter is not empty laughter, but a ''way of placing or displacing abjection'' (Kristeva 8). His humor confronts and contains the abject of history and of the self. Spalding Gray is a comedian of crises who is not trivializing the tragic but bodying it forth. ''After all, what is this film about? Survival! Whose survival? My survival'' (*Swimming*, film version). And ours.

NOTES

1. See Todorov. On the fantastic, see also Jackson, Olsen, Siebers, and Swinfen.

2. Unless otherwise noted, I refer to the film version of *Swimming to Cambodia*. Later in the essay I refer to *The Terrors of Pleasure* as it was performed at the Wexner Center for the Visual Arts, February 25, 1990.

3. Nevertheless, Mark Poster's critique of Lasch is important. See *Critical Theory and Poststructuralism* (143–69).

WORKS CITED

Artaud, Antonin. *The Theater and Its Double*. Trans. Mary Caroline Richards. New York: Grove, 1958.

Auslander, Philip. ''Going with the Flow: Performance Art and Mass Culture.'' Unpublished manuscript.

———. ''Toward a Concept of the Political in Postmodern Theater.'' *Theater Journal* (March 1987): 20–34.

Baudrillard, Jean. ''The Implosion of Meaning in the Media and the Implosion of the Social in the Masses.'' *The Myths of Information*. Ed. Kathleen Woodward. Madison, Wis.: Coda Press, 1980. 137–48.

———. ''The Precession of Simulacra.'' *Art & Text* 11 (September 1983): 3–47.

Bauman, Richard. *Story, Performance and Event*. New York: Cambridge University Press, 1986.

Benjamin, Walter. *Understanding Brecht*. Trans. Anna Bostock. London: NLB, 1977.

Birdwhistell, Ray L. *Kinesics and Context*. Philadelphia: University of Pennsylvania Press, 1970.

―――. "Kinesics: Inter- and Intra-Channel Communication Research." *Essays in Semiotics*. Ed. Julia Kristeva, Josette Rey-Debove, and Donna Jean Umiker. Paris: The Hague, 1971. 527–46.

Brecht, Bertolt. *Brecht on Theatre*. Ed. and trans. John Willett. New York: Hill and Wang, 1964.

Brook, Peter. *The Empty Space*. New York: Atheneum Books, 1968.

Ekman, Paul, ed. *Darwin and Facial Expression*. New York: Academic Press, 1973.

Elam, Keir. *The Semiotics of Theatre and Drama*. New York: Methuen, 1980.

Gitlin, Todd. "Hip-Deep in Post-modernism." *New York Times Book Review* 6 Nov. 1988: 35–36.

Gray, Spalding. *Sex and Death to the Age 14*. New York: Vintage Books, 1986.

―――. *Swimming to Cambodia*. New York: Theatre Communications Group, 1987.

Grotowski, Jerzy. *Towards a Poor Theatre*. New York: Simon and Schuster, 1968.

Hume, Kathryn. *Fantasy and Mimesis: Responses to Reality in Western Literature*. New York: Methuen, 1984.

Hutcheon, Linda. *The Poetics of Postmodernism: History, Theory, Fiction*. New York: Routledge, 1988.

Huyssen, Andreas. *After the Great Divide: Modernism, Mass Culture, Postmodernism*. Bloomington: Indiana University Press, 1986.

Jackson, Rosemary. *Fantasy: The Literature of Subversion*. New York: Methuen, 1981.

Kristeva, Julia. "Le geste: pratique ou communication?" *Semeiotike: recherches pour une semanalyse*. Paris: Editions du Seuil, 1969. 90–112.

―――. *Powers of Horror: An Essay on Abjection*. Trans. Leon S. Roudiez. New York: Columbia University Press, 1982.

Lasch, Christopher. *The Minimal Self: Psychic Survival in Troubled Times*. New York: Norton, 1984.

Leverett, James. "Introduction." *Swimming to Cambodia*. Spalding Gray. New York: Theatre Communications Group, 1987. ix–xiii.

Olsen, Lance, *Ellipse of Uncertainty: An Introduction of Postmodern Fantasy*. Westport, Conn.: Greenwood Press, 1987.

Pavis, Patrice. "Problems of a Semiology of Theatrical Gesture." *Poetics Today* 2 (Spring 1981): 65–93.

Poster, Mark. *Critical Theory and Poststructuralism*. Ithaca, N.Y.: Cornell University Press, 1989.

Rothstein, Mervyn. "A New Face in Grover's Corners." *New York Times*. Review of Spalding Gray in Thorton Wilder's *Our Town*. Sunday, 4 December 1988: 10.

Schechner, Richard. *The End of Humanism: Writings on Performance*. New York: Performing Arts Journal Publications, 1982.

Shawcross, William. *Sideshow: Kissinger, Nixon and the Destruction of Cambodia*. New York: Simon and Schuster, 1979.

Siebers, Tobin. *The Romantic Fantastic*. Ithaca, N.Y.: Cornell University Press, 1984.

Spiegel, John P., and Pavel Machotka. *Messages of the Body*. New York: Macmillan, 1974.

Suleiman, Susan Rubin. "Redundancy and the 'Readable' Text." *Poetics Today* 1 (Spring
    1980): 119–42.
Swinfen, Ann. *In Defence of Fantasy: A Study of the Genre in English and American
    Literature since 1945*. Boston: Routledge, 1984.
Todorov, Tzvetan. *The Fantastic: A Structural Approach to a Literary Genre*. Trans.
    Richard Howard. 1973. New York: Cornell University Press, 1975.

12

The Shock of the Actual: Disrupting the Theatrical Illusion

Theodore Shank

Traditionally the theater presents an illusion that may resemble actuality or may be fantastic. Whether the performance presents the fairy world of *A Midsummer Night's Dream* or the estate of Madame Ranevskaya with its cherry trees, the audience is expected to focus on the illusion being presented—that is, on the characters rather than on the actors, makeup, and costumes used to create them; on magical forest, drawing room, or orchard, not the paint, flats, and theatrical lighting used to project an illusion of place. Unless there is an accident—say an actor forgets his or her lines or a piece of scenery falls over—we typically focus on the illusion. But we are not deluded. We do not mistake this illusion for efficacious actuality; we recognize it as an illusion. We have become so accustomed to this way of perceiving in the theater that theatrical illusions coincide with our expectations. One of the ways of presenting something startling or fantastic in the theater is to direct the audience to focus on actuality, which is something we do not expect to see on the stage. When such a focus is accomplished purposefully, rather than by accident, actuality is framed as art by the circumstances of performance, and we perceive it in a different way than we perceive actuality outside the theater. Much of the experimental work in the theater since the 1950s has involved disrupting the theatrical illusion by framing actuality in various ways that cause us to perceive it as fantastic.

Most definitions of fantasy contrast the illusion presented by an art work with actuality—that is, the fictional world presented by the work of art is juxtaposed against what we have come to accept as normative empirical reality. Ann Swinfen says, for example, that the essential ingredient of fantasy is the marvelous which is anything outside the normal space-time continuum of the everyday world (5). William R. Irwin considers fantasy in fiction to be "a story based on and controlled by an overt violation of what is generally accepted as possibility"

(4). So our expectations, based on our experience, compose the backdrop against which the fantastic is startlingly presented.

While this essay[1] is specifically concerned with theater performances that incorporate a focus on actuality, it is worth noting that experimental art is often perceived as fantastic even when the focus is exclusively on illusion. Since theater performances are a part of the experience about which we have formed certain expectations, it follows that when we attend the theater the fantastic can result from the use of experimental expressive means that are at odds with the expected theatrical conventions. The experimental approach to creating art is distinctly different from the conventional approach that aims to create a performance according to the existing theatrical conventions coinciding with audience expectations. Truly experimental works are based on experience rather than convention; they derive from the attempts of the artists to create perceptual forms to express their subjective experience of the world. For the most part, they ignore or deconstruct theatrical conventions because such conventions are no longer capable of expressing the emotive concepts of the artists. While newly invented forms and techniques may, through repetition, become conventions and lose their expressiveness, the original use of such forms and techniques, invented to express an artist's emotive experience, will often stand out sharply against the conventional expectations of the audience and be perceived as fantastic.

Finally, the fantastic can be achieved in a performance by presenting actuality on the stage instead of, or in addition to, illusion. A theater performance typically creates an illusory reality of characters, time, place, and action. Although this world may seem bizarre in contrast to the culturally perceived world, we accept it as the reality of the play whether it be *Endgame* or *M. Butterfly*. We have become accustomed to accepting the illusion presented by the performance as the artistic event when we go to the theater. Against this expectation, the work of certain experimental theater artists may be considered fantastic when they present actuality instead of an illusion; or they combine illusion and actuality, and sometimes blur the line between the two resulting in an ambivalent sense of reality; or they create an illusion and disrupt it with actual images or events. In each instance actuality is framed as art and made to seem fantastic in contrast with the expected theatrical illusion.

No matter how fantastic a theatrical illusion, framing actual images and events in a performance is often even more startling not only because they go against expectations but because illusions lack the efficacy of actuality. Take, for example, Chris Burden's *Shoot* (1971), a performance consisting of Burden being shot in the arm by a friend with a rifle. Or consider the London performances of *Passionate Positions* (1977) by Lumiere & Son which presented an illusion but disrupted it with actual events such as the performers sticking their fingers down their throats until they retched spontaneously. We realize that the retching is not mimetic but an actual physiological reaction. And we know that Chris Burden's gunshot wound is actually painful while Hedda Gabler's suicide is only an illusion.

One may be tempted to explain the fantastic aspect of such work in the light of Eric Rabkin's comment that "the truly fantastic occurs when the ground rules of a narrative are forced to make a 180° reversal, when prevailing perspectives are directly contradicted" (12). Rabkin, however, is dealing only with fiction that, being a nonperceptual art, cannot frame actuality. No matter how accurately a writer may describe an actual event or person or setting, what the reader perceives is not actuality but an illusion created by the writer. The only actuality in literature is the physical means by which the illusion is conveyed—the ink and paper—but these are not being framed as art. Although the nonperceptual art of literature cannot frame actuality, such framing is possible in the perceptual arts whether or not they involve performance. Duchamp's ready-mades are examples, as are some of the compositions of John Cage which frame naturally occurring sounds.

There is another potential source of confusion. In literature and in the theater it is possible to shift from one illusion, or one layer of illusion, to another. An example in theater is the work of Pirandello. In *Six Characters in Search of an Author*, some of the actual performers play characters who are actors playing characters. As originally written by Pirandello, both character layers are illusions. If the fictional actor drops the fictional character she is playing, what is left is not actuality but the fictional actor. In a recent production of the play by Soviet director Anatoli Vasiliev, however, the illusion is disrupted by actuality when performers physically interact with spectators. For example, one of the women in the cast sits on the lap of a male spectator caressing him and declaring her love. The caress is actual both for that spectator and those watching—we realize she could have sat on our laps—but she is probably only pretending to love the spectator who seems to have been chosen at random. So while the caress is actual, the performer is playing a role.

Such disruptions of illusion or shifts between actual and illusion differ from the sort of distancing associated with Brecht. Like Pirandello, Brecht may disrupt one illusion and replace it with another as when Victoria's messenger comes riding in to save Macheath at the end of *Threepenny Opera*; Brecht may use various techniques to remind the spectators that they are in a theater, but these techniques do not frame actuality as art. The audience may intentionally be made aware of the theatrical means of creating the illusion of characters, time, place, and action, but the illusion they create is the work of art. Similarly, although we may focus briefly on our own world when we are made to see the relationship between the events of Brecht's play and our knowledge of the world, actual world events do not become a part of the performance. By contrast, one of the unique aspects of some recent experimental theater performances is that actual images, tasks, events, and means are incorporated into the work of art sometimes alongside created illusions.

The framing of actuality as art began early in this century when visual artists created collages and assemblages incorporating objects from the world in their painting or sculpture. In 1913 Marcel Duchamp attached a bicycle wheel to a kitchen stool and exhibited it in a gallery. The Happenings of Allan Kaprow beginning in 1959 consisted of performing tasks with no intention of creating a fiction. The most basic of the rules he set down for Happenings in his *Assemblage, Environments & Happenings* (188–207) was that the "line between art and life should be kept as fluid, and perhaps indistinct, as possible." The Living Theatre used task performance similar to that of the Happenings as the basis for most of its work beginning with *Mysteries and Other Pieces* in 1964 and continuing for more than a decade. The performers enacted predetermined tasks with no attempt to create an illusion of character or a fictional event. Such task acting became the typical mode of performance used by formalist directors such as Robert Wilson, Michael Kirby, and Alan Finneran throughout the 1970s and 1980s.

The Happenings of the 1950s are examples of tasks being framed as art. In some respects, these are perceived by performers and spectators in much the same way as certain planned nonartistic events, such as a wedding or a baseball game. Rules and tasks are determined in advance and the scenario is followed. Performers do not play characters and do not intend to create any sort of illusion. The aesthetic principle involved is much like that of found art where an object such as a concrete block might be placed on a pedestal in a gallery and thereby be framed as art. The main difference is that a Happening has a time dimension. *Yellow Suitcases*, a performance presented in the late 1960s by People Show, is an example of work that grew out of the Happening idea. Eighteen spectator-participants were each given a yellow suitcase and instructed to carry it around in the Soho area of London. When one participant met another, they were to introduce themselves, bolt their two suitcases together end to end, and continue walking until they met another yellow suitcase carrier. Eventually, all eighteen suitcases were joined and the participants and suitcases marched off to Trafalgar Square.

Similar, but more complex, structuring of tasks without illusion is found in the work of the French company Atelier Théâtre et Musique (ATEM). The performers observe behavior in a particular environment and then structure selected gestures and sounds they have seen and heard, using them as if they were notes in a musical score. For example, *Sans Paroles* (1978) used nonverbal sounds, gestures, and frequently repeated words the company had observed in a sidewalk cafe; organized them into a formal structure; and performed them in a cafe where they were surrounded by unsuspecting customers. The performers did not imitate the people observed; they did not attempt to create characters. They instead presented a composition consisting of structured tasks which were as precisely scored as a piece of music.

Other examples of performances that create the fantastic by putting focus on actuality rather than illusion are those involving objects rather than people. Puppets, of course, are objects, but most often they are used to create the illusion of people or animals. On the other hand, the machines constructed by Mark

Pauline, the director of Survival Research Laboratories in San Francisco, are used to create performances without illusion. Pauline builds his self-propelled, radio-controlled machine performers, some as large as elephants, from disused industrial equipment and discarded parts. In performance the machines battle and destroy each other using specific actions such as stomping, slashing, jumping, and crawling. While these actions may resemble those of animals and spectators may project certain qualities on them—they may seem vicious, threatening, lumbering, and so forth—there is no intention on the part of the director to create an illusion. The actions of the machines are efficacious—they really do destroy one another in a kind of gladiatorial combat.

In some other performances illusions are created, but the nonillusory means used to create them are also part of the art work. By contrast, in the tradition that dominates our theater, care is taken that the spectator's focus is not drawn to materials and techniques but is kept on the illusion. Yet Alan Finneran, the director of SOON 3 in San Francisco, considers the means used to create the illusion an important part of his performances. As in the case of the French company ATEM, the SOON 3 performances consist of tasks. A performer may move a projector into position to project an illusory image, but this task is at least as important as the image projected. In *Renaissance Radar* (1981), Finneran was concerned with the illusions of violence presented by Hollywood films and the means used to create these illusions. In the performance, a woman is "killed" three times. In one instance her nude body is covered with many tiny explosive devices used in motion pictures to create the illusion of gunshots. Usually these would be placed under the actor's clothing, but in Finneran's production they are open to view and are wired to an onstage electric control panel. When the switches are pulled, the devices explode and spew "blood" over the woman's body. A voice-over explains how these devices are made and used in Hollywood films. Although the performer in this SOON 3 performance does not enact a character and is simply performing tasks, an illusion is created, but at the same time we see the means used to create it. While illusion and actuality are presented side by side and both are part of the work to be perceived, there is no confusion between the two.

John Fox, the director of Welfare State International in England, is not concerned with showing how illusion is created, but his environmental productions incorporate both created illusion and actual surroundings into the fictional frame of his environmental productions. Welfare State's first large work in 1972 was a one-month tour that traced in reverse the legendary route of King Arthur. The company's fictional hero, the hermaphrodite Lancelot Quail, led his bizarre entourage to the coast of Cornwall where they bade farewell to England and boarded a fishing boat which carried them to a rendezvous with an actual submarine of the Royal Navy which surfaced offshore. The group boarded the submarine, which disappeared into the depths thus ending the performance. Such combining of actual and fictional elements has continued as an important technique in nearly all of the subsequent productions of the company. By framing these actual elements as art, it is hoped that the spectators will see their world afresh and result in their wanting to change it.

Some recent theater companies have intentionally created a confusion between illusion and actuality. They blur the line between the two so that at times the spectator does not know which is which. Such ambivalence is an expression of the uncertainties of life as experienced by the Squat Theatre when it emigrated from Hungary and settled in New York City. The theatricality of chance events of the street may make them seem deceptively ineffectual while in fact they can be a matter of life and death. The company found a unique way to express this ambivalence. For several years after arriving in New York, the company performed in a storefront theater on West 23rd Street. Performances presented in this space had two audiences. There was the paying audience inside and the sidewalk audience outside looking in. In addition to the images and action created by the company, each of the audiences became part of the performance for the other audience. In Squat Theatre's *Andy Warhol's Last Love* (1978), the sidewalk audience looks in to see a naked obese woman being interviewed by Andy Warhol and being watched by a paying audience seated in chairs. The inside audience sees and hears the same naked woman (she insists that she is a witch) being interviewed by a performer wearing a lifelike mask of Andy Warhol. The spectators also observe the antics of the street audience as they drink, laugh, and gawk at the naked woman. Sometimes a police car drives up and questions a spectator or two. In one performance a crazed street person wanders in and the audience discovers he has a gun tucked into the top of his pants. The spectators begin to scatter from the unpredictable threat then realize, as the gun slips down the man's pant leg and onto the floor, that the man is a performer. As the interview continues, the inside audience watches a television set in the performance area which is showing live images from a video camera on the sidewalk. It presents cars and closeups of people on the street with the same sense of distanced reality conveyed when it shows what appears to be the Empire State Building (actually a model) on fire and toppling over. Such mixing of actual and fictional leaves one with a sense of ambivalent reality. The inside audience realizes the interviewer is not really Warhol, but is the witch really a witch? Is there such a thing as a real witch? Which of the people on the street are performers playing characters and which are passersby stopping to have a look? It becomes evident that the hold we have on what we like to think of as reality is indeed tenuous. The productions of Squat Theatre seem to coincide with Lance Olsen's understanding of the fantastic even though he is specifically concerned with fiction. The fantastic, he says, is "hostile toward anything static, rejecting any definitive version of 'reality' or 'truth.' Hence it is a mode that is hyper-self-reflective, continually calling attention to itself" (20).

In the work of several companies, including Welfare State International, SOON 3, and Squat Theatre, the spectator's focus may shift back and forth from illusion to actuality. Sometimes the artists attempt to control these shifts, but

Exhibit 12.1. Squat Theatre, *Andy Warhol's Last Love* (1978). For the audience on the sidewalk outside, the paying audience inside is part of the performance experience. Photo: Theodore Shank.

most often the circumstances of the performance do not allow such control. Some
of the interrelated techniques affecting these shifts or disruptions are environmental staging; involving the spectator physically; presenting startling images
or events or introducing unusual sense stimuli such as smell, taste, or touch;
and creating a perception of actual risk to performer or spectator.

Environmental productions place the spectators and the performers in the same
environment rather than the performance being presented in a fictional environment and the audience being in a space outside it. The environmental productions
of Welfare State International usually incorporate into the artistic frame the
natural environment where the performance takes place, whether this be the
beach from which Lancelot Quail sets out to sea to board a submarine or the
rubbish tip and surrounding villages of the company's *Beauty and the Beast*
(1973). For several years in the 1970s, the Welfare State members lived on a
rubbish tip in northern England. For *Beauty and the Beast* they constructed a
small village from debris found there. Lancelot Quail, now transformed into
Lancelot Icarus Quail, leads the spectators through this village telling them that
when his spaceship fell from the sky he was held captive by the villagers; he
also points out actual villages in the distance as if they were no more real than
the theatrical one. In one of these villages, he says, the people worship electricity
(the chief industry in the village is the manufacture of electric stoves); he points
out another village, a former coal-mining town, and tells us it was the home of
the now extinct Black Faces. We are aware simultaneously of the fictional village
constructed for theatrical purposes and the actual villages that have been incorporated into the performance. As in the previous work of Welfare State International, audience members are made to focus on aspects of their world to which
they have become inured through familiarity. By framing actual villages as
fiction, spectators may be led to imagine life as it may have been in the coal-
mining town before the mines were closed, and they may begin to ask questions.
Why were they closed? What were the political reasons for the shift from a
mining economy to a manufacturing economy? What are the social ramifications?

Awareness of the actual in environmental performances is increased when
spectators are physically involved. In *Beauty and the Beast*, the audience must
walk through the constructed village and climb a nearby hill. In performances
of Théâtre du Soleil's *1789* (1970), the spectators are surrounded by performance
platforms similar to medieval mansion stages, and they move toward the different
stages depending on where the action takes place. The National Theatre and the
Royal Shakespeare Company (RSC) in England have used similar techniques.
The Passion, assembled from York and Wakefield mystery plays, was presented
in 1977 at the Cottesloe Theatre with a large part of the audience standing and
physically following the action. *The Dillen*, produced by the RSC at Stratford
(1983), was performed at several locations along the river Avon with the spectators being led from place to place.

The environmental performances of northern California's Antenna Theatre,
directed by Chris Hardman, not only involve the spectator physically, but each

Exhibit 12.2. Welfare State International, *Beauty and the Beast* (1973). The audience is led through the village constructed from the material found in the rubbish tip. Photo: Theodore Shank.

spectator becomes the central character in the fictional story. Spectators are provided with headsets and tape players which guide them, one by one, through a mazelike structure. In *Etiquette of the Undercaste* (1987), the maze represents several environmentals important in the life of the central character. The spectator's journey begins with birth in a hospital room in the slums and continues through a number of places and experiences including juvenile court, a reform school, a boxing match, jail, and homelessness; it ends with a wino's death on a park bench. As we are guided through these events in the character's life, we hear over the headset the voices of people who have actually been through these experiences or who are familiar with them because of their occupations as social workers, nurses, police, prostitutes, prison guards, drug dealers, petty thieves, and so on. While spectators follow the story and its social implications, their physical participation is an equally important part of the experience of the work. In fact, the journey through the maze makes one relate to the work as a kind of game. There is little emotional involvement with the fictional even though the spectator is physically a part of it.

The production of *The Masque of the Red Death* by the London-based Pip Simmons Theatre Group in 1977 involved the audience as costumed guests at the masked ball of Edgar Allan Poe's story. On entering the performance space, the spectators put on robes and masks; as the performance progresses, they participate by walking from room to room as they follow the action, and at times they are encouraged to dance. In addition to this physical activity, there are instances when the audience is made to focus on actual elements framed within the work. Lights come up on a clear plastic cage where more than 80 rats are nibbling at the carcass of a skinned rabbit, spectators are given pieces of fruit to eat, and some of them are touched and caressed seductively by the performers. These images and events are perceived as actual because they are sufficiently startling visually or because they stimulate the senses of taste or touch not usually involved in the perception of art. While the spectators recognize these elements as part of the performance, they do not respond to them as fictional illusions but instead respond as they would to similar events outside the theater. The fictional illusion is intentionally disrupted. A similar reaction was expected by the audience attending performances of *Passionate Positions* by Lumiere and Son. In the fictional action the Narrator cuts out the hearts of four performers who have been made into zombies. The hearts (actually raw lamb hearts) are placed on sticks like lollipops and offered to the audience. When the spectators decline, they are eaten by the four performers, blood running down their arms.

Other performances may seem to put the performers or the audience at actual risk and thereby shift their focus to the actual circumstances of the events. Such a mode of perception is similar to that of watching a trapeze performance without a net. For several years the Japanese Butoh dance group named Sankai Juku performed a Hanging Dance in which performers, with ropes around their ankles, hung upside down from the tops of tall buildings. The perceived risk turned out

Exhibit 12.3. Lumiere and Son, *Passionate Positions* (1977). The performers eat their hearts (actually raw lamb hearts). Photo: Theodore Shank.

to be actual when a rope broke while they were performing in Seattle and a performer fell to his death.

A Catalan group from Barcelona puts the audience at risk as well as themselves. This company, La Fura dels Baus (The Vermin of the Sewers), presents *Suz O Suz* in a warehouse environment with spectators standing and attempting to escape being hit by rolling platforms or metal objects swung by performers like truncheons. Evidence of the danger became clear at the performance I attended when a spectator was hit in the knee by one of these objects. The spectators are also in danger of being hit by animal viscera and buckets of "blood" which the performers throw at each other as they run through the audience. Other images that are taken as actual rather than fictional include naked men submerged in plexiglass tanks of water being poked by poles and the frenzied eating of animal innards. Near the end of the performance, two men are suspended from scaffolds and like pendulums are swung through fire. By the end of the performance the space looks and smells like a slaughterhouse. While there is a metaphorical meaning to these events which might suggest the tortures depicted in medieval scenes of Hell or the tortures perpetrated by the Franco regime, the performers do not enact characters. While there may be illusory elements in the performance—for example, the red liquid in the buckets represents blood—the performance is perceived as consisting principally of the enactment of violent tasks rather than the creation of illusion. We perceive the events as actual rather than illusory in part because we perceive them as having the efficacy of actual events. We and the performers are in danger.

It has been suggested by Christine Brooke-Rose in *A Rhetoric of the Unreal* (4) that, if empirical reality has come to seem unreal, it is logical for us to seek the real in the fantastic. Perhaps we can also say that as fantastic fictions become commonplace in the theater (the absurdists, for example), actual, nonfictional images and events framed as theater may seem fantastic. Being framed as art, they are given a significance that is lacking in similar images and events outside the theater. By presenting actuality as art in the theater works mentioned here, certain aspects of our world are put into focus and become events and objects for perception. While in our everyday living these aspects may be ignored as mere ambiance or acknowledged only for their efficacy, when framed as art their phenomenological presence is rediscovered. This epiphanic response may indeed make actuality seem more fantastic than fiction.

NOTE

1. The factual information in this essay is from performances seen by the author and from interviews and conversations with the artists involved. Some of the performances mentioned are discussed at greater length in the author's writings listed in this volume's selected bibliography.

WORKS CITED

Brooke-Rose, Christine. *A Rhetoric of the Unreal: Studies in Narrative and Structure, Especially of the Fantastic*. New York: Cambridge University Press, 1981.

Irwin, William R. *The Game of the Impossible: A Rhetoric of Fantasy*. Urbana: University of Illinois Press, 1976.

Kaprow. Allan. *Assemblage, Environments & Happenings*. New York: Abrams, 1966.

Olsen, Lance. *Ellipse of Uncertainty: An Introduction to Postmodern Fantasy*. Westport, Conn.: Greenwood Press, 1987.

Rabkin, Eric S. *The Fantastic in Literature*. Princeton: Princeton University Press, 1976.

Shank, Theodore. *American Alternative Theatre*. 1120 photographs. 1982. Rpt. New York: St. Martin's, 1988.

———. *California Permanence: Volume One / San Francisco Bay Area. Interviews and Essays*. 157 illustrations. Claremont, Calif.: The Mime Journal, 1989.

———. "Framing Actuality; Thirty Years of Experimental Theatre, 1959–1989." In *Around the Absurd*. Ed. Enoch Brater and Ruby Cohn. Ann Arbor: University of Michigan Press, 1990.

———. *Theatre in Real Time; Materiali per uno studio sul Nuovo Teatro. America—Inghilterra dal 1968*. 500 photographs. Milano: Studio Forma Editrice, 1980.

Swinfen, Ann. *In Defence of Fantasy: A Study of the Genre in English and American Literature since 1945*. Boston: Routledge, 1984.

13

Playing at the End of the World: Postmodern Theater

Veronica Hollinger

SETTING THE POSTMODERN SCENE

> There is nothing more illusory in performance than the illusion of the un-
> mediated. It can be a very powerful illusion in the theater, but it *is* theater,
> and it is *theater*, the truth of illusion, which haunts *all* performance, whether
> or not it occurs in the theater, where it is more than doubled over.
>
> Blau 164–65

In *Mona Lisa Overdrive* (1988), the third volume of William Gibson's cyberpunk trilogy, we find Slick Henry at the Factory in Dog Solitude, obsessively
constructing gigantic and grotesque "robots" with names like the Witch, the
Corpsegrinder, and the Judge. It is worth noting that the source of Gibson's
inspiration for Slick Henry and his robots is the performance art of Mark Pauline's
San Francisco–based Survival Research Laboratories (SRL), whose productions
have themselves been influenced by the image-field of contemporary science
fiction (SF). Within the terms of my present discussion,[1] SRL performances may
be read as particularly extreme responses to the problematization of the concept
of theatrical presence in contemporary theater: these productions, which collapse
the traditional boundaries between the organic and the technological, have effectively removed the human body altogether from the space of performance.
As described by John Shirley, SRL productions also exemplify the integration
of a science fiction mode of imaging into a theater attempting to re-present
aspects of life at the fin-du-millenium:

[F]ierce-looking dark machines . . . move like giant scorpions to smash at other machines
with a spiked mace on a chain; . . . stalk one another with hammers and flame throwers
and machine-guns firing pellets. They are strikingly martial stylizations contrived with

the stripped-down elegance of automatic weapons, their parts of black metal sometimes fused with bone and bits of mummified animal, expressing a stomach-churning actualization of the inter-breeding of organism and machine. (61)

THE CRISIS OF RE-PRESENTATION

Postmodern theater not only rejects many of the conventions of the realist stage but also, in many cases, replaces what we commonly think of as theatrical convention with the more amorphous and indeterminate forms of performance art. In order to appreciate the extent of this revisionary activity, however, it is useful to examine what, in retrospect, appears to be the unavoidable failure of dramatic realism in Western drama.[2]

Of the many forms of cultural production available for contemplation at this moment in our history, none has invested more completely than the theater in the concept of presence, presence as it is embodied by actors on a stage. This embodiment, this fact of live performance, is perhaps the essence of Western theater, serving, for example, to differentiate it from electronic forms of dramatic representation such as the cinema. It is in the theater of realism that we see the most striking results of such an investment, in the theater that is—inevitably and in spite of itself—also the theater of illusion.

Herbert Blau has suggested that "what is universal in performance is the consciousness of performance" (171). Every performance is, in this sense, always already a re-presentation, a re-production, and a doubling. In fact, it can be argued that nothing is less capable of guaranteeing presence than performance. From this perspective, the anxiety of representation that has always haunted Western theater may be read as paradigmatic of that already rather clichéd condition termed the "postmodern," which for better or worse is a metatheatrical condition, a condition of self-reflexive performance.

Antonin Artaud's vision of a "theatre of cruelty," which would "break through language in order to touch life" (13), arose at least in part from his passionate desire to realize the kind of presence on stage that realist theater had seemed to promise but failed to achieve. The crisis of representation in the realist theater can be conceptualized as a crisis of authenticity originating in the unavoidable gap between actor and role, which realist performance seeks to overcome but which always threatens to undermine the "truth" of performance. Because absolute presence is exactly what is rendered impossible by the very fact of performance, the failure of the promise of realist theater arises from its own ineluctable schizoid condition.

Just as "postmodern theater" is the absent presence waiting in the wings of this discussion, so dramatic activity functions as a kind of stand-in for the presence that is both enacted and deferred on the stage. What Jacques Derrida has termed *différance* is at work here; *différance* is the gap, both spatial and temporal, that comes to exist in any activity of mediation, in this case the mediation of performance, the space for "play," for example, between actor

and character. It is *différance*, therefore, that serves not only to create the
impression of the full presence of the character but also—paradoxically and
ironically—to maintain its absence. Even Artaud recognized the impossibility
of ever actualizing his "theatre of cruelty"; he admitted that "As much as I
love the theatre, / [So] much am I, for that very reason, its enemy . . . " (quoted
in Esslin 89).[3]

RE-PRESENTING MIMESIS

> . . . the purpose of playing, whose end, both at the first and now, was and
> is to hold, as 'twere, the mirror up to nature, to show virtue her own feature,
> scorn her own image, and the very age and body of the time his form and
> pressure.
>
> *Hamlet* III.ii.20–24

In his *Poetics*, Aristotle observes that drama arises from "the instinct of
imitation" (55), and his theory of *mimesis* was one of the most powerful of the
historical forces that aimed the trajectory of Western theater toward the theater
of illusion. Now that we find ourselves on the far side/to one side of this trajectory,
however, we might reread Aristotle and conclude that he has always been right
about the mimetic function of drama. The theater of illusion, for example,
"mirrors" a world in which language is reliable, in which the "real" may lie
buried but can be unearthed, in which the "self" is more or less at one with
itself. An early modernist play like Henrik Ibsen's *Hedda Gabler* (1891), shaped
as it is by the influence of realism, relies on the certainty that, while language
may not always speak the true, it nevertheless can be made to speak the real.
We are not so naive as to believe much of what Hedda says in dialogue with
other characters like her benighted husband, George Tesman; instead we are
invited to delve beneath the surface of appearances to the realities of her complex
dramatic personality (in a kind of Freudian excitement, we set out to answer the
"meaningful" question at the "center" of the play: "What does Hedda want?").

Several characteristics of realist theater can be isolated here: the reliance on
language as a signifying system, and its close (even if oblique) relationship to
that which it signifies; the surface/depth opposition upon which much of realist
drama models itself (we can call it "getting to the bottom of things");[4] and the
conviction that dramatic character is a unified (however complex) structure that
can and will reward analysis (so that both containment and closure are products
of this analysis).

In its own very different way(s), postmodernist theater is also involved in a
mimetic enterprise. It too endeavors to mirror the real. Within the postmodern
cultural field, however, there has occurred a drastic alteration in the ways in
which aspects of the real have come to be defined. Language is an arbitrary
system of signs which are culturally produced and which undergo constant transformation; the mediation of language and other culturally defined codes creates

a permanent division between the real and our interpretation of it, so that, in Derridean terms, "il n'y a pas de hors-texte" (*Of Grammatology* 158); and the self is a fragmented and unstable entity, created in language, never identical with itself, continually in process.

THE POSTMODERN (AND THE) FANTASTIC

While it would be both naive and reductive to equate postmodernism with the fantastic *tout court*, one can nevertheless isolate certain features of both that go far to explain the assimilation of various strains of antirealism into the aesthetic productions of postmodernism. It is worth noting, for example, that postmodernism is frequently associated with the breakdown, or at least the weakening, of the barriers previously separating the products of an elitist "high" culture from those of "mass" or "popular" culture; for many cultural analysts, these barriers are a *sine qua non* of high modernism. According to Andreas Huyssen, for example—as the title of his study *After the Great Divide* suggests—the progressive blurring of previously unquestioned hierarchical distinctions between various levels of aesthetic production is *the* defining property of postmodernism; in Huyssen's words, "[t]here are many successful attempts by artists to incorporate mass cultural forms into their work, and certain segments of mass culture have increasingly adopted strategies from on high. If anything, that is the postmodern condition in literature and the arts" (xi).[5]

The contemporary inclination to question the distinctions conventionally taken for granted between reality and fantasy has also had a significant impact on contemporary aesthetic production. As Victor Burgin, James Donald, and Cora Kaplan observe in the introduction to their *Formations of Fantasy*, "in popular understanding, 'fantasy' is always opposed to 'reality.' In this definition, fantasy is the *negative* of reality" (1; emphasis in original). They argue, however, that, from a psychoanalytical perspective, fantasy is as constitutive of "reality" as are the more fact-based or experiential aspects of our lives; rather than functioning as a supplement to empirical reality, therefore, fantasy must be conceptualized as a significant feature of its constitution.

Taken together, the blurring of the traditional boundaries between high and low culture and the deconstruction of the fantasy/reality binary go far to explain the increasingly privileged positioning of anti-realist forms of aesthetic production within the postmodern field. Realism, which must now be conceptualized as merely one among many competing fictional discourses, no longer seems to provide appropriate forms for many artists who wish to evoke the experience of life in the late-industrial West.

Cristopher Nash, who has traced the "anti-realist revolt" in the literature of the past several decades, points out that this turning away from realism has resulted in a new commitment to the multiplex forms of the fantastic. Nash identifies two prominent positions taken up by the producers of such fictions; according to his analysis, "[t]hey'll try to show us 'what else there is' by breaking our conventional relations with 'this world,' or by moving us to other hypothetical worlds altogether'' (47). Although his study does not mention, SF, SF obviously has a role to play within the latter of these two functions of anti-realist fiction.

In fact, some theorists of postmodernism situate SF in a particularly influential position within the context of this new valorization of the fantastic. In his introduction to *Postmodern Fiction: A Bio-Bibliographical Guide*, editor Larry McCaffery argues that ''the most significant evolution of a paraliterary form [within the context of postmodernism] has been that of science fiction'' (xvii). In his *Postmodernist Fiction*, Brian McHale suggests, ''We can think of science fiction as postmodernism's noncanonized or 'low art' double, its sister-genre in the same sense that the popular detective thriller is modernist fiction's sister-genre'' (59). McHale bases this conclusion on what he identifies as a central difference between modernist and postmodernist literature—that is, a shift from epistemological to ontological concerns. And David Harvey concludes, in his own discussion of McHale's analysis, that ''the foregrounding of questions as to how radically different realities may co-exist, collide, and interpenetrate'' leads to the effective dissolution of ''the boundary between fiction and science fiction'' (41).

There can be little doubt that the fantastic seems now to be an aesthetic mode extremely compatible to postmodernism's various interpretations of the ''real.'' When contemporary theater, for example, turns to the fantastic, it does so not in opposition to reality; rather, the fantastic has become the new *mise-en-scène* of that reality. In a parallel movement, we can also note a renewed interest in, and the subsequent proliferation of, various forms of performance art, experiments that attempt to break with traditional notions of linear plot structure and conventional character development.

It seems appropriate as well that irony, the trope of absence, has become a privileged trope of postmodernist drama. Paul de Man's comment on irony in ''The Rhetoric of Temporality'' neatly encapsulates the divisiveness of the ironic stance and, by analogy, may also be read as a commentary on the divided self of performance:

[I]ronic language splits the subject into an empirical self that exists in a state of inauthenticity and a self that exists only in the form of a language that asserts the knowledge of this inauthenticity. This does not, however, make it into an authentic language, for to know inauthenticity is not the same as to be authentic. (197)

It is impossible to resist juxtaposing de Man's statement against Samuel Beckett's concern with ''the expression that there is nothing to express, nothing with which to express, nothing from which to express, no power to express, no desire to express, together with the obligation to express'' (*Three Dialogues* 103). For good reason, Beckett is considered both the last of the modernists and the first of the postmodernists of twentieth-century theater. Janus-like, he faces toward both the wordless alienation of an exhausted high modernism and the decentered fragmentation of a burgeoning theatrical neo-avant-garde.

STAGING THE END OF THE WORLD

Clov: Do you believe in the life to come?
Hamm: Mine was always that. (Beckett, *Endgame* 49)

Beckett's *Endgame* (first performed in 1957 as *Fin de partie*) suggests so many intriguing facets of the postmodern swerve to the fantastic—most notably in its dramatization of what I will discuss below as the postmodern "sense of an ending"—that I will introduce it here as a kind of working paradigm for the whole field. *Endgame* dramatizes a situation very familiar to SF readers. Four characters—blind Hamm, crippled Clov, and Hamm's "accursed progenitor[s]" (9) Nell and Nag—appear to be the only survivors of a disaster that has destroyed the rest of humanity and depleted the earth beyond restoration, a situation spelled out in the conventional SF figuration of the terminal beach (Hamm: "Outside of here it's death" [9]). As the play unfolds, however, this situation becomes more and more complex and ambiguous, demonstrating a degree of semantic indeterminacy that is the frequent hallmark of postmodernist aesthetic production.

The point here is that *Endgame* is not SF; it functions as a kind of allegory which appropriates the icons and images of SF as a way of commenting not on time future but on time present. As such, it is an early example of a growing body of postmodern fiction and drama that I have named "specular SF." Craig Owens, in his discussion of the "allegorical impulse" of postmodern art, writes that "in allegorical structure . . . one text is *read through* another, however fragmentary, intermittent, or chaotic their relationship may be; the paradigm for the allegorical work," he suggests, "is thus the palimpsest" (73; Owens' emphasis). In specular SF, it is the *present* that is read through the *future*, and the two, in effect, become one and the same.[6]

Endgame as specular SF provides its audiences with the semiosis of a future that has already arrived, a future collapsed back onto the present. And it does so in terms that are unremittingly, if complexly, apocalyptic. *Endgame* is perhaps *the* emblematic re-presentation on the stage of our postmodern "sense of an ending."[7]

Within the brief theatrical event that is *Endgame*, we seem to encounter the end of the world, but also an end endlessly deferred, as well as the suggestion that the end has always already occurred. There seems no way to make any choice about what the situation actually is. The title of this pre-post-apocalyptic vision provides one way into the indeterminacy of the play's often conflicting "meanings," resonating as it does with significances beyond its immediate reference to the final moves in games of chess. Repeatedly, for example, we see Beckett's characters "rehearsing" an end to their situation, playing out the apocalypse, as it were, while at the same time dreading its arrival. Hamm, for example, acts out his own death near the end of the play:

> Perhaps I could throw myself out on the floor.
> [. . .]
> Dig my nails into the cracks and drag myself forward with my fingers.
> [. . .]
> It will be the end and there I'll be, wondering what can have brought it on and wondering what can have . . . (he hesitates) . . . why it was so long coming.
>   (69)

His extremely melodramatic (ham-like?) monologue culminates in the desire to "get it over!" (70). But just as Clov's constant threats to leave the shelter come to nothing, so Hamm is merely playing at one version of the End; he is never ready for the finality of death.

Endgame dramatizes the apocalypse with irony rather than nostalgia. Beckett's characters do not desire any kind of renewal. It is the cessation of process, the End, that alone will draw the curtain on their sufferings, guaranteeing that the whole nasty cycle will not recur. Hamm rather grandiosely suggests that "it won't all have been for nothing" (33), but only the fact of its ending can confer significance on this long, agonizing winding down. It is no wonder that Hamm fears to leave the last flea alive: "If he was laying we'd be bitched" (34). The fear of renewal is even more emphatically (and metadramatically) expressed when Clov seems to see a boy outside their shelter:

> *Clov*: Bad luck to it!
>
> *Hamm*: More complications!
>
> [. . .]
>
> Not an underplot, I trust.
>
> [. . .]
>
> *Clov*: A potential procreator? (78)

This figure, a rather conventional symbol of hope, is in this context also a threat, precisely because he represents a potential future which would continue the farce/ tragedy of human life. In its steadfast renunciation of the future, *Endgame* pronounces "the end of science fiction" as the literature of extrapolation.

THEATRICAL MILLENNARIANISM

> The last few years have been marked by an inverted millennarianism, in which premonitions of the future, catastrophic or redemptive, have been replaced by senses of the end of this or that (the end of ideology, art, or social class; the 'crisis' of Leninism, social democracy, or the welfare state,

etc., etc.): taken together, all of these perhaps constitute what is increasingly
called postmodernism.

Jameson 53

Beckett's choice of what is by now a typical SF scenario emphasizes that, at
least since Hiroshima, our postmodern image of apocalypse is a nuclear one.
His "endgame," both feared and desired, is the ultimate postmodern "climax."
As stage event, the end of the world suggests some of the ways in which the
apocalyptic imagination plays itself out here at the fin-du-millenium.

One reason for its appearance on the postmodern stage, I would suggest, is
its potential for simultaneously realizing and undermining exactly the kind of
closure that has been so ubiquitous a feature of Western drama. The yearning
for closure, however, is no longer "innocent" and to stage apocalypse is to
ironize and subvert the very notion of closure even as we dramatize its allure.
Catherine Belsey, for instance, has defined "classic realism" in part as "an
illusionist mode which . . . depends on a structure of enigma leading to closure
which is also a disclosure" (87). The conventional structure of dramatic narrative—which we see already in place in Aristotle's *Poetics*—builds to a climax,
which is also a revelation, and concludes on a note of resolution. And, as so
many Renaissance tragedies assure us, the one dramatic event that can most
satisfactorily guarantee this combination of resolution and revelation on the stage
is death.

As Belsey's pairing of closure and disclosure implies, the moment of death
has conventionally been the moment of revelation. Death as "the moment of
truth"—of disclosure—supports the humanist notion that truth resides within
the self. For this reason, characters speak from a position of truth in their final
moments, and their last words serve as beacons for those who live on after them.
The chilling power of Lear's final vision of the void—"Thou'lt come no more,
/ Never, never, never, never, never!" (V.iii.307–08)—arises at least in part
because it must be accepted as the truth, even if this is a truth of absolute
negativity.

On the contemporary stage, the apocalypse functions as a kind of collective
death scene. In part, this seems to be a dramatization of our tendency to con-
ceptualize the postmodern condition as a *critical* condition. The function that
death traditionally played, however, has taken on different configurations, because one of the projects of postmodernism has been to drive a wedge between
closure and disclosure, so that apocalypse—whether individual or collective—
no longer contains within itself the promise of presence and revelation that was
for so long an integral part of the structure of Western drama. Because this is
not an age of traditional millennarianism, it is also no longer an age in which
our sense of endings includes within itself the promise of meaning, of the
resolution of conflicts, of completed patterns. We might therefore characterize
postmodernism as somehow "irresolute," in the sense of unresolved or open-
ended.

AMERICAN APOCALYPSES

The postmodern sense of an ending is an essential component in Sam Shepard's *Action* (first performed in 1975), a play that is, in many ways, a kind of reprise of Beckett's *Endgame*, one with a particularly American flavor. Indeed, the influence of American popular culture is one of the most marked features of Shepard's work and SF is an important element not only in *Action* but, as I will discuss below, in several of his other plays.

The situation dramatized in *Action* inevitably recalls that of *Endgame*. Shepard introduces us to four characters—Lupe, Liza, Jeep, and Shooter—who are isolated in what is perhaps a cabin, cut off from a world that seems to be in the throes of some "crisis" (178). Like the "game" in *Endgame*, the "action" in *Action* goes nowhere; in the process, it self-reflectively calls attention to itself as a series of events played out on a stage.

In a very brief space of playing time, the four characters prepare and consume what might be a Christmas dinner; they argue, sometimes violently; they attempt to find their place in a book they have been reading to each other; they reenact various dreams and memories; and they wait. An unnamed but self-conscious dread permeates this play, recalling from *Endgame* not only the paranoia but also the ironic absorption in role-playing. In a monologue that may or may not be of particular relevance to the overall "action," Shooter concludes that

Just because we're surrounded by four walls and a roof doesn't mean anything. It's still dangerous. The chances of something happening are just as great. Anything could happen. Any move is possible. I've seen it. You go outside. The world's quiet. . . . Then you go inside. It's a shock. It's not like how you expected. You lose what you had outside. You forget that there even is an outside. The inside is all you know. You hunt for a way of being with everyone. A way of finding how to behave. You find out what's expected of you. You act yourself out. (178)

Like *Endgame*, *Action* seems to imply that some apocalyptic event has cut these characters off from the world of everyday reality. Their understanding of events, however, is even less clear-cut than Hamm and Clov's; consequently, the action in *Action* amounts to inaction, the kind of time-passing familiar to us both from *Endgame* and from *Waiting for Godot*: "Sometimes I have the idea I know what's happening to us. Sometimes I can't see it. I go blind. Other times I don't have any idea. I'm just eating" (178).

Repeated references to the mysterious book that is so important to the four characters seem especially significant: Liza calls attention to a sequence in which "they've [no antecedent supplied] returned to earth only to find that things are exactly the same. Nothing's changed" (172); the characters' continuing and frustrating failure to find their "place" leads Lupe to ask: "Was it near the place where the sky rained fire?" (184). Shepard's references to standard SF scenarios serve at once to construct a familiar frame for *Action* and to render its "meaning" even more indeterminate. Its ending is fully as inconclusive as the final moments of *Endgame* and we find ourselves deeply implicated in a postmodern ironization of "last things," as concepts like presence and closure continue to elude both Shepard's characters and the audience that watches them in action/*Action*.

In his early play *Icarus's Mother* (first performed in 1965), Shepard ironically dramatizes another seductive feature of the apocalypse as theatrical event—that is, its potential as "spectacle."[8] The "spectacular" value of the end of the world is clearly spelled out in the description of a fireworks display which is also an airplane crash which is also the nuclear holocaust. These scenarios are played offstage against the ecstatic commentary of one of the characters:

You guys have missed the fireworks altogether. You should have seen—this is something to behold, this is. . . . If only the weather and the atmospheric conditions had been better than they were it would have beaten the Hindenburg by far more than it did. . . . By that I mean to say a recognized world tragedy of the greatest proportion and exhilaration to make the backs of the very bravest shudder with cold sensations and the hands moisten with the thickest sweat ever before known, ever. And the eyes to blink in disbelief and the temples to swell with pounds and the nose run with thick sticky pus. Oh you guys should have come, you guys should have. What a light! (57)

In plays like *Icarus's Mother* and *Action*, Shepard demonstrates a postmodern proclivity for allegory which clearly aligns his work with that of the Beckett of *Endgame* and *Waiting for Godot*. This allegorical bent is even more evident in one of his most accomplished plays, *The Tooth of Crime* (first performed in 1972), which is also his most science-fictional play, albeit of the "specular" kind. In *The Tooth of Crime*, Shepard revises the convention of individual-death-as-personal-apocalypse within the context of postmodern irony.

The Tooth of Crime dramatizes the dissolution of the essential self of traditional Western theater within the framework of an SF Western. Its characters allude to a dramatic world that looks forward to the fictional worlds of the cyberpunk writers whose work appeared in the following decade. As one of them explains: "The streets are controlled by the packs. They got it locked up. The packs are controlled by the gangs. The gangs and the Low Riders. They're controlled by cross syndicates. The next step is the Keepers" (219).

In this ambiguously futuristic setting, two rock star/killers, Hoss and Crow, compete for first place in the "charts." As befits a play that has been interpreted as "a kind of allegorical conversation—or rather confrontation—between modernism and postmodernism" (Wilcox 564), their contest climaxes in a showdown of language and style, won by the younger, more flexible Crow, who warns Hoss that "[w]e gotta break yer patterns down, Leathers. Too many bad habits. Re-program the tapes" (245).

The central action in *The Tooth of Crime* is, finally, a confrontation between Hoss's outdated reliance on absolutes, on codes of behavior, on myths of origins,

and Crow's cynically ironic acceptance that the self is all style and surface, a
simulacrum. Shepard's play seems to conclude, however regretfully, that this is
all the reality we are likely to experience in our contemporary moment. Repeating—as if in quotation marks—the narrative resolution which has conventionally guaranteed a return to full presence, *The Tooth of Crime* ends with
Hoss's suicide: "The mark of a lifetime. A true gesture that won't never cheat
on itself 'cause it's the last of its kind. . . . It's mine. An original. It's my life
and my death in one clean shot" (249).

While for Crow, the postmodern everyman as SF punk killer, "the image is
my survival kit" (249), Hoss stakes his life—and his death—on a reality that
is not just illusion. He offers the audience his death—"a true gesture"—as an
event that at once resolves the dramatic action and reveals its final truth. But
what is the truth of this truth invoked by Hoss? Shepard's play seems to require
us to ask this question. While suicide means for Hoss that he can "take [his]
life in [his] hands . . . in death" (249), those of us who have watched the play
unfold are uncomfortably aware that this has been a play about performers and
performances, about surface style and theatrical gesture. Hoss's "true gesture,"
the play seems to suggest, is itself a performance, one that ironically recalls the
heroic suicides of earlier tragic heroes at the same time as it calls into question
the possibility of such "heroic" action in the present. As an audience of one,
Crow's only reaction to Hoss's apocalyptic gesture is a rather ironic appreciation
of its theatricality: "Perfect, Leathers. Perfect. A genius mark. I gotta hand it
to ya' " (249).

THE TERMINAL STAGE

While *The Tooth of Crime* stages the death of the individual as theatrical
spectacle, Robert Wilson's *Einstein on the Beach* (first performed in 1976) once
again invokes the spectacular appeal of the collective apocalypse, eschewing,
apparently, the ironic overtones embedded in *Icarus's Mother*. Wilson's "post-
Wagnerian" operas, of which *Einstein on the Beach* is probably the most well
known, exemplify a tendency in postmodern theater—which we see also in some
postmodern fiction—to move away from conventional character, dialogue, and
narrative.

Because theater is less reliant on words than is fiction, its attempts to achieve
an immediacy of re-presentation—a kind of post-Artaudian effort to close the
breach between performer and performance—have often resulted in a perhaps
inevitable displacement of verbal language by the language of spectacle. As
such, Wilson's operas more properly belong to performance art than to conventional theater. Deconstructing traditionally rigid separations between theater and
other kinds of performance, Wilson's productions are imposing collages of dance,
music, song, the spoken word (as opposed to dialogue), setting, and high-tech
stage machinery. Wilson literally decenters the human on his stage: "actors"
are overshadowed by towering sets; and dialogue is replaced by dreamlike se-

quences of vocal repetition, pure sound, gesture, and movement. Here, for example, is the beginning of one "speech":

Will it get some wind for the sailboat. And it could get for it is. It could get the railroad for these workers. And it could be were it is. It could Franky it could be Franky it could be very fresh and clean. It could be a balloon. Oh these are the days my friends and these are the days my friends. It could get some wind for the sailboat.

In *Einstein on the Beach*, Wilson stages the apocalypse as postmodern spectacle; the beach of the title is the terminal beach of the nuclear age. For all its recognition of our situation within technology, however, *Einstein on the Beach* avoids any real engagement with history. As Bonnie Marranca writes:

[I]t remains a meditation on the modern age rather than an attempt to explore the life of Albert Einstein. Einstein is both inside (as a presence) and outside (playing his beloved violin from a position between stage and orchestra pit) the work, witness to history on trial. Or is the opera offering a grotesque pun: the earth burned while Einstein fiddled? ("Robert Wilson," 119)

This is, finally, the dilemma of what Marranca has named the "theater of images." It indicates a tendency in some postmodern performance art to fiddle with spectacle instead of critically engaging our contemporary situation, allying itself to, rather than resisting, the postmodern cult of the simulacrum, becoming in the process a neo-avant-garde that is in fact neo-conservative. Poised within the hypnotic repetitions of Philip Glass's minimalist score, the images of scientist and spaceship on the stage of *Einstein on the Beach* are, finally, passive, drained of their ability to "mirror" any reality outside their own reality as pure image.

Glass himself produced an SF "spectacular" in 1988–the evocatively titled *1000 Airplanes on the Roof*, scripted by David Henry Hwang. Here we have perhaps the ultimate replacement of "content" by spectacle on the postmodern stage, as Glass's beautiful score and Jerome Sirlin's breathtakingly high-tech sets completely overwhelm the rather weak narrative line concerning the capture of a character, "M.," by aliens. While the plot resembles something we might read about in the *National Inquirer*, the production *as production* is exquisite. As one reviewer notes, "[t]he triumph of the production lay in its overwhelming effect" (Kosson 209).

NUCLEAR THEATER

When SF is appropriated to the allegorical aims of the postmodern stage— that is, when it becomes "specular"—the result tends to be a foregrounding of the present at the expense of the future. This tendency may well be a result of the nature of theater itself as a cultural form devoted to presence and immediacy (however illusory such devotion has proven to be).

The theater of images carries postmodern self-reflexivity to one logical extreme: it re-presents nothing but itself and demands only that we submit ourselves to its seductive "spectacularity." At the same time, ironically, it might be said to have at least partially satisfied the overarching desire of Western theater for unmediated presence in the space of performance. Because it eschews self-consciousness, however, repudiating the metatheatricality of works like *Endgame* and *The Tooth of Crime*, the theater of images must also refuse to engage with its own historical moment; it remains unconscious of itself, and its invitation to audiences is to participate in exactly this same form of unthinking spectatorship.

As productions from *Endgame* to *Einstein on the Beach* attest, there is something intensely and perversely appealing, here at the fin-du-millenium, in the notion/nature of the nuclear climax, an event billed by feminist theorist Zoë Sofia as "the ultimate science-fiction spectacular" (58) and by Jacques Derrida as "a fabulous specularization" ("No Apocalypse, Not Now" 23). Given, however, that—like the Elizabethan world—all the postmodern world is indeed a stage, it makes a very great difference whether we submit to the seductions of the imagery of resolution or manage to maintain an ironic distance from our own (onstage and offstage) productions.[9] This is the distance that is maintained, for example, in the lack of closure of plays such as *Endgame* and *Action*, in the ironic treatment of spectacle in *Icarus's Mother*, in the subversion of the notion of "the moment of truth" in *The Tooth of Crime*.

These issues are central to any discussion of theater at the present moment for cultural as well as for political reasons. As Herbert Blau insists, "Whether or not the consciousness of performance is to be forgotten is perhaps the major issue of the history of performance, as it certainly is of postmodernism" (179).

NOTES

1. This is a revised and expanded version of an earlier essay, "Theater for the Fin-du-Millenium: Playing (at) the End," *Journal of the Fantastic in the Arts* 1 (Winter 1988): 29–38. I would like to thank the editors of *JFA* for their permission to reprint this material here.

2. It is hindsight, of course, that allows me to construct this cause-and-effect narrative, a narrative imbued with the kind of historical inevitability that should be received with a certain skepticism; under the sign of the postmodern, the critic as well as the performer stands at a certain ironic distance from her own productions.

3. Constantin Stanislavski's "system" of actor training, developed in Russia when realism was the privileged theatrical mode, is a form of actor training aimed at closing—to the fullest extent possible—exactly this space between performer and role. Like Newtonian physics, however, its value as a "scientific" system was eventually discovered to be appropriate to only a very specific set of theatrical conditions, and its usefulness as a "scientific paradigm" wanes when performers are faced with "interpreting" other theaters, such as Bertolt Brecht's epic theater or the absurdist theater of Samuel Beckett.

4. As Robert W. Corrigan notes:

We should remember that the idea of a "subtext" was first presented by Stanislavski at the end of the last century. This idea only makes sense if there is an underground action, which must be given expression, which has a beginning, middle, and end once you find the hidden thread. (159)

5. Fredric Jameson also identifies

the effacement . . . of the older (essentially high-modernist) frontier between high culture and so-called mass or commercial culture, and the emergence of new kinds of texts infused with the forms, categories and contents of that very Culture Industry so passionately denounced by all the ideologues of the modern, from Leavis and the American New Criticism all the way to Adorno and the Frankfurt School. (54–55)

6. For a more detailed discussion of the concept of "specular SF," see my forthcoming essay, "Specular SF: Postmodern Allegory."

7. I have appropriated this very useful term from the title of Frank Kermode's important study of the apocalyptic impulse in literature, *The Sense of an Ending: Studies in the Theory of Fiction* (New York: Oxford University Press, 1967).

8. In many ways. *Icarus's Mother* is even more elusive than *Action*. Ross Wetzsteon has suggested that, while Shepard's early plays in particular do not "seem to be 'about' anything," they are in fact "actually about their highly charged atmospheres. . . . [T]heir surreal dislocations perfectly [convey] Shepard's sense of the psychic pressures of contemporary life" (4).

9. Marranca, for example, has noted the tendency of the American military complex to appropriate the metaphors of theater and performance for their own dubious ends. She argues:

The kind of imagery rehearsal that is taking place all around us elaborates a profoundly disturbing mode of thinking because it regards history only in terms of spectacle: Europe as a 'staging ground.' Not only does it abstract war, it aestheticizes war and our feelings towards it to the point of anaesthesia. ("Nuclear Theatre" 148)

WORKS CITED

Aristotle. *The Poetics*. Trans. S. H. Butcher. Introd. Francis Fergusson. New York: Hill and Wang, 1961.

Artaud, Antonin. *The Theatre and Its Double*. 1938. Trans. Mary Caroline Richards. Rpt. New York: Grove, 1958.

Beckett, Samuel. *Endgame*. New York: Grove, 1958.

———, and George Duthuit. *Three Dialogues*. 1949. Rpt. in *Proust and Three Dialogues*. London: Calder, 1965. 97–126.

Belsey, Catherine. *The Subject of Tragedy: Identity and Difference in Renaissance Drama*. New York: Methuen, 1985.

Blau, Herbert. "Universals of Performance; or Amortizing Play." *Sub-Stance* 37/38 (1982): 140–61. Rpt. *The Eye of Prey: Subversions of the Postmodern*. Bloomington: Indiana University Press, 1987. 161–88.

Burgin, Victor, James Donald, and Cora Kaplan. "Preface." *Formations of Fantasy*. Ed. Burgin, Donald, and Kaplan. New York: Methuen, 1986. 1–4.

Corrigan, Robert W. "The Search for New Endings: The Theatre in Search of a Fix, Part III." *Theatre Journal* 36 (May 1984): 153–63.

de Man, Paul. "The Rhetoric of Temporality." *Interpretation: Theory and Practice*. Ed. Charles S. Singleton. Baltimore: Johns Hopkins University Press, 1969. 173–209.

Derrida, Jacques. "No Apocalypse, Not Now (Full Speed Ahead, Seven Missiles, Seven Missives)." Trans. Catherine Porter and Philip Lewis. *Diacritics* 14 (Summer 1984): 20–31.

————. *Of Grammatology*. 1967. Trans. Gayatri Chakravorty Spivak. Rpt. Baltimore: Johns Hopkins University Press, 1976.

Esslin, Martin. *Artaud*. London: Fontana, 1976.

Glass, Philip, and Robert Wilson. *Einstein on the Beach*. New York: Dunvagen Music Publishers, 1976.

Harvey, David. *The Condition of Postmodernity: An Enquiry into the Origins of Cultural Change*. Cambridge, Mass.: Basil Blackwell, 1989.

Hollinger, Veronica. "Specular SF: Postmodern Allegory." *State of the Fantastic: Studies in the Theory and Practice of Fantastic Literature and Film*. Selected Essays from the Eleventh International Conference on the Fantastic in the Arts, 1990. Ed. Nicholas Ruddick. Westport, Conn.: Greenwood Press, 1992. 29–39.

Huyssen, Andreas. *After the Great Divide: Modernism, Mass Culture, Postmodernism*. Bloomington: Indiana University Press, 1986.

Jameson, Fredric. "Postmodernism, or the Cultural Logic of Late Capitalism." *New Left Review* 146 (July/August 1984): 53–94.

Kosson, Robert M. "*1000 Airplanes on the Roof*. By Philip Glass, David Henry Hwang, and Jerome Sirlin." *Journal of Dramatic Theory and Criticism* 3 (Spring 1989): 209–11.

McCaffery, Larry. "Introduction." *Postmodern Fiction: A Bio-Bibliographical Guide*. Ed. McCaffery. Westport, Conn.: Greenwood Press, 1986. xi–xxviii.

McHale, Brian. *Postmodernist Fiction*. New York: Methuen, 1987.

Marranca, Bonnie. "Nuclear Theatre." 1982. Rpt. *Theatrewritings*. New York: Performing Arts Journal Publications, 1984. 147–49.

————. "Robert Wilson, the Avant-Garde, and the Audience: *Einstein on the Beach*." 1977. Rpt. *Theatrewritings*. New York: Performing Arts Journal Publications, 1984. 116–22.

————. "The Theatre of Images: An Introduction." 1977. Rpt. *Theatrewritings*. New York: Performing Arts Journal Publications, 1984. 77–82.

Nash, Cristopher. *World-Games: The Tradition of Anti-Realist Revolt*. New York: Methuen, 1987.

Owens, Craig. "The Allegorical Impulse: Toward a Theory of Postmodernism." *October* 13 (Summer 1980): 67–86.

Shakespeare, William. *The Complete Works*. Ed. G. B. Harrison. New York: Harcourt, 1952.

Shepard, Sam. *Action*. 1976. Rpt. *"Fool for Love" and Other Plays*. New York: Bantam, 1984. 167–90.

————. *Icarus's Mother*. *"Chicago" and Other Plays*. 1969. Rpt. Boston: Faber, 1982. 25–60.

————. *The Tooth of Crime*. 1974. Rpt. *Seven Plays*. New York: Bantam, 1984. 201–51.

Shirley, John. "SF Alternatives, Part One: Stelarc and the New Reality." *Science-Fiction Eye* 1 (August 1987): 56–61.

Sophia, Zöe. "Exterminating Fetuses: Abortion, Disarmament, and the Sexo-Semiotics of Extraterrestrialism." *Diacritics* 14 (Summer 1984): 47–59.

Wetzsteon, Ross. "Introduction." *"Fool for Love" and Other Plays*. New York: Bantam, 1984. 1–15.

Wilcox, Leonard. "Modernism vs. Postmodernism: Shepard's *The Tooth of Crime* and the Discourses of Popular Culture." *Modern Drama* 30 (December 1987): 560–73.

14

"Infinity in a Cigar Box": The Problem of Science Fiction on the Stage

Joseph Krupnik

With the possible exception of Karel Capek's frequently anthologized *RUR* or the recent, much publicized Philip Glass and David Henry Hwang collaboration *1000 Airplanes on the Roof*, most readers of science fiction would be hard pressed to name a work of science fiction written in the form of a stage play. It is widely assumed by readers that not many science fiction plays have been written; moreover, those few that have been published and perhaps eventually produced are thought to be mere curiosities, brief experiments by playwrights who will in time move on to "serious" themes and formats. Furthermore, the belief that science fiction requires properties, sets, and special effects that are too technically demanding for the stage underscores reservations about the effectiveness of presenting science fiction in the theater. In his unpublished paper "The 'No Science Fiction on the Stage' Hypothesis," presented at the Ninth International Conference on the Fantastic in the Arts, George J. Annas states that "the media of the theater is not comfortably compatible with the message of science fiction" (3). Annas also contends that "in the entire history of the theater in the United States it is difficult to find more than a handful of plays that even qualify as science fiction" (1).

But many plays can qualify as science fiction. To be science fiction a work does not have to display dazzling lights and technological paraphernalia. In Robert Scholes' *Structural Fabulation* (the term Scholes prefers over science fiction), he explains that science fiction's "favorite themes involve the impact of developments or revelations derived from the human or the physical sciences upon the people who must live with those revelations or developments" (41–42). Indeed, in his definition of science fiction, Scholes appears to foreground psychological and social implications of scientific and technological developments rather than the scientific systems themselves. Given this definition, many works of science fiction are capable of being presented on the stage.

Nevertheless, prejudice against science fiction on the stage still exists even among those who seem to champion it. For example, in his collection *Six Science Fiction Plays*, Roger Elwood includes three plays written expressly for the stage: Theodore and George Rae Cogswell's *Contact Point*, John Jakes' *Stranger with Roses*, and Paul Zindel's *Let Me Hear You Whisper*. But the others are written for other media: Tom Reamy's *Sting*, a film script; Fritz Leiber's *The Mechanical Bride*, a short television play; and Harlan Ellison's *The City on the Edge of Forever*, the original teleplay for what is perhaps the most famous episode of *Star Trek*. Elwood feels that science fiction is thematically too big and too complex for the stage:

There are not a great many science fiction plays available. The two forms do not meld easily. It is difficult to translate the imaginative leap characteristic of science fiction writing into the hard reality of dialogue between articulate characters. Writing a science fiction play is a bit like trying to picture infinity in a cigar box. (vii)

Obviously, science fiction theater still labors strongly against the assumptions that only film is large enough to contain science fiction themes.

Theoreticians of science fiction as a genre are captivated by the power of media other than the stage. For example, in his article "The Fantastic in Theater and Cinema," Julius Kagarlitski argues that theater is a "conditional art," one whose power derives from the sense that the events on stage are happening now, at the moment of presentation (10–11). Curiously, for Kagarlitski, such immediacy becomes a liability in science fiction on the stage. In a stage presentation, the members of the audience must simultaneously suspend disbelief and accept the drama before them, while disregarding the mundane surroundings of the theater. Consequently, for Kagarlitski, cinema is "an ideal instrument of the fantastic" (11), for it "excludes any possibility of interference"—in effect offering viewers the sense that "what has been put on film, has, as it were, already happened" (11). Kagarlitski implies that it is difficult for a theatrical production to "project" such a sense of historicity and thus validate the content of drama. Given this viewpoint, audiences expect less from a production of science fiction in a theater.

A similar argument is developed by Samuel R. Delany in his lengthy article "*Flow My Tears . . . :* Theater and Science Fiction" for the September 1988 *New York Review of Science Fiction*. Delany implies that science fiction on the stage is by its very nature a contradiction in terms. Delany's essay is basically a review of the Mabou Mines elaborate, mixed-media presentation of Linda Hartinian's adaptation of Philip K. Dick's *Flow My Tears, The Policeman Said*. Noting that "science fiction on the stage has certainly had a rather dicey career" (1), Delany insists that "materiality," or the display of "the technology of a particular historical epoch" (13), is the necessary characteristic of convincing science fiction. For Delany, theater simply cannot fulfill this function. In the theater, "there are no close-ups to convey the intricacy and coherence of detail that suggest the greater world outside the frame, the world beyond the proscenium" (13).

There have been some serious theatrical productions—such as *Via Galactica*, *1000 Airplanes on the Roof*, and, most recently, the London production of *Metropolis*—that have sought to win audiences by massive sets, by intricate stage props, and occasionally by large casts. *Via Galactica*, a huge 1972 Broadway musical, used six trampolines and a number of actors on trapezes to simulate the weightlessness of space travel, but the play closed after seven performances. In addition to such circuslike devices, the play relied upon huge sets, complex props, and the then popular music of Galt MacDermot, who was also the composer of the score for *Hair*. Critics argued that the intricate props and "interstellar" sets had overwhelmed the actors, a serious miscalculation in a play whose major theme was the struggling reemergence of the individual spirit in a future, heavily conformist society. Thus in the *New York Times*, Walter Kerr described the actors as frozen, imprisoned by the play's complex theatrical machinery: "A giant crane moved the [spaceship] slowly about the vast stage, portal to portal. But the people inside it were as good as strapped to their seats, unable to do anything" (344). The London production of *Metropolis*, Joe Brooks's intense musical reworking of Fritz Lang's 1927 film, drew much the same critical reaction. Peter Holland, in his review for the *Times Literary Supplement*, quickly dismissed the play by writing "the music is adequate, the lyrics dire, the acting appalling and the sets magnificent" (279).

With the rare exception of a self-mocking, campy presentation, such as Bob Carlton's *Return to the Forbidden Planet*, plays that rely upon spectacle do not work on the stage. Actors are easily lost amid grandiose sets that ultimately minimize character development and distract the audience. Recognizing this, the more successful science fiction theatrical productions, I would argue, often invert audience expectations and employ restricted, even confined playing areas and use stylized language, sets, and special effects. In effect, serious authors of science fiction on the stage write "intimate" science fiction.

On a practical level is the experience of the Moebius Theatre. In their history of this group, Jane Bloomquist and William McMillan describe how this professional troupe, which presents short plays at popular science fiction conferences, came to believe that "less achieves more." This realization occurred when actor and director Michael Blake attended an overly decorated, elaborately costumed production of Cordwainer Smith's *Lords of the Instrumentality*. This production was a failure. According to Bloomquist, "The setting, costuming, and lighting tried physically to recreate Smith's imaginative world. In trying to give everything it gave nothing" (81).

When Blake later established the Moebius Theater, he decided that "big sets and elaborate costumes could never compete with the images the imagination of a well-read science fiction fan generates" (83). Since the Moebius Theatre often works upon platforms in hotel conference rooms, by necessity it must "strip the performance down to its essentials: actors and the script" (83). Moreover, because these performances have proven to be popular, one might take it as a general standard that since the physical boundaries of the theater limit spectacle, science fiction in the theater must be kept simple if it is to succeed as drama.

In his important book *The Empty Space*, Peter Brook suggests that the power of theater arises from the stage's essential bareness. The visual neutrality of the stage allows the playwright "to roam the world [giving] him free passage from the world of action to the world of inner impressions" (87). Obviously, few stages are completely bare of scenery or props. Thus, playwrights may resort to minimalized and stylized sets to stimulate their audience's imagination, for "the closer we move towards the true nakedness of the theatre, the closer we approach a stage that has a lightness and range far beyond film or television" (878). As Martin Esslin observes in *The Field of Drama*, "In the theatre, paradoxically, real human beings—the actors—can convincingly interact with highly stylized or abstract representations of their environment" (74). There are few distractions. "Intimate" science fiction on the stage focuses not on the display of technology but on the drama of characters.

Indeed, many effective and provocative science fiction plays do exist in intimate form, and they present a strong challenge to the conclusions drawn by Annas, Elwood, and Delany about the paucity of science fiction on the stage. The number of science fiction plays that are available in published versions is sizable, well over 100. They include one-act dramas, verse plays, children's productions, musical parodies, traditional three-act dramas as well as adaptations of science fiction short stories and novels. While a few of these plays have been produced on Broadway, more have been presented by regional companies, summer theaters, and high school groups. Unfortunately, some have never been staged.

Science fiction plays vary greatly in literary quality and in playability. In the following annotated list, I have chosen to discuss individual plays, including a number by "mainstream" authors, that offer interesting and creative attempts to capture "infinity in a cigar box." In many cases, both the playwrights and their science fiction plays deserve wider and more serious recognition than they have so far received. This list can only serve to indicate the amount and variety of the material yet awaiting critical attention.

WORKS CITED

Annas, George J. "The 'No Science Fiction on the Stage' Hypothesis." Paper presented at the Ninth International Conference on the Fantastic in the Arts. Ft. Lauderdale, Fla., 16 Mar. 1988. 1–14.

Bloomquist, Jane, and William McMillan. "Science Fiction Theatre the Moebius Way."

Patterns of the Fantastic. Ed. Donald M. Hassler. Mercer Island, Wash.: Starmont, 1983. 81–90.

Brook, Peter. *The Empty Space*. New York: Atheneum, 1968.

Capek, Karel. *RUR: A Fantastic Melodrama*. Garden City, N.Y.: Doubleday, 1923.

Carlton, Bob. *Return to the Forbidden Planet*. London: Methuen, 1985.

Delany, Samuel R. *"Flow My Tears . . . :* Theater and Science Fiction." *New York Review of Science Fiction* Sept. 1988: 1, 11–17.

Elwood, Roger. "Introduction." *Six Science Fiction Plays*. New York: Pocket, 1976. vii–x.

Esslin, Martin. *The Field of Drama: How the Signs of Drama Create Meaning on Stage and Screen*. New York: Methuen, 1987.

Holland, Peter. Review of *Metropolis*. *Times Literary Supplement* 17 March 1989: 279.

Hwang, David Henry, Philip Glass, and Jerome Sirlin. *1000 Airplanes on the Roof: A Science Fiction Music-Drama*. Salt Lake City, Utah: Peregrine Smith, 1988.

Kagarlitski, Julius. "The Fantastic in Theater and Cinema." *Extrapolation* 22.1 (1981): 5–12.

Kerr, Walter. Review of *Via Galactica* by Christopher Gore, Judith Ross, and Galt MacDermot. *New York Times* 10 Dec. 1972: 3.

Scholes, Robert. *Structural Fabulation: An Essay on Fiction of the Future*. Notre Dame, Ind.: Notre Dame University Press, 1975.

ANNOTATED BIBLIOGRAPHY

Anderson, Robert. *Solitaire & Double Solitaire*. New York: Random House, 1972.

Solitaire and *Double Solitaire* are two loosely linked one-act plays written by Robert Anderson, author of *Tea and Sympathy, You Know I Can't Hear You When the Water's Running*, and *I Never Sang for My Father*. *Double Solitaire* consists of a series of short sketches that portray the slow death of a contemporary marriage. Reflecting a general uneasiness toward science fiction on the stage, critics gave the more favorable reviews to *Double Solitaire*. *Solitaire*, however, is not without merit.

In *Solitaire*, Anderson envisions an overpopulated, highly regimented future society. Sam Bradley checks into a Servocell, an automated motel room that provides its customers with the illusion of every convenience. Only 50, Sam lives in a society that requires mandatory "self-disposal" at age 60. Tired, lonely, and bored, Sam elects early self-disposal and thus is rewarded with Servocell's most attractive feature—a "Call Family." Not sexual in nature, the services that are offered are a type of emotional prostitution in which the hired "family" recreates the warmth of a vital family. Caught up in the simulation of family togetherness, Sam decides he wants to live; however, it is too late to renege on his decision. Once begun, the self-disposal process cannot be stopped.

Ayckbourn, Alan. *Henceforward*. London: Faber, 1988.

Alan Ayckbourn has written a disturbing comedy about technology's control of the creative spirit and about the death of love. Jerome, an experimental composer, has barricaded himself in an apartment crammed with electronic equipment: amplifiers, synthesizers, keyboards, security systems, and video phones. The most unusual piece of equipment though is Nan, a malfunctioning female robot. Surrounded by such technology,

Jerome lacks human contact and human warmth. His neighborhood is patrolled by the "Daughters of Darkness," a roving pack of women who have taken a dislike to Jerome and periodically hurl objects at Jerome's shuttered windows. Moreover, Jerome is besieged by doubts about his creative powers. Frustrated in his search for the perfect sound, he has not been able to compose since his wife departed, taking their daughter with her. His memories of his daughter are idealized.

In a bizarre plan to gain custody of his daughter, Jerome hires an actress to pretend to be his fiancée and thus convince the Department of Child Wellbeing that he is a stable, loving man. When the actress runs out on him, Jerome desperately turns to Nan and attempts to pass her off as his fiancée. Of course, Jerome's plot fails as Nan's behavior becomes erratic and uncontrolled. Moreover, Jerome finds that his daughter has grown into a bully and has joined the "Daughters of Darkness." In coping with the monster their child has become, Jerome and his estranged wife, Corinne, come to a reconciliation and, near the play's end, plan to leave the cluttered apartment. As they do, Jerome accidentally hears a previously recorded tape of Corinne's voice speak the word "Love." It is in this recorded word that Jerome finds the perfect sound for which he has been searching. Totally engrossed in his technological manipulation and amplification of this single word, Jerome forgets his waiting wife.

Bergen, Candice. "The Freezer." *Best Short Plays 1968*. Ed. Stanley Richards. Philadelphia: Chilton, 1968. 49–58.

This slight (about 10 minutes) play was written by film and television actress Candice Bergen. Clinging to his sense of individuality and espousing an unfashionable death wish, Bergen's nameless hero, simply called Man, resists undergoing entrance in "The Freezer." A compulsory process mandated by the "State," "The Freezer" rejuvenates the body and in effect grants immortality to the citizens of the State. However, Man wants to die, to experience the unknown. Forced into "The Freezer" by the State Physician, Man is given his wish. The freezing process masks a murder plot hatched by the State Physician and Man's wife. They were having an affair. Glibly excusing his act of murder, the State Physician states that the murder was actually sanctioned by the State, for Man was obviously a "corrosive force" (58).

Birnkrant, Samuel. *The Termination*. Denver: Pioneer Drama Service, 1976.

This one-act satire is set in the Termination Office of the Bureau of Over Population. The Bureau's motto is "We Lead You Gently into that last Good-Nite!" The action begins as Miss X, an officer for the Bureau, interviews Emily Schlumberger, a woman who has elected to die because she can find nothing (human beings, animals, or even plants) to love her. Emily's decision to kill herself is prompted by her failure to meet a blind date, a man wearing a red carnation.

After choosing electrocution and signing numerous release forms, Emily suddenly changes her mind. The sight of a parakeet collected by Miss X as partial payment of another client's execution fees, brings back memories of Emily's childhood joy. Emily reneges on the agreement and attempts to leave. Until this point, *The Termination* is a farce that uses rapid dialogue and outrageous puns. The play turns horrific, however, as Miss X, desperately trying to meet her death quota, suddenly and efficiently kills Emily. As Miss X disposes of Emily's body, a new customer, a man wearing a red carnation, walks into the bureau office.

Bowen, John. *After the Rain*. New York: Random House, 1968.

Bowen's play, actually a play within a play, begins in a lecture hall. It is 200 years after the Rain of 1969. As part of an illustrated demonstration, a group of men and women reenact episodes that dramatize the lives of the last six men and women on Earth. These six are survivors of a world-wide flood, and they cling to life on a large raft.

An uneasy collection of personality types, this small group is dominated by Arthur Henderson. Before the flood, Arthur was an accountant, a small man dismissed by society at large. On the raft, Arthur has developed into the most assertive of the group. He establishes himself first as a dictator over the group and then later as its god. The survivors willingly accept Arthur in these roles. Yet, as a god, Arthur is so petty and vindictive that some of his companions eventually revolt and kill him.

Arthur's totalitarian, conformist principles, however, have endured. His ideas, recorded in a fragmentary manuscript called the "Book of Arthur," have formed the basis of the society which has flourished in the 200 years after the flood. The actors in the demonstration are actually criminals who have violated the codes of this repressive society. As part of a rehabilitation program, they have been hypnotized into playing the roles of the survivors.

After the Rain, presented on Broadway in 1967, had a short, 67 performance run. Bowen adapted this play from his 1958 novel, published as "A Ballantine Science Fiction 'First.' "

Bradbury, Ray. "Kaleidoscope." *Pillar of Fire and Other Plays*. New York: Bantam, 1975. 65–93.

Utilizing a basically simple plot, *Kaleidoscope* depicts seven astronauts who are thrown from a ship that has been struck by a meteor. The men, in space suits, drift away in different directions to their deaths. The audience sees the astronauts' faces and hears their voices as they communicate with each other. The actors, either dangling by harnesses or poised on scaffolding, mimic the astronauts' drift through space.

Bradbury's script offers a fuguelike interplay of the astronauts' comments as they face death with either desperation or stoicism. Most of the astronauts want to die in the company of others, except for one named Applegate. Correctly perceiving that he is a misfit, he prefers to die alone. In the course of the play, Applegate murders one of his fellow astronauts. Applegate had been insensitive to beauty. Yet, as he drifts, he becomes entranced, touched, and humbled by ethereal radio signals still traveling across space from the twentieth century as well as by the kaleidoscopic beauty of a meteor swarm that is sweeping him out of the solar system.

Bradbury, Ray. *The Pedestrian*. New York: Samuel French, 1966.

In this dramatization of his well-known short story, Ray Bradbury depicts a city of the near future in which even walking is a crime. Dominated by an authoritative, highly automated government, the citizens pass their leisure time sitting in their darkened houses watching television. Leonard Mead, a writer, has convinced his anxious neighbor, Robert Stockwell, to join him for a nighttime walk through the city. Mead has been secretly walking for years—enjoying the starry sky, the smell of fresh air, the song of the crickets, and the taste of a blade of grass. Initially nervous, Stockwell too begins to enjoy these simple pleasures as the two men roam the deserted streets.

As they return to their homes, they are suddenly stopped by a police car, the only one patrolling 50 square miles of the city. The police car, completely automated, interrogates Mead and Stockwell and finds no satisfactory explanation for their presence in the street. Protecting Stockwell, Mead asserts that the two men were just beginning their walk. He also contends that he convinced Stockwell to accompany him. Finally, Mead confesses that he is a habitual walker, a misfit who does not like to stay at home and who has not even bothered to fix his broken television set. Reacting to this confession, the car commands Mead to enter a holding cell in the back of the vehicle. Ordering Stockwell to return home, the car then whisks Mead off to the Psychiatric Center for Research on Regressive Tendencies.

Shaken, Stockwell limps down the empty street where he sees Mead's house all aglow with light. Terrified, Stockwell intends to turn off all the lights, for "someone might *notice*" (20).

The Pedestrian is an effective play that relies heavily on sound and lighting effects. The automated police car is easily suggested by recorded voices and bright, searching lights. In spite of the theatricality of the play production, Bradbury's original short story is perhaps a more moving piece of writing. In the short story, there is only one character. But in reworking the story into a play, Bradbury introduced the figure of Robert Stockwell, perhaps to create more dramatic tension. The story, however, still holds more impact. It is the tale of a pedestrian wandering the bleak, colorless city—isolated in his enjoyment of nature and isolated in the terror of his capture.

Bradbury, Ray. "Pillar of Fire." *Pillar of Fire and Other Plays*. New York: Bantam, 1975. 1–64.

In *Pillar of Fire*, Bradbury suggests that it is better to be fearful than to be incapable of fear, that without fear the imagination dies. In this extremely poetic work, the major character, William Lantry, has been reborn after 200 years in the grave. The future society into which he emerges is one in which people lack imagination. All works of fiction have been destroyed; libraries house only books of factual information. There is no natural death in this world. In fact, all references and reminders of death have been banished. The earth's graveyards have been emptied; corpses have been burned in incinerators. Without a vision of death, the people of the future do not fear the darkness and they have no use for the supernatural.

Newly resurrected, Lantry believes that it is his mission to instill these fears in the society by introducing violence and death: "It's William Lantry against the whole vampire-disbelieving, body burning, graveyard-annihilating world" (11). Lantry hopes to revive the real and imagined terrors that plagued authors such as Hawthorne, Melville, Dunsany, Lovecraft, and, most of all, Poe by strangling people indiscriminately and by blowing up incinerators.

Lantry is eventually captured by an agent named McClure. McClure hints that Lantry, the resurrected dead, is not supernatural, that he is a medical miracle, a survivor of a cryonics experiment. McClure's logical, patient arguments almost convince Lantry, but in a brief moment McClure confesses that Lantry almost frightened him. Lantry proclaims, "I am all that is left of Edgar Allan Poe, and I am all that is left of Ambrose Bierce and Lovecraft" (59). Perceiving Lantry to be a mad prophet of the dark night of the soul, McClure is forced to take him to the incinerator. As he dies, Lantry sees himself as

Dracula, the Phantom of the Opera, the Raven, and all the other figures who have instilled fear in the minds of men.

Bradbury, Ray. "To the Chicago Abyss." *The Wonderful Ice Cream Suit and Other Plays for Today, Tomorrow and Beyond Tomorrow*. New York: Bantam, 1972. 128–61.

To the Chicago Abyss, Bradbury's play about a compulsive talker, is set in a bleak, desolate city in the near future. Much like his play *The Pedestrian*, in which walking alone was a crime, here talking and listening to descriptions of the past are criminal acts. A group of citizens gather in secret to listen to an old man whom they have hidden from the "special police." The old man is a compulsive talker who can never resist speaking to strangers of his memories of the past. In a hidden room, the old man, endowed with a memory that retains the most minute of details, describes useless, trivial artifacts. The "special police" are willing to offer a week's rations for the capture of the old man who can describe the most commonplace of objects that once existed.

As though reciting a litany, the man recalls a world abundant with bicycles, antimacassars, automobile dashboards, and all "the third-rate-hand-me down, useless and chromed over slush and junk of a racetrack civilization" (153). The old man diverts his listeners from thinking of the sordidness of their present-day lives. He is an entertainment, "almost like the theatre [or] motion picture houses" (149).

One of the grateful listeners warns the old man always to keep moving and never to speak aloud in public. To help the old man escape, the listener gives the old man a ticket to the Chicago Abyss. There, near the bomb crater that was once Chicago, the old man may find new listeners.

Leaving his newfound friends, the old man boards a crowded train for the Chicago Abyss. In the crammed car late at night, the old man spies a young boy traveling by himself. In spite of the public setting, the old man is unable to remain silent or to remain isolated. He beckons the boy to come to him and whispers "Once upon a time . . . " (161).

Bradbury, Ray, "The Veldt." *The Wonderful Ice Cream Suit and Other Plays for Today, Tomorrow and Beyond Tomorrow*. New York: Bantam, 1972. 73–125.

As with all the plays written and produced by Bradbury, *The Veldt* relies heavily upon the use of light and sound. Two indifferent but well-to-do parents, George and Lydia Hadley, install a Happylife Electrodynamic Playroom for their neglected children, Peter and Wendy. The playroom can create scenes that completely surround the occupants with convincing and entertaining displays of exotic locations. Much to the distress of George and Lydia, their children become fixated upon an African plain complete with vultures and lions. Disturbed by the sounds of animals preying upon one another that seep through the house, Lydia becomes convinced that the playroom has developed a "psychological set" (100). Indeed, this seems to be so for the room display can no longer be changed. The parents, believing that the scenes of death were actually created by the children, consult a psychiatrist who hypothesizes that "the room has become a channel *toward* destructive thoughts rather than a release away from them" (111). The father destroys the control panel of Happylife Electrodynamic Playroom. The next night, George and Lydia hear their children calling for help. Believing the children have broken into the playroom, the parents rush in to discover they are trapped on the veldt with hungry lions approaching.

Briggs, Raymond. *When the Winds Blows*. London: Samuel French, 1983.

When the Wind Blows is a tragicomedy about the effects of nuclear war upon a retired middle-class English couple. The play follows the weeks during which Jim and Hilda Bloggs prepare for—and survive—a nuclear attack.

A practical and literal-minded man, Jim has collected many government leaflets such as *Protect and Survive* and *The Householder's Guide to Survival*. Doggedly following the leaflet recommendations down to the last detail, Jim builds and stocks a rickety bomb shelter in their small cottage. Jim and Hilda have a firm resolve gained in part from having lived through World War II bombings. They have now survived a nuclear attack and emerge from the shelter to find a completely desolated world. There is no sound except the constant blowing of the wind.

Nevertheless, Jim and Hilda innocently believe that government aid will soon come. With unshaken optimism, they do not doubt that they will live in "A New World Perjured [*sic*.] of all the old vices—like London after the Fire of London! The New Elizabethan Age will dawn! Britannia will rise again with fresh fields and Pastures new to conquer" (34).

Their implacable optimism is the source of much of the play's dark humor. Yet the play becomes increasingly somber. Against an eerie background of constantly blowing wind, Jim and Hilda must struggle more desperately to live. Their rations diminish and they slowly grow ill. Suffering from radiation sickness, they retire to their shelter at first still hoping for the government to save them. Finally, they lie next to one another— quietly comforting one another, now praying and waiting for death.

Capek, Karel. *RUR: A Fantastic Melodrama*. Garden City, N.Y.: Doubleday, 1923.

As the play that introduced the word *robot*, *RUR* is the most famous title annotated here. The play is set in an unspecified future on an island where robots are efficiently manufactured by the factory of Rossum's Universal Robots. Initially designed to replace people in doing manual labor, the robots are purchased in large quantities by nations of the world to fight as soldiers. In fact, these militaristic robots have been altered by Dr. Gall, head of the physiological department of the Rossum company, to hate all that is human. Believing that they are superior, the robots demand the extinction of humankind. Coincidentally, humankind has become sterile, and no human children are being born. The robots mass together and begin a systematic killing of humankind. The victory of the robots over humankind is gained, however, at too great a cost. The robots will be worn out in 20 years and there is no formula for making new ones.

Spared because the robots respect him for working with his hands is Alquist. It is he who notices that two robots, Primus and Helena, have fallen in love. Intending to dissect one of the couple in order to find the causes of their emotions, Alquist is surprised to discover that each offers to substitute for the other in the experiment. Recognizing that Primus and Helena are a new Adam and Eve, Alquist encourages them to leave the island and take possession of the Earth.

The word *robot* has become so aligned with the mechanistic and the metallic that it is a surprise to read that the Rossum process is biologically and chemically based.

Carlton, Bob. *Return to the Forbidden Planet*. London: Methuen, 1985.

First presented in 1983, Bob Carlton's spoof of Shakespeare's *The Tempest* and the 1956 MGM film *The Forbidden Planet* has been often revived in England. Advertised as "Shakespeare's forgotten rock-and-roll masterpiece," this clever, enjoyable play moves easily from the "grace" of pseudo-Shakespearean verse to the driving, basic rhythms of 1950s rock. In the well-known plot, the square-jawed Captain Tempest, his love, Miranda, and the robot Ariel battle once again the mad Doctor Prospero and his "monsters from the Id."

Catron, Louis E. *At a Beetle's Pace*. New York: Samuel French, 1971.

A simply plotted, elegiac play that does not preach, *At a Beetle's Pace* dramatizes the condition of the old in a future society in which aging does not occur. The play centers around Ben Hest, an old man who is a survivor from a previous age that knew death. Because of medical science, Hest's body is active, flexible, and physically spry. Hest, however, is emotionally and intellectually alienated from the new generation that surrounds him. The eternally youthful are not hostile to the old; indeed, they want to welcome the old into their community, into their celebrations of life. In spite of the young's good intentions, Hest feels that he is tolerated because he is a medical curiosity and consequently rejects all attempts by the new generation to be integrated into their social structure.

Cogswell, Theodore R., and George Rae Cogswell. "Contact Point." *Six Science Fiction Plays*. Ed. Roger Elwood. New York: Pocket, 1976. 250–81.

The *Arcturus* is returning from the first successful landing of a spaceship on a plane in another solar system. But the *Arcturus* is a plague ship, for its crew has been infected by a radioactive, living "green dust" that invades all the cells of the body. The disease is slow growing, having an incubation period of 15 to 20 years.

Contact Point is primarily a psychological study of Kurt Benster, the ship's pilot. Originally believing that Earth scientists would easily find a cure for the disease, Benster selfishly intends to land his ship on Earth, thus risking contamination of the planet. Benster learns that his government, waging another of its interminable wars, is only interested in military exploitation of the knowledge the crew has gathered during its voyage. In spite of this realization, Benster decides to land the contaminated ship. He hopes that his action will force all the nations of the Earth to redirect their use of the resources they now spend on waging wars, directing their energies instead to finding a cure for this new plague.

Congdon, Constance. "Tales of the Lost Formicans." *American Theatre* May 1989: 1–15.

Tales of the Lost Formicans focuses upon the plight of the McKissik family. Living in a middle-class development in Colorado, the McKissiks are a family in crisis. The grandson is in rebellion—a school dropout and runaway. His mother has returned to live with her parents after her divorce. Her father is suffering from Alzheimer's disease. These domestic crises are witnessed by friendly, curious aliens from outer space who also transmit their observations to the theater audience, assumed to be aliens as well.

The aliens, engaged in an anthropological study, move freely and invisibly among human beings. The aliens, however, have a consistently off-center vision of human life in the suburbs. They often misinterpret the function of everyday objects as well as the purposes of human actions and motivations.

The actors alternate between human and alien roles. The only visible sign of their status as aliens is that the actors wear sunglasses. Through this technique, Congdon establishes a double perspective that gently satirizes suburban living but also points out its malaise and quiet desperation.

Elliott, Paul. *The Legacy*. New York: Samuel French, 1974.

Unrelentingly bleak, *The Legacy* offers a nightmarish look into a future totalitarian state. This state is patrolled by the Zeppons, robotic squads that exterminate the sick, the wounded, and even those luckless individuals who are caught out after curfew.

The play depends upon a few complicated light and sound effects to simulate the Zeppon presence. But Elliott concentrates essentially upon emotions—anguish and fear. A young couple, Marion and William, plan to escape the sector to which they have been assigned. Marion has secretly borne their child into a world in which no children are permitted. They hide their infant in a trunk that contains a complex life support system which sustains the child's body in a comalike state. In their maneuvers to achieve freedom, Marion and William betray to the Zeppons another couple also assigned to share their quarters.

In the play's emotional and harrowing climax, William slashes through the dead couple's duffel bag with a knife, only to discover he has killed the betrayed couple's child.

Guare, John. *Marco Polo Sings a Solo*. New York: Dramatists Play Service, 1977.

The action of Guare's intricate, bizarre, often funny play occurs in the early spring of 1999 on the iceberg island of Trollenthor off the coast of Norway.

At the century's end, Stony McBride, a movie director, attempts to make a comeback film for his father, a fallen-out-of-fashion actor, on the life of Marco Polo; at the same time, his friend, astronaut Frank Schaeffer, has been traveling through space for the past five years. Stony remarks that Frank has been "Giving us dreams. Giving us legends" (10) and indeed Frank seals his position as humankind's benefactor, for he has discovered "a green planet so fertile [that] it looks like a ball of manure popped out of a black hole in space" (17). With the problem of world hunger so easily solved, Frank attempts to impregnate his wife, Skippy (he has also named the new planet for her), from space through bolts of lightning. As bolts of lightning hit the ground, Stony inexplicably appears in Frank's space suit and flies (without rocketship) into space. He is searching for Frank's new planet where he can have "union with this green planet" and thus escape the solipsistic isolation that separates him from the other characters. At the play's end, Stony holds up his two hands and achieves an apotheosis as he states "My plant nature. Our plant nature. I celebrate that" (51). Out of his hands grow two green plants.

Marco Polo Sings a Solo opened on Broadway on February 5, 1977, with a strong cast that included Madeline Kahn, Joel Grey, Anne Jackson, Chris Sarandon, and Sigourney Weaver; nevertheless, most critics found its characterization murky and its plot turns obscure and puzzling. With the 1986 revival of *The House of Blue Leaves* and the critical and popular success of the Broadway production of *Six Degrees of Separation* (1990), critics would surely find it profitable to reexamine Guare's earlier, often neglected plays.

Gurik, Robert. *API 2967*. Trans. Marc. F. Gelinas. Vancouver: Talonbooks, 1974.

Gurik's play projects a scientific utopia where all aspects of human life are monitored and shaped by the government. Meals are taken in capsule form, conversation between individuals is rationed, weather on the Earth and other planets is regulated, and the birth rate is strictly controlled. The citizens of the society gladly accept such policies for the system rewards them and runs, for the most part, smoothly.

No one can account, however, for the mysterious appearance of an apple in this self-satisfied, scientifically created paradise. A nameless professor, male, and his female assistant E3253 are assigned to analyze the apple, called by them API. In so doing, they become a new Adam and Eve, reenacting the history of humankind through rediscovering passion, hatred, jealousy, love, and death.

First performed in Montreal in 1967, *API 2967* is a technically complex play requiring the use of slides, film, and television.

Guyer, Murphy. *The American Century: A Joke in One Act*. New York: Dramatists Play
    Service, 1985.

Marginal science fiction, *The American Century* uses time travel (briefly mentioned in the play) as a springboard for an absurdist comedy that attacks the American Dream of the "big house," the "big car," and the "best schools, the best doctors" (9).

Tommy Kilroy, a borderline schizophrenic in his own time, travels back to 1945 in a drug-induced 40-minute therapy session. Following the advice of his "Neo-Freudian Geneticist" analyst (41), he hopes to see the moment of his conception and reexperience and thus purge himself of his "fertilization trauma" (14). He meets his parents before they have made love. In his narcissistic self-absorption, Tommy describes in detail the events of his parents' future life together. Tommy's account of future disaster after disaster for the family convinces his father to leave. The play ends with Tommy, having in effect prevented his own conception, running after his father, trying to convince him that all he said was only a joke.

Hale, John: "Decibels." *Prompt Three: Five Short Modern Plays*. Ed. Alan Durband.
    London: Hutchinson, 1976. 47–63.

A witty critique of the "Me Generation," *Decibels* begins with a single clock ticking in a basement flat; soon, this lone sound builds to a sustained cacophony of blowing horns; squealing brakes; wailing jets; and the blaring of ambulance, police, and air raid sirens. In Hale's vision of this future, overcrowded world, there is no silence. To help control population, the government encourages voluntary use by 60-year-olds of the "rest-in-peace" pill. Vanessa and Marcus, young and upwardly mobile, serenely go about the day's business insensitive to the noise (and other forms of pollution) that surround them. Vanessa and Marcus communicate at close range by reading each other's lips or even by resorting to bull horns to overcome the noise.

Grateful that her father has voluntarily killed himself to make room for her new child, Vanessa is at the present moment irked by her mother's refusal to give the couple her house and move into a government-controlled home. Her optimistic husband believes, however, that in a short time all elders will heartily follow the suggestion of the latest government campaign for population control. He soon convinces Vanessa that her moth-er's stubbornness is a temporary aberration. To amuse his wife at dinner, Marcus presents Vanessa with a gag gift, earmuffs for both of them. But the unnatural silence from wearing the muffs ruins the meal for them. Both quickly discard the earmuffs to luxuriate in the surrounding noise.

Howatson, Rob. "The Hard Sell." *Interplay '85: Eleven Plays by Young People*. Sydney, Australia: Currency, 1985. 67–73.

Howatson takes the improbable premise that a group of 328 real estate salesmen have been erroneously selected by a malfunctioning computer to be passengers on a spaceship fleeing the Earth destroyed by nuclear war. Without a flight crew, the salesmen are trapped in space, aimlessly orbiting the Earth.

By luck, the ship meets a passing ship of agreeable aliens. True to their professional natures, the salesmen sell the ruined Earth to the aliens in return for improvements (such as Jacuzzis) to the Earth ship.

The Hard Sell is played for broad comedy, but a serious tone is introduced by the main character, Roy Gibwater, a disenchanted salesman who is going mad. He thinks he is Zeus, having dominion over the dead earth. He alone mourns the destruction of the planet.

Hwang, David Henry, Philip Glass, and Jerome Sirlin. *1000 Airplanes on the Roof: A Science Fiction Music-Drama*. Salt Lake City, Utah: Peregrine Smith, 1988.

A thematically rich, one-character drama written by David Henry Hwang, *1000 Airplanes on the Roof* relates the adventures of M., a young man from the country who is newly arrived in New York City. While out on a date, M. is asked, "Are you a psychopath?" This question unsettles M. and apparently triggers an episode in which he sees his apartment house begin to disappear. Not knowing whether this disappearance is a hallucination or an actual event, M. explores his memory for a solution to the puzzle. His most vivid memory is that of a night when the sky above his farmhouse burst open with a humming sound, like 1,000 airplanes landing on his roof.

M. believes that the humming sound signaled an alien presence, and indeed M. is convinced that he was once abducted by aliens in a spaceship. The humming sound returns once again and M. finds that he has, for the second time, been carried off by aliens. He travels with these aliens across five dimensions and sees the faces of his ancestors as well as those of his unborn children. M. finally comes to understand why the aliens travel. They hope to find a confirmation of their existence through their recognition by another: "We all hope one day, looking into the eyes of another, to find part of an answer" (48).

Awakening after his trip, M. discovers that he cannot account for four days of his life. Traumatized, he faints and then finds himself under the care of an inquisitive doctor. Saying nothing of the abduction to his doctor, M. realizes that his memory of the space journey is fading. Seemingly cured of his hallucinations, M. is released from the hospital, but he still has one problem. In his mind, he hears a constant throbbing. As he says in the last speech of the play, "The throbbing grows. It threatens to become sound. There is a universe in my mind, struggling to break out. And I'm a normal man. A normal man running" (63).

1000 Airplanes on the Roof is a collaborative work with music by Philip Glass and brilliant set designs and projections by Jerome Sirlin. In fact, the difficulty of constructing Sirlin's three-dimension projected backdrops will hinder later productions.

Jakes, John. "Stranger with Roses: A Science Fiction Entertainment in One Act." *Six Science Fiction Plays*. Ed. Roger Elwood. New York: Pocket, 1976. 283–327.

After entering an experimental time machine called the "warp phase effector," Vincent Deem steps from 1979 into the year 1997. He finds himself in a world where no flowers grow because of the contamination from nuclear war. The roses of the title refer to two buds that Deem's young daughter put in his coat pocket. Deem unknowingly carries them into the future and leaves them there.

Deem's purpose is to find a cure for his daughter who is ill with Parkinson's disease. During his search, which is eventually successful, he meets Sari, a young wife who has recently suffered a nervous breakdown. Sensing that Deem does not belong in her time, that his oddness is more than just eccentric behavior, Sari begins to fear that she may be again slipping into madness. In his play, Jakes explores the tension that grows between these two strangers, both suffering great anguish because of illness.

Lengyel, Cornel. *The Master Plan*. Georgetown, Calif.: Dragon's Teeth, 1978.

Cornel Lengyel's neglected *The Master Plan* is a remarkable, highly theatrical play. The action takes place in Deep Haven, a fallout shelter one mile beneath the earth's surface. Here a group of aging scientists, led by a visionary businessman named Cyrus Kane, attempts to breed a superior species, Homo Novo, "the Star-Bound Man" (14). Kane is, of course, mad—a dictator who is selfishly motivated by meeting the impossible challenge of his dream.

His niece Stella has courageously ventured out of Deep Haven and discovered on New Easter Island 51 mutant survivors of a series of earlier, unsuccessful Deep Haven experiments. These mutants have been led to New Easter Island by Albert, Kane's rebellious brother, who pities them. Albert has assumed the responsibilities that the indifferent "father" Kane has not even recognized. The island itself is covered by a blanket of volcanic smoke which apparently filters out most of the harmful radiation and allows the exiles to survive. Yet in this desolation is born a superior member of a mutant species, Omega. He is brought to Deep Haven by Albert and Stella to beg Kane for shelter for himself and the other survivors.

The actor portraying Omega is costumed in scales and webbed flippers; he wears a "dark green helmet-like mask which makes him resemble a sea horse" (30). Omega is a "strange and majestic figure" (36), the personification of a life force that survives the most hostile of environments. Growing in nobility and in charity, Omega sets the standard by which we finally judge Kane. Having ignored Albert's argument that Omega is Kane's spiritual if not biological son, Kane orders his assistants to perform a detailed and painful examination on Omega. Omega survives the examination, and Kane, responding to Albert's persistent arguments, grants Omega a hearing before the board of Deep Haven. This hearing forms the dramatic core of the play; in seven brief but theatrically rich episodes, Omega dramatically reenacts the history of his race. Here, the actor playing Omega is given, through dance, mime, and chanting, great latitude in expression.

Lengyel requires only one set for his play. All of the play's action occurs in front of Deep Haven's computer. Its stylized design and pulsating lights suggest not only the tumultuous colors of nature destroyed by nuclear war but also the impersonal, dehumanizing "Light" of Kane's plan.

Kane orders Omega's execution. In order to protect himself, Omega mimes a ritualistic gesture which apparently triggers a force exceeding the power of Deep Haven. Realizing that the shelter is to become a tomb, Kane kills himself. All of the other characters die, with the exception of Stella and Omega. Conditioned by his exposure to radiation, Omega survives—as does, somewhat inexplicably, Stella. The play closes as Omega and Stella, a new Adam and Eve, leave Deep Haven to return to the island. Omega promises Stella, "We'll find our garden together, as in the beginning" (68).

Nicholson, Norman. *Prophesy to the Wind*. London: Faber, 1950.

Commissioned in 1947 by the Little Theatre Guild of Great Britain. *Prophesy to the Wind* is a play in verse. In a brief prologue, the hero, John, describes how during an atomic war he was blown "up the chimney of time" (7) into the future. He reappears in an England that is no longer industrial. Rather, this postwar society, settled by migrants from Iceland, knows nothing of machinery and technology. One character, for example, thinks that an automobile mudguard is a knife blade used by a giant.

Initially, John is content to live in this simple, pastoral world. He falls in love with Freya, even though she is promised to marry another. John soon finds himself exploring ruins of the civilization he once knew. In a mine, he finds an old, broken dynamo which he repairs. John hopes to impress Freya's father, Hallbjorn, with his technological knowledge. Hallbjorn, however, is instead frightened by the thought that the dynamo's power will lead humankind once more to worldwide destruction. After John refuses to destroy the machine, Hallbjorn, with much regret, arranges to have John killed.

Oboler, Arch. *Night of the Auk*. New York: Horizon, 1958.

Arch Oboler's *Night of the Auk* is a free verse play that utilizes a stylized set to depict the return journey of the Alfred Rohnen Foundation–Associated Newspapers' Expedition to the Moon. The expedition, more of a publicity stunt than a legitimate scientific undertaking, will win a huge cash prize if—and only if—one of the crew sets foot on the moon. Oboler uses complex patterns and disturbing references to sound, especially oxymorons, to criticize the influence of mass media upon the ambition and the idealism of the crew.

As the play's ominous, awkward title suggests, this work is not about heroism and victory. The play is actually about the loss of self-mastery and the loss of moral direction. Lewis Rohnen, heir to the Rohnen Foundation, has tricked one of his shipmates into stepping onto the radioactive surface of the moon. Rohnen then blasts off from the moon, stranding his shipmate.

A megalomaniac, Rohnen is motivated by the desire for worldwide recognition; in fact, he boasts from space to his worldwide audience that he had claimed the moon as new territory for the United States. With radio contact with Earth becoming garbled, Rohnen learns that an enemy nation of the United States has misinterpreted his boasts. Assuming that the moon will become a launching platform for missiles, the enemy has attacked the United States and so plunged the world into nuclear war. Trapped between a dead moon and a planet now engulfed in total war, the survivors on the ship decide to return to Earth. This decision is the lone moment of heroism in the play.

Night of the Auk was produced on Broadway in 1956 with a cast headed by Christopher Plummer and Claude Rains. It was revived in New York in 1963. Neither production was a critical or a popular success.

Olson, Elder, "The Illusionists." *Plays and Poems, 1948–58*. Chicago: University of Chicago Press, 1958. 72–120.

Written by the well-known literary critic, *The Illusionists* is an interesting play that takes place on a planet governed by a small group of aesthetes. They are visited by Forsell, the leader of the "world state" that controls the Earth. Proud of the industry and productivity of the conformist society he heads, Forsell is at first repulsed by the petty bickering and self-indulgence that he sees. He discovers, however, that the aesthetes also have developed a conformist society, one that is actually more efficient than his. The aesthetes have enslaved the millions of their population by attaching them to "'illusion machines." In their dreams, these slaves are fully satisfied, experiencing all they could desire. The aesthetes, psychological vampires, are the managers of the system. Attracted to this world of pleasurable conformity, Forsell willingly attaches himself to an illusion machine.

Ressieb, George. *Danger from the Sky*. New York: Samuel French, 1957.

Reflecting the optimism in science that characterized the early 1950s, *Danger from the Sky* is a curious play that mixes domestic comedy, a murder mystery, and a scientific adventure. Nominally depicting the effect visitors from another planet have upon an American family living in a small western town, the play ultimately offers a rather heavy-handed discourse on free will and the nature of God.

The play begins lightly, focusing on the social problems of the two Brandon girls, a teenager who is inquisitive about virtually everything and a 22-year-old who is juggling two boyfriends. Their father, Lucius Brandon, is a top physicist conducting experiments for the military on Project Milky Way. Although he is being pressured to complete his work, Brandon is actually stalling. He hesitates in completing his research because he questions the morality of the project. As he tells an overly patriotic government official, "I'm a scientist—I must think of other countries, other people—I must think of people first and countries second" (50).

All of the play's action takes place in the Brandon living room; in fact, Brandon's laboratory is in his home. Into this domestic scene comes the glamorous Countess Fras-chetti, a new neighbor whose appearance has provoked much speculation in the community. Coincidentally, there have been sightings of flying saucers among the local people, especially among the native Americans living in the area.

As a neighbor, albeit an exotic one, she is welcomed into the Brandon home as a guest. The audience learns, however, that the Countess is from another planet and has come to stop Brandon, warning him that scientific inquiries such as Project Milky Way will destroy "the balance of the entire cosmos" (71).

Outwardly charming and still maintaining her pose as a neighbor, the Countess is in reality vicious. Realizing that native Americans can sense an alien presence, the Countess gives little thought to killing a maid who works for the Brandons. Then the Countess coldly plans to kidnap Brandon because her people "understand the necessity of adding new strains from time to time, of improving and refining our lines" (69).

When her kidnapping plot fails, the Countess reveals to Brandon who she is. Hoping to appeal to Brandon's sense of intellectual superiority, she describes her society—one of leaders and workers. But her boast that her society simply dispenses with the workers when they are no longer needed horrifies Brandon. Brandon, the intellectual, the astute scientist, finally invokes religious imagery. In refusing the Countess, Brandon vows to

continue with his research because "God made us free, and gave us the will to be free.
. . . I'll keep going ahead, doing what I have to do, as long as God will let me" (76).

Richards, I. A. "A Leak in the Universe." *Playbook: Five Plays for a New Theatre*.
    Ed. John Bernard Myers. New York: New Directions, 1956. 243–93.

Presented in 1954 as a home entertainment by Richards for the Poet's Theatre of
Cambridge, *A Leak in the Universe* was aired on the BBC Third Programme in 1955.
While the editor of *Playbook* labels this play a "science fiction fantasy," its science
fiction overtones are minimal.
    Set in the Institute for Advancing Studies, this play concerns a conjuror who is puzzled
by the disappearance of various objects when they are placed in a mysterious box he has
discovered. These disappearances cause the conjuror to speculate on the instability of
matter and its relationship to energy. Yet the conjuror finds that the box also absorbs
energy; consequently, he fears that if the box were broken, its mysterious "properties"
would spread and contaminate the universe. His speculations cease when the box itself
disappears.

Schulman, Charlie. "The Ground Zero Club." *InterPlay '85: Eleven Plays by Young
    People*. Sydney: Currency, 1985. 115–24.

Taking place on the observation deck of the Empire State Building in the half hour
before a nuclear attack, this play brings together a disparate group of New Yorkers (and
one tourist) who variously discover and reveal their secret fears, unfulfilled ambitions,
and unrecognized desires before the End. The play is clever, witty, and absurdist in tone.
    In the play's surprise ending, there is no final nuclear war. In an unplanned but
simultaneous action, each of the warring sides has sabotaged the other's missiles. The
play ends with a deactivated missile crashing into the observation deck—killing only the
tourist. The survivors—a few with realigned relationships—continue on as before.

Shepard, Sam. *Operation Sidewinder*. Indianapolis: Bobbs-Merrill, 1970.

Requiring a large cast, *Operation Sidewinder* is a sprawling, episodic play about a
supercomputer shaped like a snake. Created by the Air Force for $2 billion, the computer
was intended to trace UFOs. The snake, however, having a mind of its own, has escaped
into the desert and seized in its coils a hapless tourist named Honey. It is through this
improbable beginning that Shepard critiques the military establishment and its fascination
with death machines. In contrast, Shepard positions the desert Hopi culture as one that
reaffirms life. The snake, having been decapitated in the course of the progressively
absurd events of the play, becomes the central symbol of the ritual that concludes the
play. As the Hopis perform their snake dance, a dance that will unite the snake's head
with its body, military forces intervene. The religious ritual is invaded by desert tactical
troops who reclaim the snake, accidentally tearing the head from the body once again.
At this moment, amid bolts of blue lightning and huge gusts of wind, the Indians become
transcendent and disappear into the cosmos, leaving behind the blinded and puzzled
tactical troops.
    This play was first presented in 1970 by the Repertory Theatre of Lincoln Center.

Shepard, Sam. "The Tooth of Crime." *Seven Plays*. New York: Bantam, 1984. 201–51.

Without direct references to science or technology, Sam Shepard, through his brilliant use of language, creates in *The Tooth of Crime* a futuristic, cyberpunk world drawn from contemporary images of race car drivers, cowboys, criminals, and rock stars. Large areas of the country are controlled by warring gangs and competing syndicates. This is not a totally chaotic world, however, for there is an implicit hierarchical structure. Ultimate power rests in the hands of a shadowy group called the Keepers who control the "game."

The Tooth of Crime centers on Hoss, an aging rock star and "killer" who was once a winner in the "game." Unfortunately, Hoss has not had a recent kill. Utilizing the western motif of the showdown, Shepard has Hoss meet a young rival named Crow in a "face-off" where the two literally fight with words. The contest between Hoss and Crow requires the control of performance technique, the perfection of style, and the artful manipulation of language. Hoss still clings to an antiquated code that celebrates a warrior existence. In contrast, Crow is arrogant, cynical, and adaptable, for as he says, "The image is my survival kit" (249). Unable to follow fashion, to live outside of the code, Hoss loses the match. His final gesture is to kill himself. In Hoss's words, this is an act that "can't be taught or copied or stolen or sold. It's mine. An original" (249).

Shepard, Sam. "The Unseen Hand." *The Unseen Hand and Other Plays*. New York: Bantam, 1986. 1–32.

First performed at the La Mama Experimental Theatre Club in 1969, *The Unseen Hand* is an arresting mixture of science fiction and Old West motifs. Periodically very funny, the play naively celebrates the freedom and individualism of the Old West.

The action occurs in and around a 1951 Chevrolet convertible, which is the home of Blue Morphan. One hundred and twenty years old, Blue is the last of the Morphan brothers, once a band of outlaws. Blue is now content to live in squalor, disdaining the present and reminiscing about the excitement of the old days.

Fleeing the Silent Ones of the High Commission, Willy the Space Freak suddenly appears near the Chevy and disrupts Blue's life. Willy hopes to enlist Blue and his brothers, Cisco and Sycamore (whom Willy resurrects from the dead), to go with blazing six guns to his planet Nogoland and fight the repressive Silent Ones. Though they are almost pure intellect, the Silent Ones, Willy maintains, would not know how to respond to six guns.

Willy is controlled by the unseen hand, a repressive force, which causes excruciating pain whenever he thinks of freedom. Lapsing into a trance and speaking in glossolalia the ancient language of Nogoland, Willy frees himself from the power of the hand. Convinced that the Silent Ones are dead, Willy returns to his planet. As he leaves the Morphan brothers, he tells them that they too have the power to do whatever they want. Nonetheless, all three brothers feel lost and displaced in the twentieth century. With vague intentions of simply moving on, Blue and Cisco wander off. Alone, Sycamore takes up residence in the Chevy.

Sinclair, Upton. *The Enemy Had It Too*. New York: Viking, 1950.

Written by the author of *The Jungle*, this curious, almost unplayable drama is primarily set in a Manhattan all but destroyed by bacteriological warfare. Hoping to awe his audiences with scenes of a city completely devoid of human life, Sinclair requires back-drops that are detailed and realistically painted. Sinclair's purpose in writing *The Enemy Had It Too* is serious. In his dedication, he states, "I would like to have this play circulated inside the Soviet Union, and I dedicate it to anyone who will make the attempt." Unfortunately, his characters are superficial and their motivations improbable.

Into a deserted Manhattan wander the Angell family (anthropologist father, daughter and son saved from contamination by their previous isolation in the jungles of Colombia). Blowguns in hand, the family wanders from Wall Street to Grant's Tomb, encountering hostile survivors of the plague. With a heavy-handed allusion to Ezra Pound, Sinclair quickly presents the most improbable of these survivors—Ebenezer Ounce, "the most modern poet." Delighting in the solitude of a world decimated by plague, Ounce informs the Angells that he was once declared insane by the government and was subsequently imprisoned. Now he gloats that he has survived all the disasters of modern civilization—even the critics (51–52).

Sadly, Ounce is the play's only memorable character. In spite of their ironic position as innocent savages about to claim the destroyed financial capital of the world, the Angells are really an uninspired lot. Their dialogue is consistently banal; there is no sense of outrage, of amazement, or of wonder about their situation. Indifferent reporters, they merely comment upon the destruction at different sites.

In order to capitalize upon the elaborate *mise en scène* his play requires, Sinclair often has the Angell father describe the histories of the buildings that line Wall Street and then moralize upon the greed and mistrust that led to the destruction of the city. His tone, and that of his children, is flat. This flatness persists even when they meet a family from Iceland (consisting of son, daughter, and father, Leif). With such neat symmetry, romance quickly develops among the youngsters. As Leif improbably phrases it, "Here is a miracle; Arctic and the Equator have met; and out of this meeting will come a new race dedicated to peace, brotherhood, and mutual aid" (111).

These congratulations are suddenly interrupted by the returning rocket of the Harry S. Truman Expedition to Mars. It lands near Riverside Parkway and soon dispenses Captain Engstrom, his pilot, Morgan, and "two ladies from Mars": short, scaly, golden, and pregnant by the earth explorers. Equipped with digging claws instead of hands and feet, the Martians immediately burrow into the soil and disappear. Since "Martian genes [are] dominant" (118), Engstrom predicts that the Martians will soon "possess all the five continents of the earth and all the islands" (123). With the fortunes of Earth so determined, the band of human beings decides to abandon the planet and return with Engstrom to colonize Mars.

Spencer, James. "A Bunch of the Gods Were Sitting around One Day." *Playwrights for Tomorrow: A Collection of Plays.* Ed. Arthur H. Ballet. Vol. 12. Minneapolis: University of Minnesota Press, 1975. 207–67.

Presented in 1973 by the American Conservatory Theatre of San Francisco, *A Bunch of the Gods Were Sitting around One Day* concerns a group of seven space travelers who are the last survivors of a large interplanetary expedition of 46 crew members.

After the ship's computer had mysteriously shut down, the ship became trapped in orbit around an Earth-like planet. During seven generations of entrapment, the numbers of the crew steadily declined and finally stabilized at seven. Attempting to maintain this population balance, the crew determined that there could be no birth unless there was first a death.

Considering himself to be the least useful member of the crew, Sasha, an artist and poet, contemplates suicide. Some of the group encourage Sasha to kill himself. As the group argues the necessity and even the morality of such a death, each gradually comes to realize that the group is more than a loose collection of individuals. They realize that they are in essence one being, separate manifestations of a larger whole. So enlightened, the crew members each disavow the necessity for any act of violence.

Overhearing the debate, the ship's computers suddenly reengage and move the ship out of orbit. The revived computer informs the crew that it has actually been held in a type of quarantine by the computer itself. The computer's "higher consciousness" has sensed that the moral disease that afflicted the crew—namely, the failure to perceive that the whole can only benefit by the sum of its individual parts—has been cured through the process of debating and disowning acts of violence. Cured, the crew makes preparations to land on the planet.

Terry, Megan. *Megan Terry's Home: Or, Future Soap*. New York: Samuel French, 1967.

Originally written in 1967 for television and later revised by Terry for the stage, *Home* depicts an overpopulated Earth (as are the other planets in the solar system) totally encased in plastic. All people live inside the Earth having been assigned by the government to live within artificial "family" groups of nine members. One's entire life, from birth to death, is spent within a single room. Central Control regulates all aspects of life. Human instincts and spontaneous actions are minimized in this artificial environment.

A typical day is divided into formalized and controlled activities which the actors must portray in a ritualized style suggesting the authority's command over human spontaneity. Yet on this day, one family is particularly anxious, for Central Control may grant two of its members, Cynthia and Roy, permission to marry. Luckily, because the family has amassed enough work credits, they are allowed to marry.

The wedding ceremony is disrupted by the breakdown in the planet's life support system and by the appearance of a stranger at the air vent of the home. This man, who has survived the death chute, tries to crawl in. Shouting "I won't let you suck the breath from my babies," Ruth, the group's mother, kills the man. In this scene, the most effective of the play, Terry dramatizes human sponanteity amid the authority's control. Ruth illustrates the sudden emergence of instinct, of the desire to protect what one knows and loves.

Vidal, Gore. *Visit to a Small Planet*. Boston: Little, Brown, 1956.

Visit to a Small Planet is a comedy that satirizes the military and its Cold War attitudes toward the threat of invasion and war. In it, the Earth is visited by the alien Kreton. Originally planning to land in Manassas, Virginia, during the Civil War, Kreton has miscalculated and lands instead a century later in the 1950s. This error in judgment is just the first of a series that precipitates a national crisis. Kreton looks like a fully grown adult human being, but on his planet he is a child. Morally immature, he wants to start a war among the nations of the Earth for his own amusement. It is only through the last-minute intervention of an advanced representative from Kreton's planet that war is averted. A chastised Kreton is returned to his nursery.

This stage version is actually an adaptation of a television play written by Vidal for the Philco-Goodyear Playhouse. Shown on May 8, 1955, this version is much darker in tone than is the stage version. In the television production, Kreton really does start a war.

Wilson, Edmund. "The Little Blue Light." *Five Plays*. New York: Farrar, 1954. 417–541.

An interesting but ultimately unsatisfying play of ideas, *The Little Blue Light* is set in the near future. The two-party system has collapsed, and the U.S. government, now unstructured and directionless, is the focus of a political war among a number of self-interest groups. The most dominant of these is the Luke Teniakis Relief Bureau. Once a benevolent, idealistically motivated organization, the Teniakis group is now involved in political assassination.

What is most frightening about the Teniakis group is its method of assassination. The Teniakis organization possesses a secret weapon that can be disguised to look like a harmless object. The device is sensitive to human emotions and can be triggered by expressions of anger or hatred. The weapon then releases a small but powerful blue light that has the capability of killing all those who are near it.

The action of the play takes place in the New York country home of Gansvoort von Gandersheim, a liberal magazine editor. In the course of the play, Gandersheim becomes aware of the insidiousness of the Teniakis organization and crusades against it. A member of the Teniakis group hides the weapon, disguised as a flashlight, in Gandersheim's comfortable home. The play ends when squabbling among the major characters triggers the device. All but one of them die. The lone survivor is a gardener, seemingly a minor character, who reveals himself to be the Wandering Jew. He closes the play bemoaning the lack of spiritual light in humankind.

"The Little Blue Light" was first produced in 1950 by the Cambridge Summer Playhouse starring Jessica Tandy and Hume Cronyn. It later moved to Broadway in 1951 for an unsuccessful run with an impressive cast: Martin Gabel, Arlene Francis, Melvyn Douglas, and Burgess Meredith.

Zindel, Paul. "Let Me Hear You Whisper." *Six Science Fiction Plays*. Ed. Roger Elwood. New York: Pocket, 1976. 357–88.

Paul Zindel has written an engaging and humorous two-act play that comments on the controversial subject of animal experimentation.

Helen, the play's main character, has been hired to mop floors and clean the laboratories of the American Biological Association Development for the Advancement of Brain Analysis (Abadaba, for short). Helen becomes concerned with the plight of a dolphin being used in a series of animal communication studies. The dolphin has failed to communicate with the scientists and is slated to be killed.

As Helen works around the tank that houses the dolphin, it slowly begins to respond to her presence. It finally speaks to Helen in English, informing her that Abadaba ultimately intends to use dolphins in warfare—in planting mines and in attaching underwater bombs. Horrified, Helen attempts to rescue the dolphin by lifting it out of its tank and carrying it to a nearby river. She is caught, however, and fired from her job. Just before the association doctors inject the dolphin with poison, the dolphin whispers the word "Love." The excited doctors, recognizing that Helen has given them a breakthrough, encourage her to stay and continue speaking to the dolphin. Helen, sensing that the dolphin has already saved itself and disgusted by the indifference of the scientists to an animal's suffering, rejects their offer.

Zindel's play is an appropriate one with which to end this listing of science fiction for the theater, for it reflects the nature of the questions that critics pose about science fiction on the stage. Very little concern is shown by Zindel for the scientific procedure by which one attempts to communicate with dolphins. Yet, in applying Scholes' definition of structural fabulation, the play certainly illustrates the impact of science on one's life, in this instance, on Helen's.

Selected Bibliography

PRIMARY SOURCES (EXCLUSIVE OF KRUPNIK'S ANNOTATED BIBLIOGRAPHY)

Aeschylus. *The Oresteia.* Trans. Robert Fagles. New York: Viking, 1975.

Alien. Dir. Ridley Scott. With Tom Skerritt and Sigourney Weaver. 1979.

Artaud, Antonin. *Collected Works.* 4 vols. London: Calder, 1971.

————. "Production Plan for Strindberg's *The Ghost Sonata.*" *Collected Works.* Vol. 4. London: Calder, 1971. 97–105. 4 vols.

————. *The Theatre and Its Double.* 1938. Trans. Mary Caroline Richards. Rpt. New York: Grove, 1958.

————. *The Theatre and Its Double.* Trans. Victor Corti. London: Calder, 1970.

————. *Le théâtre et son double.* Paris: Gallimard, 1964.

Beckett, Samuel. "Breath." *First Love and Other Shorts.* New York: Grove, 1974.

————. "Catastrophe." *Ohio Impromptu, Catastrophe, and What Where.* New York: Grove, 1984.

————. "Embers." *Krapp's Last Tape and Other Dramatic Pieces.* New York: Grove, 1970.

————. *Endgame.* New York: Grove, 1958.

————. *Happy Days.* New York: Grove, 1961.

————. *Le Kid.* Unpublished and apparently lost.

————. "Krapp's Last Tape." *Krapp's Last Tape and Other Dramatic Pieces.* New York: Grove, 1970.

————. *More Pricks than Kicks.* New York: Grove, 1972.

————. "Not I." *Ends and Odds.* New York: Grove, 1976.

————. "Play." *Cascando and Other Short Dramatic Pieces.* New York: Grove, 1978.

————. *Proust.* New York: Grove, 1957.

————. "That Time." *Ends and Odds.* New York: Grove, 1976.

————. *Waiting for Godot.* New York: Grove, 1954.

————. *Worstward Ho.* New York: Grove, 1983.

————, and George Duthuit. *Three Dialogues*. 1949. Rpt. *Proust and Three Dialogues*. London: Calder, 1965. 97–126.

'Blaue Reiter' Almanac, The. Ed. Wassily Kandinsky and Franz Marc. New Documentary Edition. Ed. Klaus Lankheit. New York: Viking, 1974.

Borges, Jorge Luis. "A Theologian in Death." *A Universal History of Infamy*. Trans. Norman Thomas di Giovanni. Hormondsworth, England: Penguin, 1975. 103–5.

Brecht, Bertolt. *Brecht on Theatre*. Ed. and trans. John Willett. New York: Hill and Wang, 1964.

Capek, Karl. *RUR: A Fantastic Melodrama*. Garden City, N.Y.: Doubleday, 1923.

Carlton, Bob. *Return to the Forbidden Planet*. London: Methuen, 1985.

Cocteau, Jean. *La machine infernale: piece en 4 actes*. Paris: B. Grasset, 1934.

Corneille, Pierre. *Cid. The Chief Plays of Corneille*. Trans. Lacy Lockert. Princeton: Princeton University Press, 1957.

Dante. *Purgatorio*. Trans. John D. Sinclair. New York: Oxford University Press, 1979.

Duchamp, Marcel. *Opposition and Sister Squares Are Reconciled*. Brussels: L'Echiquier/ Edmond Lancel, 1932.

Ford, John. *'Tis Pity She's a Whore*. London: Benn, 1968.

Glass, Philip, and Robert Wilson. *Einstein on the Beach*. New York: Dunvagen Music Publishers, 1976.

Gray, Spalding. *Sex and Death to the Age 14*. New York: Vintage, 1986.

————. *Swimming to Cambodia*. New York: Theatre Communications Group, 1987.

Hwang, David Henry, Philip Glass, and Jerome Sirlin. *1000 Airplanes on the Roof: A Science Fiction Music-Drama*. Salt Lake City, Utah: Peregrine Smith, 1988.

Ionesco, Eugène. *Découvertes*. Geneva: Skira, 1969.

————. *Entre la vie et le rêve: entretiens avec Claude Bonnefoy*. Paris: Belfond, 1977.

————. *Fragments of a Journal*. Trans. Jean Stewart. London: Faber, 1968.

————. "L'insolite du langage." *Spirales* Mar.–Apr. 1984: 67–69.

————. "Jamais je n'ai écrit avec autant de plaisir sur des thèmes aussi sinistres." *Figaro littéraire* 7 Jan. 1972: 1 + .

————. *Notes and Counter Notes*. Trans. Donald Watson. New York: Grove, 1964.

————. *Plays*. Trans. Donald Watson, Derek Prouse, and Barbara Wright. 12 vols. London: Calder, 1958–85.

————. *Present Past Past Present*. Trans. Helen R. Lane. New York: Grove, 1971.

Johnston, Denis. *Selected Plays of Denis Johnston*. Chosen and with an introduction by Joseph Ronsley. *Irish Drama Selections 2*. Gerrards Cross, U.K.: Colin Smythe, 1983.

Kid, The. Dir. Charles Chaplin. With Charlie Chaplin, Jackie Coogan, and Edna Purviance. 1921.

Kyd, Thomas. *The Spanish Tragedy*. London: Oxford University Press, 1949.

Leivick, Halper. *The Golem*. In *Three Great Jewish Plays*. New York: Applause, 1986.

Lindsay, Kenneth C., and Peter Vergo, eds. *Kandinsky: Complete Writings on Art*. 2 vols. Boston: G. K. Hall, 1982.

Psycho. Dir. Alfred Hitchcock. With Anthony Perkins and Janet Leigh. 1960.

Röthel, H. K., and Jelena Hahl-Koch, eds. *Wassily Kandinsky's Gesammelte Schriften*. Vol. 1. Berne: Bentelli, 1980.

Shakespeare, William. *The Complete Works*. Baltimore: Penguin, 1969.

Shelley, Mary. *Frankenstein: or, The Modern Prometheus*. Ed. M. K. Joseph. London: Oxford University Press, 1969.

Shepard, Sam. *Action*. 1976. Rpt. *"Fool for Love" and Other Plays*. New York: Bantam, 1984. 167–90.

———. "Icarus's Mother." *"Chicago" and Other Plays*. 1969. Rpt. Boston: Faber, 1982. 25–60.

———. *The Tooth of Crime*. 1974. Rpt. *Seven Plays*. New York: Bantam, 1984. 201–51.

Stoppard, Tom. *Rosencrantz and Guildenstern Are Dead*. New York: Grove, 1967.

———. *Travesties*. New York: Grove, 1975.

Texas Chainsaw Massacre, The. Dir. Tobe Hooper. With Marilyn Burns and Gunner Hansen. 1974.

Walcott, Derek. "The Caribbean." *Journal of Interamerican Studies and World Affairs* 16 (1974): 12.

———. *Dream on Monkey Mountain and Other Plays*. New York: Farrar, 1970.

———. "Man of the Theatre." Interview. *The New Yorker* June 1971: 30.

Webster, John. *The Duchess of Malfi*. Cambridge: Harvard University Press, 1964.

Wilde, Oscar. *The Complete Works of Oscar Wilde*. 12 vols. New York: Doubleday, 1923.

———. "The Decay of Lying." *The Artist as Critic: Critical Writings of Oscar Wilde*. Ed. Richard Ellman. New York: Vintage, 1969.

Yeats, William Butler. *Essays and Introductions*. New York: Macmillan, 1961.

———. *The Letters of W. B. Yeats*. Ed. Allen Wade. New York: Macmillan, 1955.

———. *The Poems*. Rev. New York: Macmillan, 1989. Vol. 1 of *The Collected Works of W. B. Yeats*. Ed. Richard J. Finneran and George Mills Harper. 14 vols. 1989–.

———. *Samhain. October 1901–November 1908*. Rpt. Complete in 1 vol. with additional material. Introd. B. C. Bloomfield. London: Frank Cass, 1970.

———. *The Variorum Edition of the Plays of W. B. Yeats*. Ed. Russell K. Alspach. New York: Macmillan, 1966.

———. *The Variorum Edition of the Poems of W. B. Yeats*. Ed. Peter Alt and Russell K. Alspach. New York: Macmillan, 1965.

———. *A Vision and Related Writings*. Comp. and ed. Norman Jeffares. London: Arena, 1990.

SECONDARY SOURCES

General

Aristotle. *The Poetics*. Trans. S. H. Butcher. Introd. Francis Fergusson. New York: Hill and Wang, 1961.

Ausubel, Nathan, ed. *A Treasury of Jewish Folklore*. New York: Crown, 1948.

Bell, Hesketh J. *Obeah: Witchcraft in the West Indies*. New Haven: Negro Universities Press, 1970.

Benjamin, Walter. *Understanding Brecht*. Trans. Anna Bostock. London: NLB, 1977.

ben Joseph, Akiba. *The Book of Formation/Sepher Yetzirah*. Trans. Knut Stenring. New York: Ktav, 1970.

Bersani, Leo. *Baudelaire and Freud*. Berkeley: University of California Press, 1977.

bin Gorion, Micha Joseph, comp. *Mimekor Yisrael: Classical Jewish Folktales*. Ed. Emmanuel bin Gorion. Trans. I. M. Lask. Bloomington: Indiana University Press, 1976.

Blackmur, R. P. *Language as Gesture: Essays in Poetry*. New York: Columbia University Press, 1980.

Blavatsky, H. P. *The Key to Theosophy*. 1889. Rpt. Pasadena, Calif.: Theosophical University Press, 1972.

Bloch, Chayim. *The Golem: Mystical Tales from the Ghetto of Prague*. Trans. Harry Schneiderman. Blauvelt, N.Y.: Rudolf Steiner, 1975.

Blumenthal, David. R. *The Merkabak Tradition and the Zoharic Tradition*. New York: Ktav, 1978. Vol. 1 of *Understanding Jewish Mysticism: A Source Reader*. 2 vols.

Bottcher, Kurt, and Johannes Mittenzwei. *Dichter also Maler*. Stuttgart: Kohlhammer, 1980.

Brisch, Klaus. "Untersuchungen zur Entstehung der gegenstandslosen Malerei an seinem Werk von 1900–1921." Diss. University of Bonn, 1955.

Chipp, Herschel B., ed. *Theories of Modern Art: A Source Book by Artists and Critics*. Berkeley: University of California Press, 1968.

de Man, Paul. "The Rhetoric of Temporality." *Interpretation: Theory and Practice*. Ed. Charles S. Singleton. Baltimore: Johns Hopkins University Press, 1969, 173–209.

Derrida, Jacques. "No Apocalypse, Not Now (Full Speed Ahead, Seven Missiles, Seven Missives)." Trans. Catherine Porter and Philip Lewis. *Diacritics* 14 (Summer 1984): 20–31.

———. *Of Grammatology*. 1967. Trans. Gayatri Chakravorty Spivak. Rpt. Baltimore: Johns Hopkins University Press, 1976.

Eco, Umberto. "Producing Signs." *On Signs*. Ed. Marshall Blonsky. Baltimore: Johns Hopkins University Press, 1985. 176–83.

———. *Semiotics and the Philosophy of Language*. Bloomington: Indiana University Press, 1984.

———. *A Theory of Semiotics*. Bloomington: Indiana University Press, 1976.

———. "Towards a New Middle Ages." *On Signs*. Ed. Marshall Blonsky. Baltimore: Johns Hopkins University Press, 1985. 488–504.

Eisenstein, Sergei M. *The Film Sense*. Trans. and ed. Jay Leyda. New York: Harcourt, 1947. 113–17.

Ekman, Paul, ed. *Darwin and Facial Expression*. New York: Academic Press, 1973.

Fann, K. T. *Peirce's Theory of Abduction*. The Hague: Martinus Nijhoff, 1970.

Foucault, Michel. *This Is Not a Pipe: With Illustrations and Letters by René Magritte*. Trans. and ed. James Harkness. Berkeley: University of California Press, 1983.

Gascoyne, David. *A Short Survey of Surrealism*. 2nd ed. San Francisco: City Lights, 1982.

Glut, Donald F. *The Frankenstein Legend: A Tribute to Mary Shelley and Boris Karloff*. Metuchen, N.J.: Scarcrow, 1973.

Graves, Robert. *The White Goddess*. London: Faber, 1961.

Gunther, Herbert. *Kunstlerische Doppelbegabungen*. Munich: Ernst Heimeran, 1938. 2nd ed. 1960.

Harpham, Geoffrey. *On the Grotesque: Strategies of Contradiction in Art and Literature*. Princeton: Princeton University Press, 1982.

Heffernan, James A. W. "Resemblance, Signification, and Metaphor in the Visual Arts." *Journal of Aesthetics and Art Criticism* 44 (1985): 167–80.

Hill, Sir Francis. *Medieval Lincoln*. Cambridge: Cambridge University Press, 1965.

Holland, Peter. Review of *Metropolis*. *Times Literary Supplement* 17 March 1989: 279.

Holman, C. Hugh, and William Harmon. *A Handbook to Literature*. 5th ed. New York: Macmillan, 1986.

Hooper, Kent. *Ernst Barlach's Literary and Visual Art: The Issue of Multiple Talent*. Ann Arbor: UMI Research Press, 1987.

Huizinga, J. *Homo Ludens: A Study of the Play-Element in Culture*. Boston: Beacon, 1950.

Idel, Moshe. *Golem: Jewish Magical and Mystical Traditions on the Artificial Anthropoid*. Albany: State University of New York Press, 1989.

Innis, Robert. *Semiotics: An Introductory Anthology*. Bloomington: Indiana University Press, 1985.

Jung, C. G. "A Psychological Theory of Types." *The Collected Works of C. G. Jung*. Trans. H. G. Baynes. Rev. R.F.C. Hall. Ed. H. Read et al. Bollingen Series 20. Vol. 6. Princeton: Princeton University Press, 1971. 524–41. 19 vols.

King, Bruce. *West Indian Literature*. London: Macmillan, 1979.

Knapp, Bettina L. *French Theatre 1918–1939*. London: Macmillan, 1985.

Kristeva, Julia. *Powers of Horror: An Essay on Abjection*. Trans. Leon S. Roudiez. New York: Columbia University Press, 1982.

Lasch, Christopher. *The Minimal Self: Psychic Survival in Troubled Times*. New York: Norton, 1984.

McNerney, Kathleen. "Reinterpretations of the Classics: What's Old and What's New in Catalonia." *Studies in the Humanities* 17.2 (1990): 172–78.

Madison, Charles A. *Yiddish Literature: Its Scope and Major Writers*. New York: Frederick Ungar, 1968.

Maharishi Mahesh Yogi. *On the Bhagavad-Gita*. Harmondsworth, England: Penguin, 1969.

Nash, Cristopher. *World Games: The Tradition of Anti-Realist Revolt*. New York: Methuen, 1987.

Patai, Raphael. *The Messiah Texts*. Detroit: Wayne State University Press, 1979.

Peirce, Charles Sanders. *Collected Papers*. 8 vols. Ed. Charles Hartshorne, Paul Weiss, and Arthur Burks. Cambridge: Harvard University Press, 1935–38.

Ramchand, Kenneth. *West Indian Literature*. Nairobi: Nelson Caribbean, 1980.

Ringbom Sixteen. "Art in the Epoch of the Great Spiritual." *Journal of the Warburg and Courtauld Institutes* 29 (1966): 386–418.

Sanhedrin. Trans. Jacob Schachter and H. Freedman. In *The Babylonian Talmud: Seder Nelzikin*. Vol. 3. Ed. I. Epstein. London: Soncino, 1935.

Scholem, Gershom. *On the Kabbalah and Its Symbolism*. Trans. Ralph Manheim. New York: Schocken, 1969.

Shawcross, William. *Sideshow: Kissinger, Nixon and the Destruction of Cambodia*. New York: Simon and Schuster, 1979.

Simons, G. L. *The Witchcraft World*. New York: Harper and Row, 1974.

Stace, W. T. *Mysticism and Philosophy*. London: Macmillan, 1960.

Suleiman, Susan Rubin. "Redundancy and the 'Readable' Text." *Poetics Today* 1 (1980): 119–42.

Tolstoy, Leo. "What Is Art?" [Trans. Aylmer Maude]. *The Novels and Other Works of*

Lyof N. Tolstoï: The Kingdom of God Is within You. What Is Art? Ed. Nathan
    Haskell Dole. 22 vols. New York: Charles Scribner's Sons, 1899–1902. Vol. 19:
    337–47.
Zohar, The. Trans. Harry Sperling and Maurice Simon. 5 vols. London: Soncino, 1934.

Drama and Performance Theater

Abbott, Anthony S. *The Vital Lie: Reality and Illusion in Modern Drama.* Tuscaloosa:
    University of Alabama Press, 1989.
Ansorge, Peter. *Disrupting the Spectacle: Five Years of Experimental Theatre in Britain.*
    London: Pittman, 1975.
Bauman, Richard. *Story, Performance and Event.* New York: Cambridge University
    Press, 1986.
Belsey, Catherine. *The Subject of Tragedy: Identity and Difference in Renaissance Drama.*
    New York: Methuen, 1985.
Bentley, Eric. *The Playwright as Thinker.* New York: Meridian, 1955.
Birdwhistell, Ray L. *Kinesics and Context.* Philadelphia: University of Pennsylvania
    Press, 1970.
———. "Kinesics: Inter- and Intra-Channel Communication Research." *Essays in Se-
    miotics.* Ed. Julia Kristeva, Josette rey-Debove, Donna Jean Umiker. Paris: The
    Hague, 1971. 527–46.
Blau, Herbert. "Universals of Performance; or Amortizing Play." *Sub-Stance* 37/38
    (1982): 140–61. Rpt. *The Eye of Prey: Subversions of the Postmodern.* Bloom-
    ington: Indiana University Press, 1987. 161–88.
Brook, Peter. *The Empty Space.* New York: Atheneum, 1968.
Corrigan, Robert W. "The Search for New Endings: The Theatre in Search of a Fix,
    Part III." *Theatre Journal* 36 (May 1984): 153–63.
Dutton, Richard. *Modern Tragi-comedy and the British Tradition.* Norman: University
    of Oklahoma Press, 1986.
Elam, Keir. *The Semiotics of Theatre and Drama.* New York: Methuen, 1980.
Esslin, Martin. *Artaud.* London: Fontana, 1976.
———. *The Field of Drama: How the Signs of Drama Create Meaning on Stage and
    Screen.* New York: Methuen, 1987.
Goodman, Randolph. *Drama on Stage.* 2nd ed. Fort Worth, Tex.: Holt, 1978.
Grotowski, Jerzy. *Towards a Poor Theatre.* New York: Simon and Schuster, 1968.
Hartigan, Karelisa, ed. *Text and Presentation.* New York: University Press of America,
    1988.
Hayman, Ronald. *Theatre and Anti-Theatre: New Movements since Beckett.* New York:
    Oxford University Press, 1979.
Hogan, Robert, Richard Burnham, and David Poteet. *The Rise of the Realists 1910–
    1915. The Modern Irish Drama: A Documentary History IV.* Dublin: The Doleman
    Press, 1979.
Hogan, Robert, and James Kilroy. *Laying the Foundations 1902–1904. The Modern Irish
    Drama: a documentary history II.* Dublin: Doleman Press, 1976.
Homan, Sidney. *The Audience as Actor and Character: The Modern Theater of Beckett,
    Brecht, Genet, Ionesco, Pinter, Stoppard, and Williams.* Lewisburg, Pa.: Bucknell
    University Press, 1987.

Hornby, Richard. *Drama, Melodrama, and Perception.* Lewisburg, Pa.: Bucknell University Press, 1986.

Inverso, MaryBeth. *The Gothic Impulse in Contemporary Drama.* Ann Arbor: UMI Research Press, 1990.

Jelavich, Peter. *Munich and Theatrical Modernism: Politics, Playwriting, and Performance, 1890–1914.* Cambridge: Harvard University Press, 1985.

Kaprow, Allan. *Assemblage, Environments & Happenings.* New York: Abrams, 1966.

Kerr, Walter. Review of *Via Galactica* by Christopher Gore, Judith Ross, and Galt McDermot. *New York Times* 10 Dec. 1972: 3.

Kosson, Robert M. "*1000 Airplanes on the Roof.* By Philip Glass, David Henry Hwang, and Jerome Sirlin." *Journal of Dramatic Theory and Criticism* 3 (Spring 1989): 209–11.

Kristeva, Julia. "Le geste: practique ou communication?" *Semeiotike: recherches pour une semanalyse.* Paris: Editions du Seuil, 1969. 90–112.

McNamara, Brooks, and Jill Dolan, eds. *The Drama Review: Thirty Years of Commentary on the Avant-Garde.* Ann Arbor: UMI Research Press, 1986.

Marranca, Bonnie. "Nuclear Theatre." 1982. Rpt. *Theatrewritings.* New York: Performing Arts Journal Publications, 1984.

———. "Robert Wilson, the Avant-Garde, and the Audience: *Einstein on the Beach.*" 1977. Rpt. *Theatrewritings.* New York: Performing Arts Journal Publications, 1984. 116–22.

———. "The Theatre of Images: An Introduction." 1977. Rpt. *Theatrewritings.* New York: Performing Arts Journal Publications, 1984. 77–82.

———. *Theatrewritings.* New York: Performing Arts Journal Publications, 1984.

Mayberry, Bob. *Theatre of Discord: Dissonance in Beckett, Albee, and Pinter.* Rutherford, N.J.: Fairleigh Dickinson University Press, 1989.

Pavis, Patrice. "Problems of a Semiology of Theatrical Gesture." *Poetics Today* 2 (1981): 65–93.

Peter, John Desmond. *Vladimir's Carrot: Modern Drama and the Modern Imagination.* Chicago: University of Chicago Press, 1987.

Quigley, Austin E. *The Modern Stage and Other Worlds.* New York: Methuen, 1985.

Raben, Estelle Manette. *Major Strategies in Twentieth-Century Drama: Apocalyptic Vision, Allegory, and Open Form.* New York: Peter Lang, 1989.

Schechner, Richard. *The End of Humanism: Writings on Performance.* New York: Performing Arts Journal Publications, 1982.

Shank, Theodore. *American Alternative Theatre.* 120 photographs. 1982. Rpt. New York: St. Martin's, 1988.

———. *California Permanence: Volume One / San Francisco Bay Area. Interviews and Essays.* 157 illustrations. Claremont, Calif.: The Mime Journal, 1989.

———. "Framing Actuality; Thirty Years of Experimental Theatre, 1959–1989." *Around the Absurd.* Ed. Enoch Brater and Ruby Cohn. Ann Arbor: University of Michigan Press, 1990.

———. *Theatre in Real Time; Materiali per uno studio sul Nuovo Teatro. America—Inghilterra dal 1968.* 500 photographs. Milano: Studio Forma Editrice, 1980.

Speigel, John P., and Pavel Machotka. *Messages of the Body.* New York: Macmillan, 1974.

Worth, Katharine. *The Irish Drama of Europe from Yeats to Beckett.* Dover, N.H.: Athlone Press, 1986.

Expressionism

Denkler, Horst. *Drama des Expressionismus: Program, Spieltext, Theater*. Munich: Wilhelm Fink, 1967.

———, ed. *Einakter und kleine Dramen des Expressionismus*. Stuttgart: Philipp Reclam, 1968.

Eykman, Christoph. *Denk- und Stilformen des Expressionismus*. Munich: A. Franke, 1974.

Pörtner, Paul. "Expressionismus and Theater." *Expressionismus als Literatur: Gesammelte Studien*. Ed. Wolfgang Rothe. Bern and Munich: Francke, 1969. 194–211.

Ritchie, J. M. *German Expressionist Drama*. Boston: Twayne, 1976.

Schreyer, Lothar. *Expressionistisches Theater: Aus meninen Erinnerungen*. Hamburg: J. P. Toth, 1948.

Fantasy

Apter, T. E. *Fantasy Literature: An Approach to Reality*. Bloomington: Indiana University Press, 1982.

Brooke-Rose, Christine. *A Rhetoric of the Unreal: Studies in Narrative and Structure, Especially of the Fantastic*. New York: Cambridge University Press, 1981.

Burgin, Victor, James Donald, and Cora Kaplan. "Preface." *Formations of Fantasy*. Ed. Burgin, Donald, and Kaplan. New York: Methuen, 1986. 1–4.

Cersowsky, Peter. "The Copernican Revolution in the History of Fantastic Literature at the Beginning of the Twentieth Century." *The Scope of the Fantastic: Theory, Technique, Major Authors*. Ed. Robert A. Collins and Howard D. Pearce. Westport, Conn.: Greenwood Press, 1985. 19–26.

———. *Phantastiche Literatur im ersten Viertel des 20. Jarhunderdts*. Munich: W. Fink, 1983.

Ceserani Remo. "Genre Theory, Literary History, and the Fantastic." *Literary Theory and Criticism*. Ed. Joseph P. Strelka. *Part I: Theory*. Bern: Peter Lang, 1984. 121–38.

Clareson, Thomas D., ed. *SF: The Other Side of Realism*. Bowling Green, Ohio: Bowling Green University Press, 1971.

Coyle, William. "Introduction." *Aspects of Fantasy: Selected Essays from the Second International Conference on the Fantastic in Literature and Film*. Ed. Coyle. Westport, Conn.: Greenwood Press, 1986. 1–3.

Elgin, Don. *The Comedy of the Fantastic: Ecological Perspectives on the Fantasy Novel*. Westport, Conn.: Greenwood Press, 1985.

Fischer, Jens Malte. "Science Fiction—Phantastik—Fantasy: Ein Vorshlag zu ihrer Abrenzung." *Neugier oder Fluht? Zu Poetik, Ideologie und Wirkung der Science Fiction*. Ed. Karl Ermert. Stuttgart: Ernst Klett, 1980. 8–17.

Fredericks, S. C. "Problems of Fantasty." *Science-Fiction Studies* 5 (1978): 33–44.

Hokenson, Jan, and Howard Pearce, eds. *Forms of the Fantastic*. Westport, Conn.: Greenwood Press, 1986.

Hume, Kathryn. *Fantasy and Mimesis: Responses to Reality in Western Literature*. New York: Methuen, 1984.

Irwin, W. R. *The Game of the Impossible: A Rhetoric of Fantasy*. Urbana: University of Illinois Press, 1976.

Jackson, Rosemary. *Fantasy, the Literature of Subversion*. London: Methuen, 1981.

Kagarlitski, Julius. "The Fantastic in Theater and Cinema." *Extrapolation* 22 (1981): 5–12.

Lenk, Elisabeth. *Kritische Phantasie: Gesammelte Essays*. Munich: Mattes and Seitz, 1986.

Lovecraft, Howard Phillips. *Supernatural Horror in Literature*. New York: Dover, 1973.

Lowry, Edward. "Genre and Enunciation: The Case of Horror." *Journal of Film and Video* 36.2 (Spring 1984): 13–20.

Malekin, Peter. "Shakespeare, Freedom, and the Fantastic." *Forms of the Fantastic*. Ed. Jan Hokenson and Howard D. Pearce. Westport, Conn.: Greenwood Press, 1986. 129–42.

Manlove, C. N. *The Impulse of Fantasy Literature*. Kent, Ohio: Kent State University Press, 1983.

———. *Modern Fantasy: Five Studies*. New York: Cambridge University Press, 1975.

Marzin, Florian. F. *Die phantastiche Literatur: Eine Gattungsstudie*. Frankfurt and Bern: Peter Lang, 1982.

Mobley, Jane. "Toward a Definition of Fantasy Fiction." *Extrapolation* 15 (1974): 117–28.

Murphy, Patrick D., and Vernon Hyles, ed. *The Poetic Fantastic: Studies in an Evolving Genre*. Westport, Conn.: Greenwood Press, 1989.

Palumbo, Don, ed. *Spectrum of the Fantastic*. Westport, Conn.: Greenwood Press, 1988.

Phaïcon: Almanach der phantastischen Literatur. Ed. Rein a Zondergeld. 6 vols. to date. Frankfurt: Insel, 1974–.

Rabkin, Eric S. *The Fantastic in Literature*. Princeton: Princeton University Press, 1976.

Rottenstein, Franz. "Vorwort: Zweifel und Gewiβheit. Zu Traditionen, Definitionen und einigen notwendigen Abrenzungen in der phantastiche Literatur." *Die dunkle Seit der Wirklichkeit. Aufsatze zur Phantastik*. Ed. Rottenstein. Frankfurt: Suhrkamp, 1987.

Sartre, Jean-Paul. "*Aminadab*, or the Fantastic Considered as a Language." *Literary and Philosophical Essays*. Trans. Annette Michelson. New York: Collier, 1955. 60–77.

Schlobin, Roger, ed. *The Aesthetics of Fantasy Literature and Art*. Notre Dame, Ind.: Notre Dame University Press, 1982.

———. "Fantasy versus Horror." *Survey of Modern Fantasy Literature*. Ed. Frank N. Magill. Englewood Cliffs, N.J.: Salem Press, 1983. 2259–66.

Scholes, Robert. *Structural Fabulation: An Essay on the Fiction of the Future*. Notre Dame, Ind.: Notre Dame University Press, 1975.

Siebers, Tobin. *The Romantic Fantastic*. Ithaca, N.Y.: Cornell University Press, 1984.

Slusser, George, and Eric S. Rabkin. *Shadows of the Magic Lamp: Fantasy and Science Fiction in Film*. Carbondale: Southern Illinois University Press, 1985.

Slusser, George E., Eric S. Rabkin, and Robert Scholes, eds. *Bridges to Fantasy*. Carbondale: Southern Illinois University Press, 1982.

Swinfen, Ann. *In Defence of Fantasy: A Study of the Genre in English and American Literature since 1945*. Boston: Routledge, 1984.

Thomsen, Christian, and Jens Malte Fischer, eds. *Phantastik in Literatur and Kunst*. Darmstadt: Wissenschaftliche Buchgesellschaft, 1980. 2nd. ed. 1985.

Todorov, Tzvetan. *Introduction à la littérature fantastique*. Paris: Editions du Seuil, 1970. *The Fantastic: A Structural Approach to a Literary Genre*. Trans. Richard Howard. Cleveland, Ohio: Case Western University Press, 1973. Ithaca, N.Y.: Cornell University Press, 1975.

Tolkien, J.R.R. "On Fairy Stories." *Essays Presented to Charles Williams*. Ed. C. S. Lewis. London: Oxford University Press, 1947. 38–89.

Tymn, Marshall B., Kenneth J. Zahorski, and Robert H. Boyer. *Fantasy Literature: A Core Collection and Reference Guide*. New York: R. R. Bowker, 1979.

Vax, Louis. *L'art et la littérature fantastiques*. Paris: Presses Universitaires de France, 1960.

Wolfe, Gary K. "Symbolic Fantasy." *Genre* 8 (1975) 194–209.

Wörtche, Thomas. *Phantastik und Unschlüssigkeit: Zum Strukturellen Kriterium eines Genres. Untersuchungen an Texten von Hanns Heinz Ewers und Gustav Meyrink*. Meitingen, Wimmer, 1987.

Postmodernism

Auslander, Philip. "Going with the Flow: Performance Art and Mass Culture." Unpublished manuscript.

———. "Toward a Concept of the Political in Postmodern Theater." *Theater Journal* March 1987: 20–34.

Baudrillard, Jean. "The Precession of Simulacra." *Art & Text* 11 (1983): 3–47.

———. "The Implosion of Meaning in the Media and the Implosion of the Social in the Masses." *The Myths of Information*. Ed. Kathleen Woodward. Madison, Wis.: Coda Press, 1980. 137–48.

Blau, Herbert. *The Eye of Prey: Subversions of the Postmodern*. Bloomington: Indiana University Press, 1987.

Brater, Enoch, and Ruby Cohn, eds. *Around the Absurd: Essays on Modern and Postmodern Drama*. Ann Arbor: University of Michigan Press, 1990.

Gitlin, Todd. "Hip-Deep in Post-modernism." *New York Times Book Review* 6 Nov. 1988: 1, 35–36.

Harvey, David. *The Condition of Postmodernity: An Enquiry into the Origins of Cultural Chaos*. Cambridge, Mass.: Basil Blackwell, 1989.

Hollinger, Veronica. "Specular SF: Postmodern Allegory." *State of the Fantastic: Studies in the Theory and Practice of Fantastic Literature and Film*. Selected Essays from the Eleventh International Conference on the Fantastic in the Arts, 1990. Ed. Nicholas Ruddick. Westport, Conn.: Greenwood Press, 1992. 29–39.

Hutcheon, Linda. *The Poetics of Postmodernism: History, Theory, Fiction*. New York: Routledge, 1988.

Huyssen, Andreas. *After the Great Divide: Modernism, Mass Culture, Postmodernism*. Bloomington: Indiana University Press, 1986.

Jameson, Fredric. "Postmodernism, or the Cultural Logic of Late Capitalism." *New Left Review* 146 (July/August 1984): 53–94.

McCaffery, Larry. "Introduction." *Postmodern Fiction: A Bio-Bibliographical Guide*. Ed. McCaffery. Westport, Conn.: Greenwood Press, 1986. xi–xxviii.

McHale, Brian. *Postmodernist Fiction*. New York: Methuen, 1987.

Olsen, Lance. *Circus of the Mind in Motion: Postmodernism and the Comic Vision*. Detroit: Wayne State University Press, 1990.

————. *Ellipse of Uncertainty: An Introduction to Postmodern Fantasy.* Westport, Conn.: Greenwood Press, 1987.

Owens, Craig. "The Allegorical Impulse: Toward a Theory of Postmodernism." *October* 13 (Summer 1980): 67–86.

Poster, Mark. *Critical Theory and Poststructuralism.* Ithaca, N.Y.: Cornell University Press, 1989.

Sofia, Zoë. "Exterminating Fetuses: Abortion, Disarmament, and the Sexo-Semiotics of Extraterrestialism." *Diacritics* 14 (Summer 1984): 47–59.

Science Fiction

Annas, George J. "The 'No Science Fiction on the Stage' Hypothesis." Paper presented at Ninth International Conference on the Fantastic in the Arts. Ft. Lauderdale, Fla., 16 Mar. 1988.

Bloomquist, Jane, and William McMillan. "Science Fiction Theatre the Moebius Way." *Patterns of the Fantastic.* Ed. Donald M. Hassler. Mercer Island, Wash.: Starmont, 1983. 81–90.

Delany, Samuel R. "*Flow My Tears . . . :* Theater and Science Fiction." *New York Review of Science Fiction* Sept. 1988: 1, 11–17.

Elwood, Roger. "Introduction." *Six Science Fiction Plays.* New York: Pocket, 1976. vii–x.

Gunn, James, ed. *The New Encyclopedia of Science Fiction.* New York: Viking, 1988.

Nicholls, Peter, ed. *The Science Fiction Encyclopedia.* New York: Doubleday, 1979.

Shirley, John. "SF Alternatives, Part One: Stelarc and the New Reality." *Science-Fiction Eye* 1 (August 1987): 56–61.

Suvin, Darko. *Metamorphoses of Science Fiction: On the Poetics and History of a Genre.* New Haven: Yale University Press, 1979.

————. *Positions and Presuppositions in Science Fiction.* Kent, Ohio: Kent State University Press, 1988.

Wytenbroek, Jacqueline. "Science Fiction and Fantasy." *Extrapolation* 23 (1982): 321–32.

INDIVIDUAL PLAYWRIGHTS

Samuel Beckett

Bair, Deirdre. *Samuel Beckett: A Biography.* New York: Harcourt, 1978.

Ben-Zvi, Linda. *Samuel Beckett.* Boston: Twayne, 1986.

Cohn, Ruby. *Just Play: Beckett's Theater.* Princeton: Princeton University Press, 1980.

————, ed. *Samuel Beckett: A Collection of Criticism.* New York: McGraw-Hill, 1975.

Connor, Steven. *Samuel Beckett: Repetition, Theory, and Text.* New York: Basil Blackwell, 1988.

Duckworth, Colin. *Angels of Darkness: Dramatic Effect in Samuel Beckett with Special Reference to Eugène Ionesco.* New York: Barnes and Noble, 1972.

Esslin, Martin, ed. *Samuel Beckett: A Collection of Critical Essays.* Englewood Cliffs, N.J.: Prentice-Hall, 1965.

Fletcher, John, and John Spurling. *Beckett: A Study of His Plays*. New York: Hill and
    Wang, 1972.
Gontarski, S. E. *The Intent of Undoing in Samuel Beckett's Dramatic Texts*. Bloomington:
    Indiana University Press, 1985.
————, ed. *On Beckett: Essays and Criticism*. New York: Grove, 1986.
Hobson, Harold. Review of *Endgame*. *The Sunday Times* (London) 15 July 1973: 37.
Kalb, Jonathan. *Beckett in Performance*. New York: Cambridge University Press, 1989.
Kenner, Hugh. *A Reader's Guide to Samuel Beckett*. New York: Farrar, 1973.
Knowlson, James, and John Pilling. *Frescoes of the Skull: The Later Prose and Drama
    of Samuel Beckett*. New York: Grove, 1980.
McCarthy, Patrick A., ed. *Critical Essays on Samuel Beckett*. Boston: G. K. Hall, 1986.
Pountney, Rosemary. *Theatre of Shadows: Samuel Beckett's Drama, 1956–76*. Totowa,
    N.J.: Barnes and Noble, 1988.

Spalding Gray

Leverett, James. "Introduction." *Swimming to Cambodia*. Spalding Gray. New York:
    Theatre Communications Group, 1987. ix–xiii.
Phelan, Peggy. "Spalding Gray's *Swimming to Cambodia*: The Article." *Critical Texts:
    A Review of Theory and Criticism* 5 (1988): 27–30.
Rothstein, Mervyn. "A New Face in Grover's Corners." *New York Times* 4 Dec. 1988:
    1, 10.
Siegle, R. "Condensed Book: Performance Art and Fiction." *Suburban Ambush: Down-
    town Writing and the Fiction of Insurgency*. Baltimore: Johns Hopkins University
    Press, 1989. 250–72.

Eugène Ionesco

Bonnefoy, Claude. *Conversations with Eugène Ionesco*. Trans. Jan Dawson. London:
    Faber, 1970.
Coe, Richard N. *Ionesco: A Study of His Plays*. London: Methuen, 1971.
Coleman, Ingrid H. "Conscious and Unconscious Intent in the Creative Process: A Letter
    from Eugène Ionesco." *French Review* 54 (1981): 810–15.
Hayman, Ronald. *Eugène Ionesco*. New York: Frederick Ungar, 1976.
Lamont, Rosette C., ed. *Ionesco: A Collection of Critical Essays*. Englewood Cliffs,
    N.J.: Prentice-Hall, 1973.
Lazar, Moshe, ed. *The Dream and the Play: Ionesco's Theatrical Quest*. Malibu, Calif.:
    Undena Publications, 1982.
Lewis, Allan. *Ionesco*. Boston: Twayne, 1972.
Marcabru, Pierre. "Notre théâtre est une expérience pour demain." *Arts* 15 Feb. 1956:
    3.
Mègret, Christian. "Eugène Ionesco ou le dramaturge malgré lui." *Carrefour* 6 Mar.
    1957: 15.
Pronco, Leonard C. *Eugène Ionesco*. New York: Columbia University Press, 1965.
Sarraute, Claude. "Eugène Ionesco: '*Tueur sans gages* s'inscrit dans la ligne faussement
    classique des pièces faussement policières'." *Le Monde* 13 Feb. 1959: 12.
Schechner, Richard. "An Interview with Ionesco." *Tulane Drama Review* 7 (1963):
    163–68.

Wassily Kandinsky

Bowlt, John E. "Vasilii Kandinsky: The Russian Connection." *The Life of Vasilii Kandinsky in Russian Art: A Study of "On the Spiritual in Art."* 2nd ed. Ed. John E. Bowlt and Rose-Carol Washton Long. Newtonville, Mass.: Oriental Research Partners, 1984. 1–41.

Brisch, Klaus. "Untersuchungen zur Entstehung der gegenstandslosen Malerei an seinem Werk von 1900–1921." Diss. Bonn University, 1955.

Fuhr, James Robert. " 'Klänge': The Poems of Wassily Kandinsky." Diss. Indiana University, 1982.

Grohmann, Will. *Wassily Kandinsky: Life and Work.* Trans. Norbert Guterman. New York: Abrams, [1958].

Hahl-Koch, Jelena, ed. *Arnold Schönberg-Wassily Kandinsky: Briefe, Bilder und Dokumenter einer aussergewöhnlichen Begegnung.* Salzburg: Residenz, 1980. *Arnold Schoenberge-Wassily Kandinsky: Letters, Pictures and Documents.* Trans. John C. Crawford. Boston: Faber, 1984.

Heller, Reinhold. "Kandinsky and Traditions Apocalyptic." *Art Journal* 43 (1983): 19–26.

———. Review. *Art Journal* 39 (1980): 313–29.

Hooper, Kent. "Understanding Wassily Kandinsky's *Der gelbe Klang." C.L.A.M. Chowder: Proceedings of the Second Midwest Comparative Literature Graduate Student Conference.* Ed. Brady Axelrod et al. Minneapolis: Comparative Literature Association of Minnesota, 1983. 75–83.

Lankheit, Klaus. "A History of the Almanac." *The 'Blaue Reiter' Almanac.* Ed. Wassily Kandinsky and Franz Marc. New Documentary Edition. Ed. Lankheit. New York: Viking, 1974. 11–48.

Long, Rose-Carol Washton. "Kandinsky and Abstraction: The Role of the Hidden Image." *Artforum* 10.10 (1972): 42–49.

———. "Kandinsky's Vision." *The Life of Vasilii Kandinsky in Russian Art: A Study of "On the Spiritual in Art."* 2nd ed. Ed. John E. Bowlt and Rose-Carol Washton Long. Newtonville, Mass.: Oriental Research Partners, 1985. 43–61.

———. "Kandinsky's Vision of Utopia as a Garden of Love." *Art Journal* 43 (1983): 50–59.

———. *Kandinsky: The Development of an Abstract Style.* Oxford: Clarendon, 1980.

———. "Occultism, Anarchism, and Abstraction: Kandinsky's Art of the Future." *Art Journal* 46 (1987): 38–45.

———. "Vasily Kandinsky, 1909–1913: Painting and Theory." Diss. Yale University, 1968.

Ringbom. Sixten. "Die Steiner-Annotationen Kandinskys." *Kandinsky und Munchen: Begegnungen und Wandlungen 1896–1914.* Ed. Armin Zweite. Exh. cat. Städt. Galerie im Lenbachhaus München, 18 Aug.–17 Oct. 1982. Munich: Pestel, 1982. 102–05.

———. *The Sounding Cosmos: A Study in the Spiritualism of Kandinsky and the Geneses of Abstract Art.* Acta Academiae Aboensis, A, 38:2. Abo, 1970.

Sheppard. R. W. "Kandinsky's Abstract Drama 'Der gelbe Klang': An Interpretation." *Forum for Modern Language Studies* [St. Andrews, Scotland] 11 (1975): 165–77.

————. "Kandinsky's Early Aesthetic Theory: Some Examples of Its Influence and Some Implication for the Theory and Practice of Abstract Poetry." *Journal of European Studies* 5 (1975): 19–40.

————. "Kandinsky's *Klänge*: An Interpretation." *German Life and Letters* NS 33 (1980): 135–46.

Stein, Susan Alyson. "Kandinsky and Abstract Stage Composition: Practice and Theory, 1909–12." *Art Journal* 43 (1983): 61–66.

————. "The Ultimate Synthesis: An Interpretation of the Meaning and Significance of Wassily Kandinsky's 'Der Gelbe Klang.' " M. A. Thesis. State University of New York at Binghamton, 1980.

Tassel, Janet. "Staging a Kandinsky Dream." *New York Times* 7 Feb. 1982: 4.

Weiss, Peg. "Editor's Statement: Are We Ready to Memorialize Kandinsky?" *Art Journal* 43 (1983): 9–13.

————. "Kandinsky and 'Old Russia': An Ethnographic Exploration." *Syracuse Scholar* Spring 1986: 43–62.

————. "Kandinsky and the Symbolist Heritage." *Art Journal* 44 (1985): 137–45.

————. *Kandinsky in Munich: The Formative Jugendstil Years*. Princeton: Princeton University Press, 1979.

Sam Shepard

Marranca, Bonnie, ed. *American Dreams: The Imagination of Sam Shepard*. New York: Performing Arts Journal Publications, 1981.

Mottram, Ron. *Inner Landscapes: The Theatre of Sam Shepard*. Columbia: University of Missouri Press, 1984.

Roof, Judith. "Testicles, Toasters and the 'Real Thing.' " *Studies in the Humanities* 17.2 (1990): 106–19.

Wetzsteon, Ross. "Introduction." *"Fool for Love" and Other Plays*. Sam Shepard. New York: Bantam, 1984. 1–15.

Wilcox, Leonard. "Modernism vs. Postmodernism: Shepard's *The Tooth of Crime* and the Discourses of Popular Culture." *Modern Drama* 30 (December 1987): 560–73.

Zinman, Toby Silverman. "Sam Shepard and Super-Realism." *Modern Drama* 29 (1986): 423–30.

Tom Stoppard

Bigsby, C.W.E. *Tom Stoppard*. Harlow, England: Longman, 1976.

Brassell, Tim. *Tom Stoppard: An Assessment*. New York: St. Martin's, 1985.

Cahn, Victor L. *Beyond Absurdity: The Plays of Tom Stoppard*. Rutherford, N.J.: Fairleigh Dickinson University Press, 1979.

Dean, Joan Fitzpatrick. *Tom Stoppard: Comedy as a Moral Matrix*. Columbia: University of Missouri Press, 1981.

Feeney, Joseph J., S.J. "Fantasy in Structure: Layered Metaphor in Stoppard." *Forms of the Fantastic*. Ed. Jan Hokenson and Howard Pearce. Westport, Conn.: Greenwood Press, 1986. 233–39.

Gabbard, Lucina Paquet. *The Stoppard Plays*. Troy, N.Y.: Whitston, 1982.

Gruber, William E. " 'Wheels within Wheels, Etcetera': Artistic Design in *Rosencrantz and Guildenstern Are Dead*." *Tom Stoppard: A Casebook*. Ed. John Hartz. New York: Garland, 1988. 21–46.

Hartz, John, ed. *Tom Stoppard: A Casebook*. New York: Garland, 1988.

Hayman, Ronald. *Tom Stoppard*. London: Heinemann, 1977.

Hunter, Jim. *Tom Stoppard's Plays: A Study of His Life and Works*. New York: Grove, 1982.

Huston, J. Dennis. "Misreading *Hamlet*: Problems of Perspective in *Rosencrantz and Guildenstern Are Dead*." *Tom Stoppard: A Casebook*. Ed. John Hartz. New York: Garland, 1988. 47–66.

Jenkins, Anthony. *The Theatre of Tom Stoppard*. Cambridge: Cambridge University Press, 1987.

Keysar-Franke, Helene. "The Strategy of *Rosencrantz and Guildenstern Are Dead*." *Educational Theatre Journal* 27 (1975): 85–97.

Perlette, John. "Theatre at the Limit: *Rosencrantz and Guildenstern Are Dead*." *Modern Drama* 19 (1985): 659–69.

Robinson, Gabrielle. "Leapfrog and Ambush in Stoppard." *Forms of the Fantastic*. Ed. Jan Hokenson and Howard Pearce. Westport, Conn.: Greenwood Press, 1986. 241–50.

Rusinko, Susan. *Tom Stoppard*. Boston: Twayne, 1986.

Derek Walcott

Brown, Lloyd. "Dreamers and Slaves." *Caribbean Quarterly* 17.3–4 (1971): 39.

Colson, Theodor. "Derek Walcott's Plays." *World Literature Written in English* 12 (1973): 90–91.

Hamner, Robert. *Derek Walcott*. Boston: Twayne, 1981.

Ismond, Pat. "Self Portrait of an Island." *Journal of West Indian Literature* 1 (1986): 59–73.

Jones, Dennis. "Derek Walcott." *Dictionary of Literary Biography, Yearbook* 16 (1981): 270–77.

Oliver, Edith. Review. *The New Yorker* March 1971: 83–85.

Rodman, Selden. "Derek Walcott." *Tongues of Fallen Angels*. New York: New Directions, 1974. 233–59.

Oscar Wilde

Bloom, Harold, ed. *Oscar Wilde*. New York: Chelsea House, 1985.

Ellmann, Richard. *Oscar Wilde*. New York: Knopf, 1988.

———, ed. *Oscar Wilde: A Collection of Critical Essays*. Englewood Cliffs, N.J.: Prentice-Hall, 1969.

Ericksen, Donald H. *Oscar Wilde*. Boston: Twayne, 1977.

Hampshire Stuart. "Oscar Wilde." *New Statesman* 63 (1962): 941–42.

McCarthy, Mary. "The Unimportance of Being Oscar." *Theater Chronicles 1937–1962*. New York: Farrar, 1963. 106–10.

Peckham, Morse. "What Did Lady Windermere Learn?" *College English* 18 (1956): 11–14.

Walkley, A. B. Review of *Lady Windermere's Fan. Academy* 5 March 1892: 257–58.
Worth, Katharine. *Oscar Wilde*. New York: Grove, 1984.

William Butler Yeats

Albright, Daniel. *The Myth against Myth: A Study of Yeats's Imagination in Old Age*.
    London: Oxford University Press, 1972.
Bushrui, S. B. *Yeats's Verse Plays: The Revisions 1900–1910*. Oxford: Clarendon, 1965.
Cave, Richard Allen. "Time for a Yeatsian Revolution." *Theatre Ireland* 22 (1990):
    22–26.
Ellmann, Richard. *Yeats: The Man and the Masks*. New York: E. P. Dutton, 1958.
Finneran, Richard J., ed. *Critical Essays on W. B. Yeats*. Boston: G. K. Hall, 1986.
Flannery, James B. *W. B. Yeats and the Idea of a Theatre: The Early Abbey Theatre in
    Theory and Practice*. New Haven: Yale University Press, 1976.
Flannery, Mary Catherine. *Yeats and Magic: The Earlier Works*. Gerrards Cross, U.K.:
    Colin Smythe, 1977.
Friedman, Barton R. *Adventures in the Deeps of the Mind: The Cuchulain Cycle of W. B.
    Yeats*. Princeton: Princeton University Press, 1977.
Griffin, Christopher. "Memories and Prophecies." *Theatre Ireland* 20, 21 (1989): 5–
    11, 14–19.
Harper, George Mills, ed. *Yeats and the Occult*. Toronto: Macmillan of Canada, 1975.
Lapisardi, Frederick S. "A Most Conscious Craftsman: A Study of Yeats's *Purgatory*
    as the Culmination of His Expressed Dramatic Theories." *Eire-Ireland* 2.4
    (1967): 87–95.
McGarry, James. *Place Names in the Writings of William Butler Yeats*. Toronto: Mac-
    millan of Canada, 1976.
Moore, John Rees. *Masks of Love and Death: Yeats as Dramatist*. Ithaca, N.Y.: Cornell
    University Press, 1971.
Nathan, Leonard. *The Tragic Drama of William Butler Yeats: Figures in a Dance*. New
    York: Columbia University Press, 1965.
Pine, Richard. "Cuchulain: From Gang Leader to Hero." *Irish Times* 9 Sept. 1989,
    weekend: 5.
Skene, Reg. *The Cuchulain Plays of W. B. Yeats: A Study*. New York: Columbia Uni-
    versity Press, 1974.
Taylor, Richard. *The Drama of W. B. Yeats: Irish Myth and the Japanese No*. New
    Haven: Yale University Press, 1976.
———. *A Reader's Guide to the Plays of W. B. Yeats*. New York: St. Martin's, 1984.
Unterecker, John. *A Reader's Guide to William Butler Yeats*. New York: Noonday Press,
    1959.
———, ed. *Yeats: A Collection of Critical Essays*. Englewood Cliffs, N.J.: Prentice-
    Hall, 1963.

Index

About the Editor and Contributors

PETER N. CHETTA is Associate Professor at Iona College concentrating on modern drama and East Asian literature in translation. He has presented papers in medieval studies, American culture, and Asian studies, as well as the fantastic.

ELIZABETH C. HESSON was Associate Professor of German at Memorial University of Newfoundland. Author of *Twentieth Century Odyssey: A Study of Heimito von Doderer's Novel "Die Damonen"*, she died in August 1989 after a five-year struggle with cancer.

IAN M. HESSON is Associate Professor of French at Memorial University of Newfoundland, presently writing on the political implications of Ionesco's theater and conducting a comparative study of the theater of Ionesco and the German dramatist Peter Weiss.

VERONICA HOLLINGER teaches in the Cultural Studies Program at Trent University, Ontario, and is a co-editor of *Science-Fiction Studies*. Her publications include essays on feminist science fiction, cyberpunk, vampire fiction, and postmodern theater.

KENT W. HOOPER is Assistant Professor of German at the University of Puget Sound. He has written on German expressionism and modernism and has published a book on Ernst Barlach. Work in progress focuses on Werner Brenner and Bert van Bork.

SUSAN TAYLOR JACOBS is Director of the Scientific and Technical Writing Program at Rutgers University. Having written about fantasy in Kafka, Lady

Gregory, and heroic literature, she is currently researching Wilde's expository methods and performance theory.

JOSEPH KRUPNIK is Associate Professor of English at Indiana University of Pennsylvania where he teaches literature and film. He is currently studying Hitchcock's late films as well as analyzing the image of the feminine in the films of Maya Deren.

FREDERICK S. LAPISARDI is Literary Advisor/Dramaturg to the Annual W. B. Yeats International Theatre Festival at the Abbey Theatre in Dublin. He is currently completing *W. B. Yeats's Dramatic Theories: A Compendium* and has edited *The Collected Plays of Eva Gore-Booth*.

PETER MALEKIN has been many things to many people, most recently Senior Lecturer, Department Chair, and Eighteenth-Century Studies Director at the University of Durham. He is mainly concerned with theories of consciousness in relation to literature.

PATRICK D. MURPHY is Associate Professor of English at Indiana University of Pennsylvania. He is also Director of the Graduate Program in Literature and Criticism. He has recently published *Critical Essays on Gary Snyder* and *Understanding Gary Snyder*.

LANCE OLSEN, Associate Professor of English and Creative Writing at the University of Idaho, is author of four books on and of postmodern fiction, most recently *The Reader's Guide to William Gibson* and the novel *Live from Earth*.

JESSICA PRINZ teaches English at The Ohio State University. Her book *Art Discourse/Discourse in Art* is a study of postmodern interdisciplinarity. She has published widely on art and literature.

CARL SCHAFFER holds a position at the University of Scranton in Pennsylvania, where he teaches American and Jewish literatures. He is currently researching the influence of Jewish mysticism on American Puritan thought.

THEODORE SHANK, award-winning playwright and director, teaches contemporary theater and directing at the University of California, San Diego. His books and articles on contemporary theater have been published internationally, including the recent *American Alternative Theatre* and *California Performance*.

ROBERT J. WILLIS teaches English at East Stroudsburg University of Pennsylvania. He is particularly interested in Third World literatures and has delivered papers on Caribbean and West African authors at numerous conferences.

RALPH YARROW teaches drama and European literature at the University of East Anglia, Norwich, England. He has recently published *Improvisation in Drama* and a *Nouveau Roman Handbook* and has edited *European Theatre 1960– 90*.

ISBN 0-313-27270-0